The Government of Life

forms of living

Stefanos Geroulanos and Todd Meyers, *series editors*

The Government of Life

Foucault, Biopolitics, and Neoliberalism

Edited by Vanessa Lemm and Miguel Vatter

FORDHAM UNIVERSITY PRESS
NEW YORK 2014

Copyright © 2014 Fordham University Press

All rights reserved. No part of this publication may be reproduced, stored in a retrieval system, or transmitted in any form or by any means—electronic, mechanical, photocopy, recording, or any other—except for brief quotations in printed reviews, without the prior permission of the publisher.

Fordham University Press has no responsibility for the persistence or accuracy of URLs for external or third-party Internet websites referred to in this publication and does not guarantee that any content on such websites is, or will remain, accurate or appropriate.

Fordham University Press also publishes its books in a variety of electronic formats. Some content that appears in print may not be available in electronic books.

Library of Congress Cataloging-in-Publication Data is available from the publisher.

16   5 4 3 2

First edition

CONTENTS

List of Abbreviations ix

Acknowledgments xi

Introduction 1
Vanessa Lemm and Miguel Vatter

Part I. The *Nomos* of Neoliberalism

1. The Fourth Age of Security 17
    Frédéric Gros

2. The Law of the Household: Foucault, Neoliberalism,
    and the Iranian Revolution 29
    Melinda Cooper

3. The Risks of Security: Liberalism, Biopolitics, and Fear 59
    Thomas Lemke

Part II. Genealogies of Biopolitics

4. A Genealogy of Biopolitics: The Notion of Life
    in Canguilhem and Foucault 77
    Maria Muhle

5. Power over Life, Politics of Death: Forms
    of Resistance to Biopower in Foucault 98
    Francesco Paolo Adorno

6. Identity, Nature, Life: Three Biopolitical Deconstructions 112
    Judith Revel

Part III. Liberalism between Legality and Governmentality

7. From Reason of State to Liberalism: The Coup d'État as Form of Government   127
   Roberto Nigro

8. Foucault and Rawls: Government and Public Reason   141
   Paul Patton

9. Foucault and Hayek: Republican Law and Liberal Civil Society   163
   Miguel Vatter

Part IV. Philosophy as Ethics and Embodiment

10. Parrhesia between East and West: Foucault and Dissidence   187
    Simona Forti

11. The Embodiment of Truth and the Politics of Community: Foucault and the Cynics   208
    Vanessa Lemm

Notes   225
Bibliography   257
List of Contributors   277
Index   281

ABBREVIATIONS

Note: All titles in this list are by Michel Foucault and frequently cited in this volume. Other cited works by Foucault appear in the bibliography.

AEW   *Aesthetics, Method, and Epistemology: Essential Works of Michel Foucault, 1954–1984: Volume II*. Edited by J. D. Faubion. New York: New Press, 1998.

BB   *The Birth of Biopolitics: Lectures at the Collège de France, 1978–1979*. Translated by G. Burchell. New York: Palgrave Macmillan, 2008.

CT   *The Courage of Truth: The Government of Self and Others, II: Lectures at the Collège de France, 1983–1984*. Edited by A. Davidson; translated by G. Burchell. London: Palgrave Macmillan, 2011.

DE   *Dits et Écrits: Tome II, 1976–1988*. Paris: Gallimard, 2001.

ECS   "The Ethics of the Concern of the Self as a Practice of Freedom." In *EEW*, 281–301.

EEW   *Ethics: Subjectivity and Truth: Essential Works of Michel Foucault, 1954–1984: Volume I*. Edited by P. Rabinow. New York: New Press, 2006.

HS   *The Hermeneutics of the Subject: Lectures at the Collège de France, 1981–1982*. Translated by G. Burchell. New York: Palgrave Macmillan, 2005.

OES   "'Omnes et Singulatim': Toward a Critique of Political Reason." In *PEW*, 298–325.

PEW   *Power: Essential Works of Foucault, 1954–1984: Volume 3*. Edited by J. D. Faubion. New York: New Press, 2000.

RS	"The Risks of Security." In *PEW*, 365–81.
SMD	*Society Must Be Defended: Lectures at the College de France, 1975–1976.* Translated by D. Macey. New York: Picador, 2003.
SP	"The Subject and Power." In *PEW*, 326–48.
STP	*Security, Territory, Population: Lectures at the Collège de France, 1977–1978.* Translated by G. Burchell. New York: Palgrave Macmillan, 2007.
UP	*The History of Sexuality: Volume II. The Use of Pleasure.* Translated by R. Hurley. New York: Vintage Books, 1985.
WC	"What Is Critique?" In *The Politics of Truth*, edited by S. Lothringer and L. Hochroth, 23–82. New York: Semiotext(e), 1997.
WE	"What Is Enlightenment?" In *EEW*, 303–19.
WK	*The History of Sexuality: Volume I, an Introduction. The Will to Knowledge.* Translated by R. Hurley. New York: Vintage Books, 1990.

ACKNOWLEDGMENTS

This collection of essays is in part based on conference papers given at the International Conference "Michel Foucault: Biopolitics and Neoliberalism," which took place in Santiago de Chile at the Faculty of Social Science and the Institute of Humanities, Diego Portales University in September 2008. Earlier versions of Chapters 1, 3, 4, 5, and 9 have been published in Spanish translation in *Michel Foucault: Biopolítica y neoliberalismo*, edited by Vanessa Lemm (Santiago: Ediciones Universidad Diego Portales, 2010). Chapter 6 has been previously published in Italian as "Identità, natura, vita: Tre decostruzioni biopolitiche" in *Foucault oggi*, edited by M. Galzigna (Milan: Feltrinelli, 2008). The editors wish to thank Simon Porzak for his work on the draft translations of Chapters 1, 5, and 6; and Ely Orrego for her work on the abbreviations and bibliography.

Introduction

Vanessa Lemm and Miguel Vatter

The recently completed publication of the Courses that Michel Foucault gave at the Collège de France starting in 1971–72 and ending in 1983–84 has dramatically changed the way Foucault's thought as a whole is now understood.[1] Prior to the publication of these Courses many interpreters thought that the "last" Foucault had shifted away from the post-structural analysis of power that characterized his work from the late 1960s in order to move toward an "aesthetic" and "ethical" preoccupation with self-invention and authenticity, with the problem of subjectivity. Some interpreters hypothesized that Foucault had reinvented himself as a liberal political philosopher.[2] Today, on the evidence of the complete transcript of the Courses, it is clear that Foucault's work did undertake a "turn" in the mid-1970s, but that this was a turn toward the problem of "government" or "governmentality."[3] Foucault did not become a "liberal" political theorist in the mid-1970s, but he did turn the focus of his attention toward a genealogy of liberalism and neoliberalism as forms of "governmentality," rather than as political ideologies or forms of state. Still, what Foucault wanted to say about what it means to "govern" human beings, why "government" is not a political activity in the traditional understanding of politics, what the relation is between "government" and subjectivity (freedom, action, rule-following, self-reflection): all this remains highly contested, and indeed the systematic study of these questions in relation to the corpus of Foucault's Courses may well be said to be at its initial stages.

This volume seeks to make a contribution to these questions by focusing on the relation that Foucault established between the ideas of biopower and biopolitics and the studies of governmentality in his last Courses and occasional writings of this period. Most of the essays in this volume adopt and contribute to Foucault's analysis of biopolitics as a guiding thread to understand why liberalism and neoliberalism is a "government of life." The idea that biopolitics is somehow the core issue of governmentality is in many ways a contribution of recent Italian theory, from Antonio Negri and Giorgio Agamben to Roberto Esposito. Many of the contributions to this volume in one way or another critically engage this Italian reception of Foucault. At the same time, the originality of this collection consists in the variety of perspectives and traditions of reception brought to bear on the problem of the connection between biopolitics and governmentality in Foucault's work, showing this connection to be anything but obvious, both with regard to its textual basis as well as in its philosophical and political projections.

Although all the essays in this volume center on the biopolitical core of the question of governmentality, they reflect very different, sometimes opposed, approaches to the meaning of Foucault's term "biopolitics." The contributions of Thomas Lemke and Maria Muhle, for instance, privilege an approach to governmentality that understands it as a radical modification and deepening of Foucault's earlier thesis concerning the identity of power and knowledge. As a consequence, this approach emphasizes Foucault's continued interest in the history of systems of thought, of epistemology, as it applies in particular to the sphere of biological life and its application in the social sciences.[4] The essays by Judith Revel, Roberto Nigro, and Francesco Paolo Adorno react to the influential interpretations given by Negri, Agamben, and Esposito to the idea of biopolitics by contrasting them with what Foucault may have actually intended by biopolitics. The contributions of Paul Patton, Melinda Cooper, and Miguel Vatter engage the Anglo-

American reception of late Foucault, which approached the problem of government as a useful instrument to understand the reasons for the new hegemony of liberal political philosophy, something that Foucault perceived in advance of other thinkers. Lastly, the essays by Frédéric Gros, Simona Forti, and Vanessa Lemm approach the problem of government from Foucault's last Courses in which the engagement with Greek philosophy and its understanding of philosophy as a form of life is primordial. This collection does not presume to represent all the approaches found in current Foucault scholarship, but it does offer perhaps the most complete overview of the debates found in the current literature, in any language.[5] The aim of this introduction is to present the connection between government and biopolitics as a problem, and show in what ways this problem calls for such a varied, irreducible plurality of approaches to biopolitics. This is the very feature of Foucault's late work that has established him, for a second time since he burst into fame in the late 1960s, and for very different reasons, as the fundamental thinker of contemporary continental political thought.

Foucault famously gives the formula for government as the "conduct of conduct [*conduire la conduite*]" (*DE*, 237). The discovery of this problem, and hence of a history of governmentality, offers him a grammar through which to articulate his previous discoveries of disciplinary power and of biopower, as well as to account for their difference with respect to sovereign power. These problems had remained unsolved in *Discipline and Punish* and in the first volume of *The History of Sexuality*, raising questions among interpreters about the internal coherence of Foucault's archeological and genealogical investigations.[6] In a sense, the introduction of the concept of government settles this question. Likewise, the legend according to which Foucault underwent a conversion to liberalism that oriented his thinking toward individual self-creation and authenticity is put to rest as soon as it is realized that the governmental understanding of conduct is characterized by the element of *self*-conduct: the subject who is governed is also always a subject who governs. Thus the analysis of governmentality is inextricable from the analysis of subjectivity, of self-reflexivity; and this also explains why, with respect to power understood as government, it is always true that "where there is power, there is resistance" (*WK*, 95). The problem of subjectivity (and so of ethics), and its relation to what Foucault calls "technologies of the self," needs to be understood as an integral part of the problem of government and does not require a "break" with the prior genealogical analysis of power. We return to this point at the end.

Foucault's idea of a "conduct of conduct" is perhaps best approximated by comparing it with what Max Weber calls, in *The Protestant Ethic and the Spirit of Capitalism*, a *Lebensführung* (conduct of life), by which is meant a government of life that gives this life a "form" or an ethos. It is well-known that Weber's fundamental contribution in sociology consisted in analyzing human action in terms of what the actors think they are doing when they perform certain activities (as opposed to reconstructing causal chains operating behind their backs). The "meaning" of their actions does not refer to an abstract semantic content, to a logical connection between ideas, but to a complex of beliefs and practices that allow for a life to be governed or led along a certain path: such "conduct of conduct" is what permits an individual to have a "biography" or a social group to have a "history" without thereby having to presuppose any teleology. Weber takes this idea of *Lebensführung* directly from Nietzsche's understanding of "asceticism" in the third essay of the *Genealogy of Morals*, where the "ascetic ideal" or the "will to know" is understood as a function of disciplinary arrangements or *dispositifs* that generate "meaning" for the individual who subjects herself to them. Foucault's study of government, therefore, expands his previous uncovering of "power/knowledge" arrangements in the form of disciplinary power into an analysis of the "spiritual" preconditions of power (akin to Weber's analysis of the "spirit" of capitalism) that depend on establishing a *Lebensführung* (akin to Weber's analysis of a "religiously" informed "ethic").

Placing the accent, as Nietzsche and Weber had already done, on the "religious" origins of government as *Lebensführung* is one of the important innovations found in Foucault's Courses. Foucault introduces the very idea of government in relation to its Christian "pastoral" origins; he offers an analysis of the assumptions about "providence" in neoliberal government; he is interested in the role played by religion in the Iranian Revolution and in the dissident resistance movements of Eastern Europe. Several recent volumes have shown that Foucault had a developed "ear" for religion and religious themes.[7] But it is more likely that what caught Foucault's attention is the connection between (religious) salvation and (governmental) security, both of which refer to the conduct or circulation of life through a predetermined circuit.

Foucault's turn to the study of government opened up a new avenue of research into the Marxist project of a "critique of political economy" and the reasons for the hegemony of political economy over a politics centered on sovereign power in late modernity. As Foucault makes clear at the end of *The Birth of Biopolitics*, one of his motivations to study government is given by the task to understand the rise of "civil society" and of the *homo economicus*, that is, of a human "type" that is the product of the constant application of economic thinking in all areas of natural and social life. This human "type" is the unique product of a modern conduct of conducts which Foucault calls liberalism. The reorientation of his analysis of power toward what has been called the "economization of society" made possible the productive reception of Foucault's work by post-Marxist thought in the 1990s, primarily in the work of Negri.

The reencounter of post-Marxist thought with the late Foucault was due to Foucault's emphatic indication of an essential link between the problem of government and biopolitics. Indeed, as Negri and Michael Hardt make clear, the prevalence of "immaterial labor" which characterizes neoliberal political economy is understandable only if one assumes a "biopolitical" form of capitalist production. Hence, the recent literature on the transformations of late capitalism tend to make comparatively less use of Foucault's analyses of pastoral power whereas they strongly emphasize the biopolitical dimension.[8] It would not be exact to say that the connection between biopolitics and neoliberalism that Negri and others have theorized is a forcing of Foucault's intentions, since it was Foucault himself (not the editors of the Courses) who chose to keep the title *The Birth of Biopolitics* for a series of lectures dedicated to the history of neoliberalism in which biopolitics is hardly mentioned. This has left an unsolved puzzle as to how exactly Foucault understood the conjunction between biopower and late modern capitalism.

The essays in this collection, read as a whole, suggest that the linkage between governmentality, understood as a "conduct of conduct," and biopolitics, understood as power over biological life, is fruitfully illuminated by considering the ancient understanding of *nomos*, which is best translated neither as "law" nor as "order" but by the term "normative order": a way to regiment and govern the lives of people that brings together the religious as well as the economic dimensions of social order. All the contributions address the relationship between governmentality and biopolitics, but they do so from a variety of perspectives: some emphasize the problem of security; others the problem of managing the life of populations; others focus on the normative order of neoliberalism; still others address the way in which Foucault returns to ancient Greek philosophy and Christian and Islamic religion to understand this relationship. Despite this variety of perspectives, we suggest that one of their common threads is given by the idea of a normative order or *nomos*.

Foucault first attempts to connect governmentality to biopolitics in his Course titled *Security, Territory, Population*. These three terms can be used to translate the meaning of the archaic idea of *nomos*, which refers to the way in which a population of living beings (Nietzsche will say a "herd") is collected by another group ("shepherds") through a division of a territory (i.e., in the form of a spatial grid or network of power), for the purpose of providing "security" to the grouping, and thereby governing complexity and contingency.[9] In his later work, Schmitt drew attention to this archaic idea of *nomos*, showing how its pastoral metaphors are organized around the economic finality of justifying "an original distribution of land."[10] The grammar of *nomos* thus joins a pastoral metaphor of conduct with an economic metaphor of appropriation, reproduction, and accumulation. For this reason it seems a promising candidate to illustrate Foucault's interest for using religions and religious practices (Christianity, Shi'ite Islam, confession, mysticism, etc.) to decode logics of economic power.

The first part of the volume, "The *Nomos* of Neoliberalism," contains three essays illustrating different aspects of neoliberal governmentality as a *nomos*. The essay by Gros is intended to familiarize the reader with the idea that security has functioned as a *nomos* in four different ways in the West, from the "spiritual" security of Hellenism to the "imperial" security in the medieval social imaginary, from the early modern "state" security to our current "biopolitical" or "human" form of security. Although Gros never mentions Schmitt, it is interesting to note that his discussion of medieval security presupposes the idea that security is brought by a *katechon* (the historical agent, represented by pope or emperor, who postpones the apocalypse) just as much as modern security is brought by a *sovereign* who maintains peace through his capacity to signal who is the enemy: both figures of security are decisive in Schmitt's thinking.[11] Foucault, according to Gros, moves beyond Schmitt's political theology by thinking a new form of security that works through networks of communication flows and where security is brought by the generalized function of policing the circulation of communication, commodities, and persons which are in turn essential to capitalist relations of exchange and production.

The essay by Cooper argues that Foucault's engagement with the early phases of the Iranian Revolution shed a great deal of light on his understanding of neoliberalism as a new *nomos* of the household (*oiko-nomia*). But on Cooper's reading, Foucault's fascination with the ideology of the Iranian Revolution betrays his intention to recover the "ancient" understanding of the *nomos* of the household in order to offset Becker's neoliberal "new household economics" that threatens to destroy all sexual discipline, all substantive sexual normative order, by turning every individual into the entrepreneur of his or her own body and sexuality. Unlike Gros, Cooper sees in Foucault's brief romance with the initial stages of the Iranian Revolution a nostalgia for "economic sovereignty" not unrelated to Schmitt's anxieties with respect to the liberal world order.

Lemke's contribution is intended to show how Foucault's idea of a "technology of security" can provide the link between liberal government and biopolitics. On this reading, liberalism is a form of government which, unlike previous forms, does not "run" on obedience but on freedom. The *nomos* of security is productive of individual freedom by regulating doses of security with doses of fear into the "population" in what Lemke designates as a veritable "economy of power" that lies beneath and makes possible the "power of the economy" in neoliberal regimes.

Foucault repeatedly states that all forms of governmentality, and liberalism is no exception, appeal to a "natural" standard of conduct. In general, the Courses do not reveal a univocal, systematic answer to the question of what is the "nature" that governmentality relies on, and in particular what is "natural" about the liberal normative order in which individuals are required to conduct themselves as if they were endowed with "natural rights" to freedom and equality. Rather, Foucault's Courses seem to pursue two distinct paths that continuously cross into each other. The first path investigates the relation between *nomos* as a "natural" standard of conduct and the sphere of biological and species life (*zoe* in Greek), which is characterized by an inherent normativity. The connection between the right conduct in society and the natural order is obvious in Greek and Roman philosophy, where justice ultimately means living in accordance to nature. But early modern political thinkers sought also to find man's natural equality and liberty in those traits that they shared with all living species based on the drive to self-preservation, whether this meant emphasizing the capacity to kill (Hobbes) or the capacity to feel pity (Rousseau). The connection between biological life and the government provided by normative order in Foucault is fairly clear since he defines biopolitics as the entrance of the living species into the calculus of political rationality (*WK*, 143) and he proposes to understand liberalism, as a form of governmentality, as "the general framework of biopolitics" (*BB*, 22). In this context, Foucault is indebted to the French philosopher of science Canguilhem with respect to the idea of finding the source normativity in the biological and medical understanding of the normal and the abnormal, as he recognized in his early Course *Abnormal*, which in a sense opened the "turn" to governmentality, and then in the important essay of self-definition on Canguilhem. Additionally, in Foucault one also finds another claim with respect to biopolitics which suggests a possible affirmative biopolitics, a philosophical linkage to species life, that is extremely influential in contemporary Italian theory.[12]

The second part of the volume, "Genealogies of Biopolitics," contains essays further developing or preparing these two possible readings of affirmative biopolitics in Foucault. The essay by Muhle offers an in-depth and original treatment of Foucault's debt to Canguilhem's conception of biological normativity for his reconstruction of neoliberal biopolitics. What Lemke discusses as the oscillation between security and fear, certainty and risk, in the neoliberal *nomos* is here led back to a polarity intrinsic to biological life, which, according to Canguilhem, moves between self-preservation and self-transgression. On Muhle's reconstruction, Foucault understood neoliberal biopolitics as the attempt by power to "imitate" this polarity of life, and so achieve a "regulation" of conduct that would appear as "normal" as possible, where normality is now understood to include the occasional transgression of established patterns, the acknowledgement of the subject's "authenticity" and "creativity."

Adorno's contribution pursues this Canguilhemian approach to Foucaultian biopolitics by discussing the implications of the parallel formation of economics and biology in the eighteenth century that account for the continuous transference of medical metaphors to the economy and of economical considerations into medical well-being that is so characteristic of the neoliberal normative order. Foucault famously defined biopower as that power which has "the right to make live" in opposition to the sovereign right to "put to death." Adorno takes up this formula and attempts to give it an affirmative reading by advancing the paradoxical hypothesis that, if thanatopolitics is the product of the power to "make live," then perhaps an affirmative biopolitics ought to be found on the side of a practice of "learning how to die" which, since Socrates through Montaigne to Heidegger, has characterized the philosophical form of life.

The question of affirmative biopolitics is also what motivates the contribution of Revel, who argues that Foucault's analysis of the relation between life and power needs to be "deconstructed" in order to appreciate how Foucault's treatment of subjectivity is aimed at freeing a discourse on self-identity, nature, and life from any substantive standards. For Revel, Foucault does advance an affirmative biopolitics centered on the self-fashioning of subjectivity, but this "form of life" is attainable only if subjectivation is a function of nonidentities or singularities; if all naturalism is resolutely historicized; and, lastly, if "life" is entirely understood as *bios* and not *zoe*, as a product of sociality, of the creation of a relation to the other (rather than based on the metabolism with what is natural or nonsocial).

The second approach to the idea of *nomos* as the "natural" standard of conduct found in Foucault's Courses concerns not the biological content of "nature" but the legal content of "normative order": the aspect of any normative order that assigns substantive "rights" and "duties" to its members, the side that underpins a legal system of norms. The productivity of Foucault's later thought for rethinking the liberal system of rights was thematized in the first, Anglo-American reception of Foucault's studies on governmentality in the late 1990s.[13] But that discussion reached an impasse on the false problem of whether Foucault approved or not of liberal rule of law: it missed the point that Foucault understood the "rule" in liberal "rule of law" as an example of a *nomos* of governmentality. That initial, Anglo-American reception of Foucault's turn toward governmentality, significant as it was, ignored the biopolitical dimension that underlies the liberal system of rights. It is now possible to consider what Foucault has to say about the discourse of human rights within the wider context of his treatment of liberal arts of government, biopolitics, and the theory of sovereignty.

The essays contained in the third part of the volume, "Liberalism between Legality and Governmentality," are dedicated to Foucault's reconstruction of liberalism as a form of political rationality, and in particular to the transition from the republican tradition of politics to the early modern invention of "reason of state," and then into the liberal reversal of "reason of state" into "public reason." The contribution of Nigro offers a reconstruction of Foucault's understanding of reason of state, and its central device of the coup d'état, in the Courses by reading Foucault's lectures in the context of his complicated relation to Marxist thought and leftist politics in the 1970s. As is well-known, in *Homo sacer* Agamben attempts to reunite Foucault's biopolitics with Schmitt's sovereignty in a theory of the "state of exception" as the *nomos* of liberalism. Nigro's essay shows that Foucault approaches the state of exception from a perspective that is very different from the Schmittian defense of state sovereignty. Nigro argues that the reason Foucault does this is because, despite his severe criticism of Marxism–Leninism, he remained committed to the basic Marxist problem of understanding the conception of the state and of the law that was necessary for the primitive accumulation of capital.

Patton's essay discusses the next stage in the development of liberal governmentality, namely, the transition from reason of state to the public use of reason: from Hobbes to Kant. Like Nigro, Patton is also interested in the function of liberal governmentality as a normative order for a certain way of distributing property, and in this context he situates the interest of Foucault's reading of the liberal *nomos* by comparing and contrasting the neoliberal conception of equal distribution with that of Rawls, who advocates a normative order of "property-owning democracy" informed by a Kantian conception of public reason. If Nigro argues that Foucault remained committed to a leftist agenda in the 1970s, Patton takes seriously the claim that Foucault in the late 1970s may have been closer to certain neoliberal ideals than previously supposed, but only because such ideals, especially in the form of German Ordoliberalism, can be helpful in providing socialist ideals with a working conception of governmentality.

Vatter's essay discusses Foucault's claim in *The Birth of Biopolitics* that the neoliberal project consists in the introduction of legal principles into the economic order. Foucault's analysis emphasizes the essential role played by the system of law in the neoliberal conception of the "free market," such that this market appears to be both the most "spontaneous" or "natural" and the "best" form of coordination of expectations. Vatter illustrates this claim by offering an analysis of the neoliberal jurisprudence of Hayek and its role in his economic thinking. Whereas Hayek's jurisprudence emphasizes "judge-made law," which no longer carries any inherent reference to republican principles of constitutionalism, Vatter argues that Foucault's critique of the neoliberal "economic rule of law" is premised on Foucault's adoption of a republican conception of freedom as the constituent power of law-making belonging to a people that is irreducible to the conduct of a population.

Foucault's recovery of the Kantian idea of "public use of reason," together with his revaluation of the classical republican opposition between a "rule of law" and a "government of men," both depend on a deeper background understanding of freedom as counter-conduct or resistance; a conception of freedom that is alternative to the liberal idea of freedom as security. That Foucault opens up the possibility of another "form of life" that does not entail a liberal or neoliberal "government of life" is a point brought up by all the previous essays, but in the fourth and last part of the volume, "Philosophy as Ethics and Embodiment," this possibility is discussed explicitly and in relation to his extended treatment of the Socratic schools of ancient philosophy in his last Courses dedicated to *The Government of Self and Others*. We said at the beginning that the turn to government, to an understanding of ethics as the conduct of conduct, is inseparable, in Foucault, from the problem of subjectivity or self-government, what Foucault calls the problem of a "hermeneutics of self." The Courses on *The Government of Self and Others* indicate quite precisely the context within which Foucault wrote his famous essay on "What Is Enlightenment?" responsible for the initial confusion as to Foucault's purported conversion to liberalism or to an aesthetic sense of self-creation. This context is nothing other than his exploration of the fundamental theme of Socratic philosophy, namely, the understanding of philosophy as a form of life or a conduct of conduct that is both political and yet anti-governmental. In his transition from Kantian critique to Greek *parrhesia* (frank speech or truth-telling) Foucault seems to have been after a conception of political action as "critique" that would permit him to articulate an idea of resistance, that is very old in his thinking, with his new discovery of the problem of government. This question of what it means to do politics from within the history of governmentality is the crucial question that Foucault studies still need to explore, and to which our volume simply wants to indicate some initial hypotheses.

The last Courses taught by Foucault seem to indicate his belief that the resistance to government may be found in the Socratic practice of philosophy since—on his account—Plato thematized pastoral power but only in order to reject it, and turned instead toward an ideal of critique whose "conduct" characterizes a life lived in truth or a true life, that is, philosophy as a form of life.[14] The fourth and last part of this volume contains two essays that examine Foucault's return to Greek philosophy. The essay by Forti situates Foucault's discussion of *parrhesia*, the activity of speaking the truth to power, which is the explicit theme of *The Courage of Truth*, his last Course before his untimely death, in relation to Foucault's involvement, in the late 1970s, on behalf of the Polish *Solidarność* movement and of the Czech *Charta* 77 dissidence movement.[15] Foucault's often remarked advocacy of human rights is placed in the context of Jan Patočka's theory of resistance, which is inspired by a return to the Platonic motif of a "care of the soul." Forti argues that such care is anti-pastoral in its intentions, because by separating the soul from the body, it attempts to counteract the reasoning of the Grand Inquisitor, according to which what human beings want is not freedom and rebellion, but satisfaction of material necessities and the security of body and life.

Lemm's essay gives another perspective on Foucault's return to the Socratic practice of philosophy by focusing on the most extreme of the Socratic schools, namely, the Cynics. Whereas Forti argues that the Socratic philosophical life was one that allowed a distance to the body, in order to avoid what Lefort identified as a crucial trait of totalitarianism, namely, the closure of the political body on itself, Lemm instead reads into Foucault's fascination with the Cynics the traces left in his thinking by Nietzsche's problem of how much truth can be incorporated or embodied in a life. Cynic philosophy, for Lemm, presents itself as the most radical reduction of *bios* to *zoe* in order to unleash both the immunitary and the communitary resources of embodiment. According to Lemm, Foucault saw in the Cynic form of life an experiment to unite life (*zoe*) and philosophy (truth) so as to make possible a form of life (*bios*) that resists the very idea of a government of life.

The problem of philosophy and government remains open, but it is thanks to the work of the Courses that this problem can now begin to be treated from within a horizon beyond that of liberalism and totalitarianism.

PART ONE

The *Nomos* of Neoliberalism

ONE

The Fourth Age of Security

Frédéric Gros

In this essay I discuss what I call the four ages of security. My reconstruction of the four great ages of security owes much to the work of Foucault, and I will address the idea of biopolitics through the lens of the fourth age of security. The four ages of security refer neither to social or political practices, nor to representations or mentalities. They stand for four great historical problematizations of security that Foucault marked out, but did not fully develop. For that matter, the concepts of "security" and "biopolitics" were never objects of any sustained conceptual elaboration on Foucault's part. The schema I propose is by no means definitive, and constitutes a set of hypotheses rather than one thesis. I will describe four homogenous, relatively systematic sets of statements (*énoncés*) that have had important effects on political and ethical reality. I am describing knots of problematization.

The first age of security is the spiritual age and corresponds to the first sense taken on by the term "security" in the West. The word "security" derives from the Latin *securitas*, which can be deconstructed into *sine curae*: without troubles, without cares. The Greek equivalent, *a-taraxia*, also means without worries, without unrest. Security designates, in its first problematization, the mental state of the wise man that has attained definitive serenity through a series of appropriate spiritual exercises. Here, security has a spiritual meaning, rather than a political one. Seneca writes in the *Letters to Lucilius*, "Securitas proprium bonum sapientis est." Security is the proper goal of the wise man. A certain number of remarks can be made with respect to this first sense of security. First, Foucault describes this state of mental serenity as well as the techniques of the self that allow for its attainment, mainly in his 1982 course at the Collège de France titled *The Hermeneutics of the Subject*, which strongly emphasizes the wisdom of the Stoics. It is important to note that it is only in Hellenistic and Roman philosophy that security comes to be thought as the aim of the philosophical life. In the classical philosophy of Plato and Aristotle, the term *ataraxia* is mostly absent. However, in the works of the Skeptics, the Stoics, the Epicureans, and the Cynics, the idea of *ataraxia* takes on a capital importance, since the pursuit and attainment of this security will come to define the philosophical enterprise. Philosophy is an enterprise of security in the sense that it promises to help achieve this mental state. What varies from one philosophical school of thought to another is the means and techniques to attain *ataraxia*, as well as the quality of this mental state itself. Let me provide only a few brief indications of these differences. For the Skeptics, *ataraxia* depends on a mental conversion, called *epokhe*, through which one renounces all judgments pertaining to the truth of what happens to oneself. There follows a mental security, a serenity made up of detachment and indifference. Abandoning the illusory pursuit of some definitive truth, one learns to experience a steadiness of the soul that permits one to maintain a perpetual calm in the midst of events. For the Epicureans, instead, *ataraxia* is conceived as the securing of the simple pleasure of existing. Through regular practices of meditating on the gods, conversation with friends, contemplation of basic philosophical precepts, and actively remembering moments of joy from the past, the goal is the crystallization of the pure happiness of existence, so as to make it a feeling that is always at one's disposal. For the Stoics, *ataraxia* or *securitas* hinges on a long series of exercises, of *askeses*, of constant and highly codified tests, a series that has been studied in depth by

Foucault, as for example the sorting of representations, meditation on death, morning and evening self-examination, and so forth. The goal is to reach in this way a perfect mastery of oneself and of one's emotions, to constitute a strong ego that would be able to act in the world and confront the world's hazards without ever allowing oneself to become destabilized. This Stoic security designates the stability of a subject who does not allow him- or herself to be moved by anything and who has at his or her disposal spiritual means that are powerful enough to prevail over all of the world's misfortunes. This first sense of security as serenity, as the condition of the wise man, as steadiness of disposition has been of great importance for our culture. It returns again in contemporary philosophy, when Wittgenstein, for example, in his *Lecture on Ethics*, says that security constitutes one of the three fundamental moral experiences.[1] It is important to understand that in this first sense "security" does not refer to the feeling of being protected or to the absence of any danger, but instead to the capacity to maintain the tranquility of one's soul in the middle of these dangers and to find the source of security exclusively within oneself.

The second age of security is the imperial age, a concept that has often been suggested by Foucault, even if he never devoted any longer exploration to this problem. Still, on at least three occasions during his course at the Collège de France—for example, the lectures of March 22, 1978; January 5, 1983; and February 2, 1984[2]—Foucault evokes the famous political myth of the Middle Ages, the Empire of the last days, a myth based on Christian millenarian doctrine. This millenarian doctrine—largely founded on (re)readings of the Apocalypse of Saint John and the Pauline Epistles, particularly the letter to the Thessalonians, in which the famous expression "pax et securitas" can be found—consists in the belief in a period of a thousand years preceding the Last Judgment which will be a period of peace, prosperity, and happiness on Earth, and which idyllic era would be followed by a series of great catastrophes (climactic, political, and social) and brought to an end with a final confrontation with the forces of Evil.[3] The Church quite rapidly condemned this doctrine of one thousand years of terrestrial happiness before the Last Judgment and the end of the world. However, it has not ceased to reappear throughout history, and in particular it reappears in the High Middle Ages and takes on an important political dimension. Naturally, the simple utopia of a period of happiness, peace, and tranquility promised to humanity is not in itself particularly original and can be found in a number of cultures and historical periods. It often represents nothing more than the expression of a hope oriented toward the future which is complementary to a nostalgic longing for the golden age of the disappeared past. On the other hand, what is particularly interesting about the Christian millenarianism of the Middle Ages is the way in which this period of peace comes to graft itself on the idea of Empire and on the idea of security. This synthesis between the ideas of Empire, peace, and security had already been prepared by the Roman Empire in the time of Nero when one could find coins engraved with the motto "pax et securitas." But in the European Middle Ages this security, a propaganda theme in the Roman Empire, becomes a political program founded on a mystical hope. In millenarian doctrine, this thousand-year period before the Last Judgment will witness simultaneously the end of history and the disappearance of borders. Indeed, this period of peace and security presupposes the establishment of a single Empire, the Empire of the last days, which brings together all nations around one single faith and in one single political space. One sole flock, as these millennium texts repeat over and again, with one solitary shepherd. The great problem that confronts the medieval West is how to know who this last Emperor will be: will he be French (a new Charlemagne), German (a new Frederick), or might it even be the pope, leader of Christendom? Every successful kingly campaign to conquer foreign lands or expand the borders of the realm was typically interpreted as a possible sign of the coming of the Emperor of the last days, of the onset of an age of peace and security, and of the end of history. As if authentic security could only be obtained by the constitution of a perfectly homogenous political and cultural space, and by the exclusion or destruction of all the figures of the Other. The last great resurgence of this political myth in the contemporary world was during the first Persian Gulf War promising a New World Order, made possible by the end of the Cold War and by the faith in the immanent extension of the model of liberal democracy to the entire globe. The president of the United States thus would have been the Emperor of the last days and the *pax Americana* would have led to the reign of a definitive security. For here security is Empire; security is the unification of worlds; security is the end of history.

The third age of security corresponds to the history of Western Europe and the rise of political philosophies centered on the state of nature and the social contract, that is, Hobbes, Locke, Spinoza, and Rousseau. Foucault elaborated on this third age at length in his course *Security, Territory, Population* at the Collège de France in 1978, in his studies of reason of state (*raison d'État*) and, in particular, in the development of the diplomatic-military *dispositif*, as well as in 1976, in his interpretation of Hobbes's thought in *Society Must Be Defended*. This third age of security can be understood on the basis of the disappearance of the medieval dream of Empire, starting with the construction of a new political space composed of a plurality of sovereign states, each attempting to maintain its individual place in the midst of all the others, exemplified by Westphalian Europe. Here it is no longer a question of security as a spiritual condition, nor of the myth of an Empire of the last days. Instead, the goal is to think the consistency of a nation-state in the midst of history. Security will be defined as the consistency of the state, which is simultaneously the consistency supplied by the state to the rights of its citizens and to the existence of its subjects, and the consistency that the state provides for itself as one political subject in relation to others. Indeed, the very meaning of the word "security" is immediately divided into internal security and external security.

The great political philosophers of the modern age all thought of security as the goal of civil society, as the essential function of the state: "the virtue of a state is its security [*securitas*]";[4] "the people, who have a right to . . . provide for their own safety and security, which is the end for which they are in society";[5] "them that did institute the Common-Wealth, for their perpetual, and not temporary, security."[6] But clearly one must try to understand exactly what "security" entails in this new context. It is important to note here, that security is not simply a question of "public order," and that in no way do these philosophies simply seek to legitimate a police state. Otherwise, one could not make intelligible why these texts, which all place security at the heart of a state's legitimacy, were considered as dangerous and subversive by the ruling powers of their time. A general pattern can be found everywhere in the above-mentioned examples of modern political philosophies. Their point of departure is the description of a catastrophic state of nature, in which a certain number of natural, fundamental dispositions of man are made impossible: for example, the ownership of the fruits of one's labor, equality as well as solidarity between men, and, lastly, freedom in the authentic sense of the term. In the state of nature, ownership is fragile; violence, suspicion, and dependency are the rule. None of man's natural, fundamental dispositions are able to develop themselves. This is to say that all modern political philosophers want to give a double meaning to the word "nature": it refers either to the savage immediacy of the state of nature, or to the conformity to Reason and God (natural law or laws). The creation of society and the institution of the state have as their purpose to make possible the application of the laws of nature understood as rational and divine laws: let ownership gained through labor be guaranteed, let the equality of all before the law be respected, let public freedom be preserved, let human solidarity be maintained and encouraged. In all these texts, security does not appear as a right among others, but as the very movement through which our natural dispositions must be assured, guaranteed, maintained, and all this against the eventual abuses of power by a biased, unjust state and against the influence of pressure groups representing particular interests. Security is the process through which consistency must be given by the state and by society to the fundamental, natural dispositions of man, which, in the state of nature, are precarious and in vain.

But, soon enough, a second meaning of "security" will overlay this first meaning. Most of these authors (Hobbes, Rousseau, Spinoza) indicate, although in a purely marginal way, that states stand in relation to one another as individuals in the state of nature: a permanent state of war holds sway among them. But the situation is not entirely the same: the state of nature is less destructive, and the state of war less absolute, between states than between individuals, since this violent situation does not necessarily lead to the creation of a global society. Each state must provide its citizens with security, must give consistency to their natural rights, and also guarantee its own security as a political subject. But the term "security" cannot have the same meaning in both cases. The defining feature of "political realism" in thinkers such as Hans Morgenthau, Raymond Aron, and Henry Kissinger, to give some contemporary examples, is precisely the conception of security as external security.[7] For a state, then, external security signifies the defense of its territorial integrity, the development of its military power, the necessity of alliances (which will always be fragile and reversible), the cynical calculation of its interests, the development of a systematic suspicion of all other countries, and its ability to start wars or make peace as soon as its interests come into play. In expressions such as "nuclear security," "UN Security Council," or "collective security system" it is this sense of "security" which is predominant, and which has been predominant in Europe across the nineteenth century and up to the end of the Cold War. I refer to this sense of security as sovereign security.

Biopolitics names the fourth age of security. Thanks to Foucault's analyses of neoliberalism and biopower, it is possible to define its outlines. I am here interested in analyzing a series of statements pertaining to security so as to be able to locate transformations and ruptures. These statements constitute a discursive network that defines, for any given security *dispositif*, an object (what must be secured or safeguarded: a spiritual condition, a unified world, a sovereign state), an actor (who must perform the securing: the wise man, the emperor, the state), a modality (how to perform this securing: by means of spiritual exercises, kindly solicitude, the constant threat of war), and a scope of action (that against which something must be secured: the pains of existence, the divisions of the world, invasions by the enemy). I have shown above that the set of these definitions varies historically. I propose that the contemporary era is marked by a very profound transformation in the idea of security itself, which is visible in a new discursive network, a new series of statements such as those pertaining to "human security," "biosecurity," "global security," or even "affective security." To simplify things somewhat, I proceed by opposition, by showing first of all how the biopolitical age can be opposed to the age of sovereign security.

The object of security has changed. The great statements of political realism named, as the principal object of security, the defense of the state's territorial integrity, which may require the sacrifice of citizens. The doctrine of human security instead proclaims insistently that living populations and individuals ought to constitute the new object of security. They are what must be protected: what is sacred is no longer the sovereignty of the state, but the life of the individual. From here arises the principle of the right to interference, or what international institutions today define as the "responsibility to protect." If today, in whatever corner of the world, the life of a population or populations is directly endangered (e.g., by a bloodthirsty state), this constitutes a breach of security *as* human security. As soon as the state is no longer the first and final object of security, everything that is involved in the life of civil populations becomes an object of security. In this manner, one speaks today of "nutritional security" and "energy security." The chief characteristic of these new objects of security is that they are constituted by flows: the flow of food, of energy, but also of images and of data (and, by simple extension, one speaks of "traffic security," "information security," "internet security," etc.). On the subject of these two objects, life understood as the biological component of the human and the circulation of those objects necessary for this life, Foucault showed in his course of 1978 how, beginning in the early modern age, the police defines one part of itself as urban police, giving to itself the care over this part of life and over its circulation. This suggests that in searching for the genealogy of this new biopolitical security one must look closely at the police. While the modern age based security on the army and justice (on war and the law), the new age considerably enlarges the role of the police, as the securing of communications and the control of circulations.

This redistribution of objects also involves a redistribution of the principal actors of security. Previously, the state constituted itself simultaneously as the sole object and sole subject of security. Once the object of security is seen as constituted by civil populations, or by various flows, the principal actors of security change as well. One witnesses a double movement that leads constantly to the delegitimization of the state as sole actor of security: on the one hand, a privatization of security in which private companies and organisms present themselves as specialists in the control of a given flow, and on the other hand, a humanitarianization of security in which the protection of civil populations will fall under the aegis of humanitarian organizations that do not, unlike states, seek to protect one or more given sets of political subjects, but strive to come to the aid of civil populations that are at risk of death, no matter what the nature of this risk may be.

It is important to understand that one is here at the limits of Foucault's analysis, or better, at the heart of the aporia he encountered. In 1976, in *The Will to Knowledge*, Foucault constructs an opposition between an "anatomopolitics" understood as power over of the individual's body through discipline, at work in institutions like the school, the factory, and the barracks, and a "biopolitics" understood as power over the population in its biological dimension through a regulatory politics carried on by the state. This articulation of biopolitics through the state makes it difficult to think biopolitics together with liberalism, because the latter is defined as a governmentality of the weak state. This is why, at the end of the 1979 course, *The Birth of Biopolitics*, Foucault sketches a new paradigm which still stands in need of further elaboration. Namely, the definition of what would be a neoliberal biopolitics which is detached from the state. What is striking in this new *dispositif* of security is precisely that they are no longer governed by the imperatives of the state, but by the demands of the circulation of flows.

Thereby, the modalities of security undergo transformation. Inasmuch as security remained centered on the state, the modalities of security consisted in the threat of armed force and a *dispositif* of alliances: what Foucault called the diplomatic–military *dispositif*, that is, strength and cunning—the lion and the fox, to return to Machiavelli's images. In this new configuration, two other paradigms emerge corresponding to the protection and to the control of flows. These two paradigms are not separate. After the Second World War, through the work of Donald Winnicott and Margaret Mahler (and later through the work of Franz Veldman and the school of haptonomy), an idea took shape in contemporary psychology that security is to be defined as the internal construction of the subject: security is what allows the child to grow up successfully. From here on child psychology is redefined as a technique for making the child secure. Security is understood simultaneously as protection—that is, the child must feel surrounded by a protective barrier, safe from external threats—and as the control of flow, since security is based on the regularity of flows of food and a regulated exchange, between parent and child, of the flows of communication and affection. It is striking the way in which the question of security is no longer posed in terms of closure as in the modern age, where the two symbols of security were the prison, for internal security, and the border, for external security, but, instead, in terms of the control of circulations and exchanges. The key sites of security are no longer borders defining the spaces of states, but, within the territory itself, airports and railway stations, that is, the nodal points of communication and exchange. The problem becomes one of "traceability": the ability to determine, at any given moment, what is moving, where it is coming from, where it is going, what it is doing in its current place, and if it actually has a right of access to the network in which it is moving or if its use of the network is unauthorized. Finally, the technical groundwork enabling these acts of tracking is seen more and more as based in the biological singularity of individuals, which opens up the question of biometrics.

The fourth transformation relates to the nature of the threat. Here, the doctrine of human security can act as a guide, since the majority of its efforts lie precisely in defining the new range of threats. One might even say, instead of "defining," that this effort consists in *enlarging* this range of threats, to the greatest possible extent. What is indeed peculiar about this new doctrine is that it considers everything that might do harm to the living individual and to the good of civil populations as a threat.[8] This new definition of security thus produces a continuous stream of threats, whether these are economic, climactic, social, ecological, political, hygienic, medical, or nutritional. Everything is part of one single continuum: natural disasters, epidemics, terrorist attacks, civil wars, rivalries between crime syndicates vying for the control of illicit trafficking in arms, drugs, people, climate change, poverty and unemployment, and so on. Today, all these threats are considered as risks to society understood in the broadest possible sense. In the interior of states, this *continuum* of threats is produced through the concept of "global security" which stands to a given population as "human security" stands to the whole of humanity, and which entails, in France and elsewhere, the fusion of all those institutional security authorities that had heretofore been separate. Today, it is commonly held that national, interior, medical, ecological, and other security departments ought to work together. The globalization of the world involves the abolition of the previous divisions between interior and exterior, criminal and enemy, the political and the natural. The biopolitical age of security has led to this great equivalence of all threats. This continuity and equalization entail the effacement of figures such as the worker, the citizen, the patriot, and so forth. All of them disappear for the benefit of the living individual whose vital nucleus must be secured, and nothing exists outside of the great community of living bodies, the security of which will be the responsibility of private organisms acting with the blessing of the state.

To conclude, I will propose two figures that to my mind incarnate this new biopolitical age of security, which one could also call the *global* age of security, and which, one day, will need to be opposed to the *total* age of security where there will be no more discussion of the state's interests in an international milieu, but instead solely of the circulation of flows in a globalized world. These two figures are the suspect and the victim.

The suspect must be distinguished from the enemy, who typically belongs to the third age of security. The enemy comes from the exterior and by the very fact of his threat patches up the holes in the national community. The enemy is identifiable and definable: he is a calculating and rational agent. The suspect, however, is by definition non-locatable and unpredictable. He is here, close at hand, and his threatening presence turns me into a stranger even to my closest neighbors. We live in an age of suspicion and distrust: suspect individuals, suspicious packages, suspect food. This generalized distrust appears as the shadowy side of globalization. On the other hand, one finds the victim. The new *dispositif* of security turns the individual, rather than the state, into a sacred object. Thus it is the suffering of the individual, his victimized condition, which now becomes scandalous. This figure of the victim makes the biopolitical security function through a new regime of affects that turn on compassion, which for its part is triggered by the various stagings offered by the media. Security, pity, image: this is the new articulation, different from the old system of sovereignty which drove national security through heroism and narrative.

In this essay, I have tried to extend Foucault's analyses of biopolitics by attempting to understand what the ages of security may be, in general, and what biopolitical security may be, in particular. I believe that these four ages of security also imply four great modalities of surveillance that Foucault was able to demarcate here and there throughout his works. Spiritual security presupposes *spiritual vigilance*: the vigilance of the wise man who pays careful attention to his spiritual capacities and means of support, as well as to his possible weaknesses, as studied by Foucault in *Hermeneutics of the Subject* as one of the aspects of the care of the self. Imperial security presupposes *paternal solicitude*: the Emperor watches over his subjects like the shepherd over his flock, with that kindly care studied by Foucault in his writings on pastoral government. Sovereign security presupposes *centralized surveillance* of internal and external enemies, all submitted to the total gaze of the state as in Bentham's Panopticon, the kingdom of spies. Biopolitical security implies *flow control*: the control of movements and communications, but in a decentralized fashion, depending on competing transnational networks, which immediately raises the question of access: who will have the right of access to any given network to control or redistribute any given flow? What is left to consider for another discussion is the exact form of the relationship between this biopolitical security and two other, minority flow systems, whose reality effects are incredibly strong, and which seem simultaneously to sustain and threaten our new security: these are the flow of international finance and the clandestine flow of illegal trafficking, or, in other words, the flow of the market.

TWO

The Law of the Household: Foucault, Neoliberalism, and the Iranian Revolution

Melinda Cooper

> Economics is an atheistic discipline; economics is a discipline without God.
>
> —MICHEL FOUCAULT, *The Birth of Biopolitics*

The year 1979 precipitated an extraordinary set of events in world politics, the effects of which are still alive today. In early 1979, a tenuous coalition of Iranian Marxists, leftists, and Shi'ite clerics brought down the secular oligarchy of the American-backed Mohammad Reza Shah Pahlavi, instituting in its place the equally authoritarian and theocratic rule of Khomeini. In this, the first modern revolution to install an Islamic state, many detected the birth of a uniquely contemporary form of anti-imperialism, one that looked for inspiration in religious law and divine violence rather than the Marxist repertoire of class struggle or liberal and republican notions of democratic constitutionalism. In many respects, their assessment has been vindicated. In today's Middle East, the Islamic Republic of Iran stakes a place apart as the stronghold of a peculiarly Shi'ite incarnation of Islamist anti-imperialism. And yet the success of the revolution itself was critical in galvanizing the forces of Sunni (Salafi and Wahhabi) militancy across the Middle East, South and Southeast Asia, and North Africa, with Saudi

Arabia acting as a powerful counter pole in the shaping of Islamist doctrine over the following decades. In the aftermath of the Cold War, political Islam has emerged as one of the most powerful opposition forces to American imperialism.[1]

In the very same year, another "revolution" of sorts was underway, one which would see the principles of Chicago School neoliberalism displace Keynesianism as the reigning orthodoxy of state economic management in the imperial centers of the world economy. In 1979, Margaret Thatcher was elected to power in Great Britain and immediately implemented the monetarist anti-inflation program advocated by the Chicago School neoliberals. Later that year, a Democratic president, Jimmy Carter, appointed Paul Volcker head of the U.S. Federal Reserve, leading to the abrupt turn in national economic policy which has been referred to as the "monetarist counterrevolution." In the following year, Ronald Reagan would be elected to power, espousing an austere program of welfare reductions, deindustrialization, and anti–trade unionism which would break the back of the Fordist labor movement and pave the way for a profound restructuring of the American economy. In North America as in Britain, these austerity measures were accompanied by a sudden escalation in military expenditures and a return to Cold War belligerence.

Foucault was one of the few political philosophers to have grasped the long-term importance of these events. In late 1978, as the revolutionary movement was reaching its zenith, Foucault made two trips to Iran, under commission to the Italian newspaper *Il corriere della sera*. In the intervening weeks, he visited Khomeini in his place of exile on the outskirts of Paris. These visits resulted in a series of fifteen articles and interviews, published in *Il corriere della sera, Le nouvel observateur*, and *Le monde*, in which Foucault reflected on the unfolding events of the revolution and their wider significance for world politics. With astonishing prescience, Foucault predicted that the Iranian Revolution marked the emergence of a radically new genre of anti-imperialism, one which would have profound and enduring effects on global geopolitics:

> Maybe its [the uprising's] historic significance will be found, not in its conformity to a recognized "revolutionary" model, but instead in its potential to overturn the existing political situation in the Middle East and thus the global strategic equilibrium. Its singularity, which has up till now constituted its

force, consequently threatens to give it the power to expand. Thus, it is true that, as an "Islamic" movement, it can set the entire region afire, overturn the most unstable regimes, and disturb the most solid ones. Islam—which is not simply a religion, but an entire way of life, an adherence to a history and a civilization—has a good chance to become a gigantic powder keg, at the level of hundreds of millions of men. Since yesterday, any Muslim state can be revolutionized from the inside, based on its time-honored traditions.[2]

Upon his return from Iran, in early January 1979, Foucault delivered the first of his annual lecture series at the Collège de France. The title of the series had been designated in advance as *The Birth of Biopolitics*. The actual content of the lectures, however, had very little to do with the problematic of biopolitics as Foucault had previously addressed it. Instead, the 1979 lectures would be dedicated entirely to the subject of the new economic liberalism that had developed simultaneously in Germany (Ordoliberalism) and the United States (Chicago School neoliberalism) in the decades following World War II. Foucault was not the first to broach the subject in France— the late 1970s had seen a renewed fascination with economic liberalism in France and a flurry of publications commenting on and translating the work of significant neoliberal thinkers in Western Europe and the United States.[3] Foucault's intervention nevertheless stands out as representing the first substantive critical appraisal of neoliberalism as an economic, social, and political movement. Unlike the more skeptical of contemporary commentators, Foucault insisted that neoliberalism, as a movement, was neither homogenous nor reducible to classical liberalism. "We should not be under any illusion," he wrote, "that today's neoliberalism is, as is too often said, the resurgence or recurrence of old forms of liberal economics which were formulated in the eighteenth and nineteenth centuries and are now being reactivated" (*BB*, 117). Moreover, Foucault was keenly attuned to the singularity of American neoliberalism, with its eclectic fusion of Chicago School neoclassicism (Milton Friedman, George Stigler, Gary Becker) and Austrian romanticism (Friedrich von Hayek and Ludwig von Mises). Whereas the neoliberal reforms in France had been engineered from on high by a small cadre of political elites, the neoliberal movement in the United States represented something much larger and momentous in its consequences, fueled as it was by both extra-state institutions and corporate interests, and feeding into both leftist and conservative critiques of big government

(*BB*, 93, 218). This was a movement, Foucault implied, which could not be ignored.

By any standards, the scope of Foucault's intellectual preoccupations during this period was impressive. Between late 1978 and mid-1979, Foucault produced an entire course of lectures and an ongoing series of newspaper reports on two seemingly unrelated topics. Foucault began his lectures on neoliberalism at the zenith of the Iranian uprising, shortly before Iran was declared an Islamic Republic by referendum. His final lecture on neoliberalism preceded his last text on the Iranian Revolution by only several weeks. And yet there is little in the written archive that would suggest any interference between these two bodies of work. What connection, if any, did Foucault see between the rise of political Islam and the evolving fortunes of neoliberalism? And why, in the following year, did Foucault reorient his work on power and knowledge toward a new concern with the ethics of the self—as embodied, in particular, in the practices of a small group of aristocratic citizens in classical Greece?

This essay argues that Foucault's preoccupations of the time were indeed connected in subtle and highly consequential ways. In his lectures on neoliberalism, Foucault documented the rise of a power formation which escaped his own categories of the disciplinary and biopolitical norm. Neoliberalism, he noted, invented a novel articulation of power—one which incited toward the management of the self, through practices of self-transformation beyond the norm. Most important perhaps, neoliberalism responded to the exit of women from the Fordist household by erasing the dividing line between the transaction of labor in the market place and the transaction of services in the self. In his minute reading of the Chicago School economist Gary Becker, Foucault remarks that "pleasure" itself becomes an exchangeable service in the neoliberal labor market. This essay suggests that Foucault's focus on the work of the lesser-known economist Gary Becker provides a clue to the intellectual maneuvers that led him from neoliberalism, to the Iranian Revolution, to the sexual ethics of classical Greece. Becker, after all, is the author of the "new household economics"—he is the one neoliberal economist to have focused deliberately and consistently on the shifting politics of the familial (the articulation, that is, of sex, sexuality, race, and class) in the late twentieth century. A conservative economist, he anticipated much of the conceptual terrain that was subsequently explored by the new humanities disciplines such as women's and gender studies, queer studies, cultural studies, and critical race studies. He was, however, much more pragmatically attuned than many on the academic left to the recomposition of class, consumption, and power that was to recuperate these movements within an expansive market of nonnormative identities. This essay argues that Foucault's rapid conceptual move from neoliberalism, to the Iranian Revolution, to the ethics of the self can be read as a compressed response to what he foresaw as the newly hegemonic regime of neoliberal power relations. In the face of neoliberalism's economy of transactional pleasure, Foucault retreated, finding a radical political alternative in the form of political Islam, which was equally concerned, if not obsessed, with the idea of relegislating the sexual politics of the household. Neoliberal economics dissolves the boundaries between private and public space, reabsorbing the intimate relations of the Fordist household into the space of market transactions; political Islam seeks to reestablish the foundational value of the household by submitting the transaction of pleasure and money to the dictates of divine law. Following Janet Afary and Kevin Anderson,[4] I argue that Foucault never renounced his interest in the moral economy of political Islam but rather returned to investigate it in greater detail in his late monograph on classical Greek ethics, *The Use of Pleasure* (volume 2 of *The History of Sexuality*). Here, Foucault discovered and asserted a law of the household (i.e., an *oikonomia*) which he believed could act as a political and spiritual alternative not only to the normalizing powers of the welfare state but also to the emerging sexual economy of neoliberalism. Anticipating a move that has become increasingly prevalent on the anti-imperialist left, Foucault's final work articulates a moralist critique of capitalism in which the transactional exchanges of neoliberalism are condemned at the very moment they threaten to undo the genealogical foundations of the household and the fraternal community of transaction in public space. What he asserts in response is a renewed ethics of sexual virtue, founded on the priority of divine law, and embodied in the figures of the virginal or pious woman and the self-mastering ascetic man.[5]

In a critical move that both renews and departs from the work of Hannah Arendt, Angela Mitropoulos suggests that we displace the focus of critical attention from "biopolitics" to "oikopolitics"—the latter term, she claims, "offers something far more explanatory of the genealogical and familial than any understanding of sovereignty through a biological lens has been able to admit and far less subjectively universal than many accounts of affect and intimacy aspire to."[6] Here I follow her lead in exploring the tensions and collusions between a neoliberal economics of transaction and a neofoundational politics of restoration (in this case, revolutionary Islam), both of which are singularly fixated on the sexual politics of the household.

Shi'ite Revolution: Political Theology against the State?

Even before the ratification of the Islamic Republic of Iran and its rapid descent into a reign of terror, Foucault's reports on the Iranian Revolution were controversial. In the context of the postwar French left, dominated by the Communist Party and the Maoists, Foucault was exceptional in having consistently distanced himself from the rigors of Stalinist Russia and the Cultural Revolution; yet he demonstrated considerably less skepticism with regard to the Iranian struggle. It was the specifically messianic and religious dimension of the revolution in Iran, embodied in the ascetic figure of the Ayatollah Khomeini, which aroused Foucault's passion. Here he discerned the possibility of a political experience wholly alien to that of the modern West. In Foucault's words, "There are those who struggle to present a different way of thinking about social and political organization, one that takes nothing from Western philosophy, from its juridical and revolutionary foundations."[7] At one and the same time, Foucault attributed an irreducible otherness to the Iranian Revolution, while discerning in it the promise of a redemptive future for the West; the possibility, that is, of a new political spirituality that would save the West from its own intellectual exhaustion.[8] In this respect, Foucault's celebration of political Islam bears a striking resemblance to the philosophical tradition of revolutionary conservatism which, from Georges Sorel to Martin Heidegger, calls for a complete revolution of progressive modernism, only in order to retrieve absolute law from the depths of historical time. Reading the prophetic, futural philosophy of the later Heidegger back into the Shi'ite eschatology of the twelfth Imam, Foucault describes the political ideal of divine law as a kind of groundless ground, "something very old and also very far into the future," a "light that is capable of illuminating the law from the inside."[9]

Paraphrasing Sorel, he refers to the uprising as "a generalized political strike" and repeating a locus classicus of totalitarian political philosophies, he endows the revolutionary movement with a "collective will," undivided by the contradictions of class, ethnicity, or gender.[10] In these, the most "revolutionary" of his texts, Foucault abandons his signature historiographical method in favor of an eschatological history which closely mimics the rhetoric of the revolution itself.

Foucault was convinced that something quite extraordinary was at stake here. The revolutionary movement in Iran, he contended, paved a way for a new form of politics, one which escaped the limitations of the two most salient models of revolution in modern European history—on the one hand, the liberal revolution which had introduced parliamentary democracy, citizenship, and "the monstrosity of the state," and on the other, Marxist revolution, with its vanguardist notions of political mobilization and its tendency to reduce all conflict to class struggle (DBP, 185). It was clear to Foucault that the Iranian Revolution confounded Leninist models of political organization. "What is happening in Iran is enough to worry today's observers. In it they recognize not China, not Cuba, and not Vietnam, but rather a tidal wave without a military leadership, without a vanguard, without a party."[11] But neither did the revolution aim to liberate desire from the repressive institutions of the state, in the manner of the 1968 movement in France. Foucault was quite explicit that the Iranian Revolution was not anti-normative, much less anti-legislative. Indeed, he insisted that this was "first and foremost . . . a movement that aim[ed] to give a permanent role in political life to the traditional structures of Islamic society."[12] Foucault recognized that the Islamist wing of the Iranian Revolution was animated by an eschatological vision of historical time, that of Twelver Shi'ism, which aimed to reinstate a political theology of divine law:

> As for Shi'ite doctrine, there is the principle that truth was not completed and sealed by the last prophet. After Muhammad, another cycle of revelation begins, the unfinished cycle of the imams, who, through their words, their example, as well as their martyrdom, carry a light, always the same and always changing. It is this light that is capable of illuminating the law from the inside.[13]

Foucault, however, was convinced that the spirituality embodied in the Iranian Revolution was not comparable to the political theology of the state—that form of modern sovereignty which Carl Schmitt had theorized in the 1930s and which the National Socialist revolution had brought into power. While undoubtedly conservative (and radically so) in its desire to retrieve absolute, divine law, Foucault contended that the Islamist movement in Iran was fundamentally uninterested in occupying the institutions of the state. The Shi'ite religion, he insisted, had always played and continued to play an oppositional role in relation to state bureaucracy. "Persia," he wrote, "has had a surprising destiny. At the dawn of history, it invented the state and government. It conferred its models of state and government on Islam, and its administrators staffed the Arab Empire. But from this same Islam, it derived a religion that, throughout the centuries, never ceased to give an irreducible strength to everything from the depths of a people that can oppose state power."[14] But in what constitutional form was the political theology of the Iranian Revolution to be realized, then? And how would the "invisible law" of Shi'ite eschatology manifest itself in practice?

It is true that in the decade preceding the revolution, the clerical establishment came into direct conflict with the Pahlavi regime on the question of law and its source of authority—divine or secular. After a period of close political alliance during the 1950s, the clerics turned against the regime when it instituted a series of law reforms which threatened both the economic and spiritual power of divine law. Importantly this conflict turned on the question of sexual politics and the law of the household. In 1963, the shah ceded to pressure from the U.S. Democrats to introduce a series of modernizing reforms into the Iranian constitution. What was known as the White Revolution included both agrarian reforms, which threatened to undermine the economic basis of clerical power, and women's suffrage, a move that could only be symbolic in the radically undemocratic context of the Pahlavi regime. More alarmingly, from the point of view of the clerics, was the patronage accorded by the Pahlavi regime to the Women's Organization of Iran, an association that supported both women's education and antiviolence projects. In 1967, the Ministry of Justice, under advice from the Women's Organization of Iran, introduced a Family Protection Law (revised in 1975), which overturned some of the more egregious sexual inequalities of sharia law and asserted the power of civil courts over and above the power of the clerics. The reforms were limited in scope, although nevertheless in direct conflict with Islamic law—they granted women the right to initiate divorce, limited men's rights to unilateral divorce, restricted but did not abolish the right to polygamy, and raised the age of consent for women to eighteen and men to twenty. In the eyes of the radical clerics, however, the reforms were an intolerable affront, provoking a tirade of antistate invective. From exile, Khomeini declared the reforms null and void, warning that any woman who divorced under civil law and remarried would be considered an adulterer and punished accordingly.[15] The Pahlavi regime ceased to be an ally from the moment it usurped the authority of divine law, undermining both the economic power of the clerical establishment and the power of men within the household.

The clerical response to the White Revolution and the Family Protection Law profoundly reshuffled the status quo of political alliance within Iran.[16] It brought to an end the dominance of the secular National Front, propelling the more religious Iran Liberation Movement to the forefront of the opposition and endowing the exiled Khomeini with an unprecedented authority among both secular and clerical political dissidents. Now that the clerics were no longer aligned with the Pahlavi regime, Khomeini fashioned a new political rhetoric which brought together the thematics of anti-imperialism and anti-capitalism with a concern for sexual morality. The civil reform of family law, which after all had been almost exclusively associated with the Pahlavi regime, could be indicted as an example of cultural imperialism, a liberation of women from the domestic sphere which would only lead to their commodification as sexual objects. At this point, the opposition between leftist and clerical movements began to break down. Finding a point of consensus on the issue of sexual politics, Islamist radicals such as Khomeini and Ayatollah Morteza Motahhari momentarily joined forces with Islamist leftists such as Ali Shariati in denouncing what they saw as the forcible liberation of women from divine law.

It is true then that the Iranian Islamists opposed the sovereignty of the state. Yet they opposed it only to the extent that it failed to defer to the higher sovereignty of the clerics. Well before the revolution, Khomeini had devised a specific blueprint for the reform of government, the *velayat i-faqi* (government of the doctor of law), which would combine the democratic elements of universal suffrage and referenda with a submission of all levels of elected government to supreme clerical rule. With its well-organized, hierarchical clergy, such a combination of theocracy and republicanism is a possibility unique to Shi'ite Islam, making the question of Islamic government much easier to resolve in practice than in Sunni-dominated contexts.[17] When the Islamic Republic was ratified by referendum in March 1979, it was precisely this vision of constitutional reform under clerical rule that was implemented. The Islamic Republic does not dispense with the methods of constitutional democracy, since it allows for the election of the president of the Republic and the representatives of the National Council by universal suffrage, and yet it places the supreme religious authority over and above these functionaries of the state, in a position of absolute sovereignty. Invested with the interpretative authority to represent the Hidden Imam, the clerical scholars hold the ultimate power of decision in government, since only they can determine whether the enactment of secular legislation is in accordance with divine law. Foucault notwithstanding, then, the Islamic Republic does not abolish the apparatus of the state but rather retains it at the service of a higher order—that of divine law. And if Islamic government cannot be described as normative, as Foucault contends, it is only in the sense that it goes well beyond the modern welfare state in its desire to oversee the intimacies of everyday life—that is, the practices of the self which unfold in the ostensibly "private" space of the household. In this respect, we could argue, using Foucault's own taxonomy of power, that constitutional theocracy replaces the relative, expansive, and inclusive logics of the norm with the absolute decisionism of divine law—and applies this legalism to the space of the household. The ambition of political Islam is not so much to regulate or normalize, as to *legislate* sexuality by reestablishing a direct line of contact between the authority of divine law and the intimate ethics of the self. It is this, according to Khomeini, that constitutes the essential difference between a secular and divine political order:

> Secular governments . . . are only concerned with the social order. What he wants to do in the privacy of his home, drinking wine, . . . gambling, or other such dirty deeds, the government has nothing to do with him. Only if he comes out screaming, then he would be prosecuted, because that disturbs the peace. Islam and divine governments are not like that. These [governments] have commandments for everybody, everywhere, at any place, in any condition.

If a person were to commit an immoral dirty deed right next to his house, Islamic governments have business with him.[18]

Was Foucault's perspective on Islamic government naive or simply ambivalent? Foucault seems to have remained consistently indifferent to the political implications of Islamic law for Iranian women. Apart from a brief passage praising the female militants who chose to don the chador as an expression of anti-imperialism, he manages only the most dismissive of references to the "subjugation of women, and so on" in his final text on Iran (UR, 265). Foucault's response to Atoussa H., an Iranian woman who critiqued the complacency of French leftists in a letter to *Le nouvel observateur*, was outright hostile.[19] At the same time, however, Foucault seems to have genuinely believed that the "traditional structures" of Islam opened up a space for homoerotic relations among men, unencumbered by the normative categories of the European social sciences. Janet Afary and Kevin Anderson recount an episode in which Foucault recoiled in shock at the assertion, by an Islamic female militant, that homosexuals would be condemned to death under the provisions of Islamic law.[20] Yet Foucault remained silent when the first male homosexuals were executed, along with female prostitutes and adulterers, after the ratification of the Islamic Republic. Distancing himself from the postrevolutionary government, Foucault would never abandon the religio-sexual utopia of male homosocial asceticism and female piousness which he had discerned in the revolutionary moment itself. Instead, he would continue to explore this utopia, through displacement, in his final monographs on the ethics of sexual life in classical Greece, Rome, and early Christianity. Far from renouncing the positions he had enunciated in his newspaper reports on the Iranian Revolution, Foucault's work subsequent to his visit to Iran and his lectures on neoliberalism would pursue and deepen them. In the meantime, however, his intuitions into the question of political spirituality were now filtered through a second problematic, that of the changing nature of power in the "West." Between his visits to Iran and his late studies of the care of the self, Foucault had delivered his 1979 lecture series on the doctrine of economic neoliberalism. Here he had encountered a formation of power that was emphatically not normalizing, a power that infiltrated social and sexual relations of all kinds, beyond the purview of the state, and a power that brought the liquefying force of the transaction into the intimate space of the "household."

The Chicago School and the New Household Economics

Between January and April 1979, Foucault delivered his annual Collège de France lectures on the topic of the new economic liberalism in Europe (German Ordoliberalism) and the United States (Chicago School neoliberalism).[21] Perhaps most surprising in Foucault's account of North American neoliberalism is the fact that he focuses on the work of the lesser-known Chicago School economist Gary Becker—going so far as to name him "the most radical of the American neoliberals" (*BB*, 269)—rather than that of his more renowned colleagues, such as Milton Friedman or George Stigler. In terms of economic methodology, Becker's arsenal of concepts would appear to be standard, with its assumptions of rational choice, maximizing behavior, and market equilibrium. Unlike the more famous of the Chicago School neoliberals, however, who directed their attention to the macroeconomic questions of inflation and monetary policy, Becker consistently and self-consciously focused his attention on the "social issues" of sex, race, migration, demographics, crime, education, and health.[22] Alone among the Chicago School economists, and unorthodox by the general standards of the discipline, Becker was interested in precisely those domains of social power which Foucault had studied through the lens of "normalization." And yet as Foucault would implicitly acknowledge, Becker was already "beyond" Foucault's analytics of "normalization" in that his theory of human capital attempted to account for, and intervene in, a field of power relations which no longer recognized the categories of the norm.

Whereas Foucault (and others) persistently describe Becker as the major theorist of human capital, a concept that has undoubtedly had a profound effect on social policy, Becker himself refers to his work as the "new household economics." In his own terms, Becker's numerous interventions into the field of social economics were prompted by what he saw as the most significant shift in economic affairs to have taken place in the late twentieth century—that is, the profound crisis in "household" relations which took place in the late 1960s and 1970s as a consequence of the massive return of middle-class women to the workforce, the decline in average family size, and the relative desegregation of social space brought about by the civil rights movement. The Fordist/Keynesian welfare state had not only established a strict sexual division of labor between the masculine sphere of formal labor and the feminine sphere of reproductive, unpaid care (to be supported through the family wage), it also relied, in the United States, on an implicit exclusion of African Americans from the normative household itself. It was the implosion of this whole architecture that Becker sought to theorize in his numerous studies on the economics of everyday life. In a collection of essays published in 1981, Becker noted that the "family in the Western world has been radically altered, some claim almost destroyed, by events of the last three decades."[23] Within Becker's account, the sociological irrelevance of notions such as deviance (the redundancy of the very category of norm) could only be understood as a consequence of the mass exit from the Fordist/Keynesian household.

Foucault both acknowledges and underestimates the centrality of the "household" to the neoliberal analysis of human capital. In the lecture of March 21, 1979, for example, he notes that the neoliberals seek to analyze "what takes place within a household" and cites at length the work of the Canadian economist Jean-Luc Migué:

> One of the great recent contributions of economic analysis has been the full application to the domestic sector of the analytical framework traditionally reserved for the firm and the consumer. By making the household a unit of production in the same way as the classical firm, we discover that its analytical foundations are actually identical to those of the firm. . . . What in fact is the household if not the contractual commitment of two parties to supply specific inputs and to share in given proportions the benefits of the household output? (*BB*, 245)[24]

Becker's specific contribution to the problematic was to suggest that the long-term marriage contract should be replaced by a series of short-term commercial contracts, in order to reflect the increasingly contingent and flexible nature of "household" relations. For Becker then, the implosion of the Fordist sexual division of labor led not only to the conclusion that the household was to be managed like an enterprise, but also that the kind of transactions previously concealed within the walls of the domestic sphere were spilling out into the realm of economic transaction per se. "What is the house, if not an enterprise?" Foucault remarks (*BB*, 148). In response to the increasing participation of married women in the actual labor force, Becker suggested the application of a transactional calculus of "services" to all intimate relations—sexual, affective, and educational. The consequence of this maneuver, as Foucault noted, was a breakdown of the division between consumption and production, indeed a rethinking of the category of "labor" itself, in terms that now incorporated all that had been relegated to the domestic sphere of reproductive (unproductive) labor—sex, care, emotion itself. Paraphrasing Becker, Foucault writes, "The man of consumption, insofar as he consumes, is a producer. What does he produce? Well, quite simply, he produces his own satisfaction" (*BB*, 229). The integration of the consumer into the production of his own pleasure, Foucault observed, rendered obsolete the Frankfurt School theme of mass consumption. In Becker's new household economics, emotion itself, that "unproductive expenditure" of theories of consumption, demanded to be counted as a productive factor in the accumulation of value. "Time spent," "care given," "affection" itself needed to be considered as investments in human capital (*BB*, 229).

Becker's "new household economics" emerges in the immediate aftermath of the social movements of the 1960s and 1970s. It responds precisely to those social movements that had taken aim at the normalizing power of the welfare state in the administration of everyday life (feminism, anti-racism, gay liberation, anti-psychiatry). Where the new left movements had decried the paternalism of the welfare state and sought to undo the effects of normalization on the very sense of self, neoliberalism responds with the imperative to self-differentiation. And where these movements had experimented with forms of self-organized living in excess of the state, neoliberalism offers the logic of self-management. The "new household economics" replaces the social contract of Fordism, in which the state plays the role of implicit third party to all transactions, with an economy of short-term contractual relations, in which everyone becomes an independent contractor in personal services. In Becker's work, "homo oeconomicus is an entrepreneur, an entrepreneur of himself," charged with both the care and valorization of "services in the self" (*BB*, 226). Whatever the ambivalence of its effects, Foucault recognized that this was a formation of power that no longer worked through the dissemination of norms or the pathologization of difference. In Becker's work, deviations from the norm appear instead as an expanding horizon of market opportunities to be included, as far as possible, within the terms of contract:

> What appears on the horizon of this kind of analysis is not at all the ideal or project of an exhaustively disciplinary society in which the legal network hemming in individuals is taken over and extended internally by, let's say, normative mechanisms. Nor is it a society in which a mechanism of general normalization and the exclusion of those who cannot be normalized is needed. On the horizon of this analysis we see instead the image, idea, or theme-program of a society in which there is an optimization of systems of difference, in which the field is left open to fluctuating processes, in which minority individuals and practices are tolerated, in which action is brought to bear on the rules of the game rather than on the players, and finally in which there is an environmental type of intervention instead of the internal subjugation of individuals.
> (BB, 259–60)

Foucault's lectures of 1978–19 can be read as auto-critique—their inescapable, if implicit, conclusion is that the analytics of power pursued by Foucault up until that point was in danger of becoming obsolete. The neoliberal formation of power demanded a renewal of critique, but in what form? What I am suggesting here is that Foucault's final philosophy takes refuge in an ethics of askesis (or non-excessive pleasure) articulated around the notion of *oikonomia*. In response to Becker's iconoclastic philosophy of household transactions, Foucault turns to the premodern tradition of Western philosophy to retrieve a deeply nostalgic ethics of the noble, patriarchal household, one which maintains a strict order of hierarchical relations between husband and wife, free citizens and slaves, and one which subordinates the destabilizing effects of trade or chrematistics to the foundational economy of the household—or *oikonomia*. Here the neoliberal imperative of self-enterprise will be countered by an intimate management of the self, which revives sovereignty while separating it from the power of the state. It is precisely this moral economy of the household that Foucault deciphers in the sexual politics of the Iranian Revolution.[25]

Interestingly, Becker (whose wife, the Iranian scholar Guity Nashat, had written on the question of sexual politics in Iran) was consistently interested in the difference between "Western" and "Islamic" views on the household. In his *Treatise on the Family*, he would cite the work of Syed Abul A'la Maududi, the Sunni Islamist and founder of twentieth-century Islamic economics, as witness to the patriarchal law of the household which he presumed to reign in Muslim societies.[26] In many respects, however, Becker's description of the "new household economics" could just as easily have applied to the Iranian context in the 1950s and 1960s, when far-reaching changes to the labor market were eroding the boundaries between women's "emotional labor" in the home and the transactional performance of feminized emotion in the service sector. It is a peculiarity of the modernization process in Iran that the service sector, employing mostly women, grew much faster than the male-dominated agricultural and industrial sectors.[27] During the last two decades of the Pahlavi regime, foreign direct investment in Iran soared, and an unprecedented number of women left the household for paid labor in the service sector, working in positions as diverse as those of secretary, hotel clerk, cinema attendant, waitress, bank clerk teacher, and prostitute. Foreign interests favored capital- not labor-intensive investment in the Iranian primary and secondary sectors, with the result that women's relative rates of employment (in services) increased at the same time that men's employment in agriculture and manufacturing declined. It was this disruption of sexual and economic relations (the two indissolubly intertwined) that the various factions of the Iranian Revolution singled out as the most egregious symptom of colonial dependence. In the face of these changes, conservative clerics, lay Islamists of the left, and Marxists momentarily overcame their differences to denounce the insidious cultural imperialism of the West, the rise of sexual immorality, and the commodification of women at the hands of Western media. Performing a conceptual slippage that is symptomatic of the moralist response to capitalism, these discourses conflated women's labor outside the home with the commodification of woman herself, all forms of female labor being equated, in the last instance, with prostitution.[28] The equation between cultural imperialism, sexual decadence, and women's mass employment in service labor was the one point of consensus between the Islamists and the Marxists.[29] It is no accident then that in the final months of the revolution, cinemas showing foreign films were smashed, the red light district of Tehran laid to waste and prostitutes assaulted.[30] These mob actions were validated by the incoming regime when, in its first months in power, it proceeded to execute convicted prostitutes, adulterers, and gay men.

In many respects, then, the linearity of conventional histories of neoliberalism is thrown into question by the process of Iranian modernization, which as early as the 1950s and 1960s favored the service sector over mass manufacture, the transaction of feminized "pleasure" over the mobilization of the industrialized male worker. Without being informed by the precepts of the Chicago School of neoliberalism, the rise of the feminized service sector under the Pahlavi regime corresponds closely to Becker's account of the "new household economics" as it emerged, a decade or so later, in the United States. In this respect, the Iranian Revolution can be read as a reactionary response to precisely the kinds of sexual–economic shifts that are only now being theorized, under the rubric of emotional labor, in "Western" contexts. In his close adherence to the rhetoric of political Islam, Foucault's late philosophy must also be understood as a compressed response to what he saw as the emerging sexual economy of neoliberalism. Moving beyond the analytics of the norm, then, Foucault will have anticipated some of the most far-reaching changes to the everyday life of power, pleasure, and formations of the self in the late twentieth and early twenty-first centuries. In his turn to a moral economy of pleasure, however, Foucault also preempted the novel forms of reaction which accompany and shape the "new household economics" of neoliberalism.

Foucault's Oikonomia: Sovereignty in the Household

Foucault never reneged on the insights he had developed in the context of the Iranian Revolution but rather returned to investigate them, by displacement, in his two last monographs on the sexual ethics of Hellenistic Greece and early Christianity. It is in the sexual ethics of fourth-century classical Greece (explored in *The Use of Pleasure*) that Foucault discovers an alternative economy of bodily pleasures, one which carefully moderates the sexual act while escaping the absolute prohibitions characteristic of the early Christian era. In Greek antiquity, Foucault suggests, sexual relations are not codified around sexual difference in the manner of Christian morality. Relations between a free man and a younger male lover are perfectly licit, indeed privileged, since they take place in a domain of extra-familial sexual practice, outside the constraints of heterosexual lineage, without in any way disrupting the order of household lineage itself. This is an economy of extra-genealogical pleasure, Foucault readily admits, which is restricted to a very small class of free, noble, male citizens—as such it constitutes a space of *restrained luxury* or *austere excess* which escapes but does not threaten the proper order of genealogical relations between the sexes: "In classical thought... the demands of austerity were not organized into a unified, coherent, authoritarian moral system that was imposed on everyone in the same manner; they were more in the nature of a supplement, a 'luxury' in relation to the commonly accepted morality" (*UP*, 21). This is an economy, moreover, which is reserved for the noble head of a household or *oikos* (the *kyrios*), who must perfect the art of self-managed freedom in order to prove his ability to govern his wealth, his wife, children, and servants:

> The same apprenticeship ought to make a man both capable of virtue and capable of exercising power. Governing oneself, managing one's household, and participating in the administration of the city were three practices of the same type. Xenophon's *Oeconomicus* shows the continuity and isomorphism between these three "arts." (*UP*, 75)[31]

The Greek word *oikonomia* (οἰκονομία) can be translated as the law of the *oikos* (οἶκος) or household: it is indifferent to the modern distinction between political, sexual, and economic relations, incorporating all these domains into the one art of household administration.

It is widely recognized that the *oikos*, or large household estate, played a foundational role in the classical Greek polis. The *oikos* was by definition a noble household, comprising the members of the family, slaves, animals, the house, land, and all that was cultivated and produced on it. As Marx noted in the first book of *Capital*, classical Greek political theory did not register the concept of "free labor" as the source of wealth for the simple reason that the use value of the slave was immediately comprised within the property of the household and was therefore deemed to belong to it, by bondage, not by contract. The *oikos* differed from the modern institution of the private family in that it functioned immediately as an economic institution—that is, as a source of independent wealth—whose success was integral to the continued survival of the state. As Sarah Pomeroy explains,

"The earliest written evidence from the Greek world indicates that *oikoi*, both royal and common, were the basis of the Greek economy: they were the most common units of production and consumption. The polis was a community of oikoi rather than of individual citizens."[32] The polis, which collected few taxes, depended on these large agrarian households to donate a portion of their wealth, in the form of "liturgies," to finance almost all public expenditures, including military campaigns. In the sense that the wealth of the large households constituted the financial foundation of the state itself, the *oikos* was considered to be an institution of direct political and economic importance. For this very reason, however, classical political philosophy also drew a sharp dividing line between legitimate and illegitimate modes of wealth creation within the household, characteristically figuring the distinction in terms of natural limits to the conduct of sexual and economic exchange. If relations between free men and their slaves of whatever sex could be tolerated, sexual relationships between free women and men outside the household were rigorously prohibited as a threat to the very foundation of the state.

It is Aristotle who provides the classic formulation of this philosophy when he distinguishes between a legitimate mode of exchange, which is defined by and limited to the finite needs of the household and another, illegitimate practice of commerce, in which money becomes both means and ends of exchange, reproducing itself without limit through the accumulation of interest. Where the first mode of exchange (chrematistics) comprises all forms of wealth that are generated within the household through the usufruct of land, crops, and the unpaid labor of slaves, the second (chrematistics as an end in itself or chrematistics proper) derives from salaried labor, foreign trade, and lending at interest or usury. In both cases, Aristotle contends, the art of exchange can be explained in terms of a preoccupation with life. But whereas the art of household management is wholly contained within the ends of the good life, whose satisfaction is not limitless, the practice of usury is inseparable from a life of excess—the production of sensation outside the discriminating mean of proportion. More precisely, the distinction hinges on the difference between two ways of getting pleasure. The good life, as Aristotle defines it, is one in which the pursuit of sensation is contained within the needs of the domestic sphere and where pleasure is regulated by the end to which it is assigned by nature—the free man's ability to master his sexual urges authorizing his sovereignty over the household. The art of acquisition, on the other hand, evokes the dangers of a pleasure escaping the ends of the household economy, a pursuit of pleasure that becomes an end unto itself and therefore without limit—self-accumulating. Following the premise that all vice lies in excess or default, Aristotle draws a direct analogy between the excessive pursuit of pleasure and that other form of reprehensible accumulation—the production of interest from exchange:

> The cause of this disposition is preoccupation with life but not with the good life; so, desire for the former being unlimited, they also desire productive things without limit. Those who do actually aim at the good life seek what brings the pleasures of the body; so, as this too appears to lie in property, their whole activity centres on getting goods; and the second type of skill in acquiring goods has come about because of this. For since their pleasure is in excess, men look for the art which produces the excess that brings the pleasure. And if they cannot procure it by means of the skill of acquiring goods, they attempt to do so by means of something else that causes it, using each of their faculties in a manner contrary to nature.[33]

Aristotle, it must be stressed, is not so much averse to surplus, as opposed to a surplus which arises solely from the act of exchange, a surplus, that is, which is not produced within the limits of the noble household. The polis, after all, is dependent on the periodic donation of surplus wealth from the large household estates in the form of liturgies. These acts of unproductive expenditure are not only permissible, they also serve to confirm the nobility of the donor. Indeed, to be a free citizen is to prove one's ability to give without return—beneficence, then, as distinct from excess, represents a legitimate form of surplus expenditure. The free man is, at one and the same time, restrained and beneficent, self-controlled and generous, in his ability to give.

Implied here is an ethics which, in Foucault's terms, is more interested in the moderation of expenditure than the codification of objects. According to Aristotle's economy of household transactions, sexual immorality resides not so much in the nature of the act as in its quantity or proportion—excessive or temperate:

> This idea that immorality in the pleasures of sex is always connected with exaggeration, surplus, and excess is found . . . in the third book of the *Nicomachean Ethics*: Aristotle explains that for the natural desires that are

common to everyone, the only offenses that one can commit are quantitative in nature: they pertain to "the more" (*to pleion*) . . . It appears, then, that the primary dividing line laid down by moral judgment in the area of sexual behavior was not prescribed by the nature of the act, with its possible variations, but by the activity and its quantitative variations. (*UP*, 45)

The classical Greek ethics of pleasure does not limit the legitimate sexual act to the heterosexual married couple but rather draws the ethical boundaries within the sexual act itself, whether heterosexual or homosexual, distinguishing sharply between male and female positions as distinct from male and female bodies. It is assumed, in classical Greek ethics, that the free man can only ever be the active partner in sex. The free man is he who "gives," never he who "receives." His ability to control and guide his partner is confirmed through his ability to master himself—that is, to exercise restraint, limitation, and self-control over his impulses and appetites. To lose control, within this schema, would be to risk unsettling the proper divisions between passive and active partner in the sexual act, and thus to forsake the very privilege of freedom. As Foucault points out, classical Greek ethics does indeed recognize a certain lawfulness (*nomos*) to pleasure (*UP*, 31). At stake here, however, is something very different from the tight imbrication of desire, law, and prohibition which emerges in the early Christian ethics of heterosexual love. The classical Greeks do not recognize the problematic of guilt and redemption which shapes the Christian morality of desire, nor do they pin the lawfulness of desire on sexual difference—the relationship of a man to a woman. Instead, the sovereignty of desire is cultivated and maintained through the relationship of free man to himself, and free men among one another. In Foucault's terms, the sexual ethics of classical Greece works through a process of "problematization," in which the sexual act functions as a test of one's ability to temper, control, and master the self in the name of greater freedom; an ascetic proof of masculine virtue rather than a submission to external law: "Interdiction is one thing, moral problematization is another" (*UP*, 10).[34] In the classical Greek economy of pleasure, moral law is not a prohibition imposed from the outside, by the state or some other political authority, but the intimate law (*nomos*) that is imposed on the self by the free citizen, as sign and confirmation of his fitness to govern others. For the household master, freedom itself is confirmed through the act of self-sovereignty.[35]

It is worth repeating at this point that Foucault's ethics of the self is concerned exclusively with an *ars erotica* developed for free men. This much Foucault concedes when he writes:

> Women were generally subjected (excepting the liberty they could be granted by a status like that of courtesan) to extremely strict constraints, and yet this ethics was not addressed to women . . . It was an ethics for men: an ethics thought, written, and taught by men, and addressed to men—to free men, obviously. (*UP*, 22)

What Foucault fails to acknowledge (or rather what he assumes and dismisses as peripheral to his analysis) is that the liberation of a space of ethical problematization for and among free men was only possible on the basis of an absolute prohibition imposed on women. This prohibition was if anything more rigorous with regard to free married women and their daughters since the very transmission of the family name depended on their faithfulness and virginity. Free marriageable women, notes the classical scholar Wolfgang Detel, were strictly sequestered within the walls of the *oikos*. He explains:

> It is only against the background of the enormous economic and social weight of the *oikos* within the ancient polis that the fundamental significance of marriage between male and female full citizens, and the legitimacy of their children, can be fully appreciated. A functioning marriage was indeed an important prerequisite for the *oikos*' property and in most cases this functionality was guaranteed by the merciless legal, cultural and sexual oppression of the wife. Girls, young women and wives were kept in almost total seclusion in their houses . . . the legitimacy of children had to be free of all doubt. What is more . . . women had no political rights whatsoever and enjoyed only an elementary education.[36]

The question of female pleasure, as Foucault concedes, does not belong within the classical Greek understanding of *eros*. It belongs rather (and this Foucault notes only in passing) to the question of familial property, inheritance, and the transmission of name—all matters which are rigorously enforced by the polis in the register of pure prohibition.[37] It is interesting then that when Foucault reflects in passing on the form that female virtue would take in a contemporary ethics of pleasure modeled on the classical Greek, he comes up with the notion of "virginity." The laws of marriage, for women, "take the form not of a voluntary ethics, but of a coercive regimentation" since it is women's virginity which underwrites genealogical law itself, that is, "lineage and the necessity of a bastardless race that can claim the distinction of a noble birth and the continuity of a genealogy that can be traced all the way back to the gods" (*UP*, 167, 171). It is a mistake then to presume that Foucault's sexual ethics implies a radical interrogation of the logic of genealogy and descent. Instead, his ethics returns to a classical Greek conception of noble beneficence and restrained luxury to open up a space of limited excess among aristocratic men, while insisting on the absolute submission of women to the intimate law of the household.

Although idiosyncratic in the context of his previous oeuvre, Foucault's interest in the ethics of the classical Greek household is by no means unique in modern political theory. As noted by the literary theorist Vincent Pecora, the return to the noble household as the site of virtuous exchange is a recurrent theme among political theorists in the aftermath of the French Revolution. In the work of Nietzsche, the utopian socialists, and twentieth-century anthropologists such as Marcel Mauss, the noncommercial use values of the classical *oikos* are held up as a model of both aristocratic virtue and magnanimous gift exchange over and against the equalizing effects of commodity exchange. It is in the highly patriarchal economy of the noble household, founded on the hidden labor of slaves and the sequestration of free women, that these theorists find a counterpoint and utopian alternative to the homogenizing, anti-aristocratic and anti-agrarian tendencies of modern societies of exchange. This utopia, notes Pecora, is more often than not projected onto the other culture, the culture that is deemed to have remained closer to the conditions of the ancient world:

> A certain stream of romantic anthropology in the nineteenth and twentieth centuries would . . . look to savage or primitive societies in an attempt to recover the virtues of noble mastery no longer supportable at home. On the whole, and quite apart from the racist superiority that remained a part of its heritage, this modern anthropology rediscovered Aristotle's noble mastery and noble oikos not in terms of Europe's own dominant position but rather as an element of "primitive," "archaic," or "traditional" society itself. Aristotle's proud, magnanimous man—whose honor rests on his power to give, his distance from the market, his freedom from need or servile labor, his attachment to an aesthetic (symbolic) rather than utilitarian mode of activity, his capacity

for great expenditure, in short, his position in a network of noble, rather than necessary, exchanges—is recovered by a variety of anthropological and sociological discourses as the basis of primitive or archaic modes of exchange.[38]

After eschewing the mystifications of state sovereignty, Foucault, in his final work, will both rediscover and reassert the ethical necessity of sovereignty, in the form of an intimate law of the household. In this respect, his conception of a new ethics of pleasure and a new law of transaction was perfectly attuned to the thinking of those Shi'ite scholars who sought to reanchor the modern science of economics in a renewed theology of the household. For these scholars, too, the modern science of economics was marked by an utter indifference to the sovereign form of power. What they sought to fashion through the very means of the Iranian Revolution was a "monotheistic economics" which would restore sovereignty not to the state but to the individual master of the household. The project of a divine economy was to replace the purely modern concept of economy, in which transaction is freed from all absolute foundation in law, with the classical sense of *oikonomia* (literally the law of the household).

Sovereignty in the Household: The Dream of a Monotheistic Economics in Revolutionary Iran

The field of Islamic economics is a twentieth-century phenomenon which encompasses both Sunni and Shi'ite variants, and bridges both utopian–socialist and free-market philosophies of wealth. Despite this heterogeneity, almost all currents within Islamic economics are marked by an anti-imperialist ethic, the Islamization of the economy being conceived as an intervention against foreign influence, in and of itself. And all currents respect, in one form or another, the various Quranic injunctions surrounding illegitimate economic transactions: the prohibition of usury (*riba*), the exclusion of contracts involving chance (*gharar*), and the imperative to participate in *zakat*, religious taxes that are intended for redistribution among the poor.

Shi'ite interpretations of Islamic economics are particularly indebted to the work of the Iraqi cleric Muhammad Baqir al-Sadr (executed by Saddam

Hussein in 1980) and the Iranian Abol Hasan Bani-Sadr, a European-educated economist whom Foucault met twice in Paris before his first trip to Iran.[39] The version of Islamic economics developed in Iran in the lead-up to the revolution differs from its counterparts in Pakistan and Saudi Arabia in that it espouses a populist ethics of state welfare. Even in the work of Bani-Sadr, first appointed deputy minister of finance (1979) then president of the Islamic Republic (1980) in the wake of the revolution, the dream of a "monotheistic economics" guided by divine law is colored by the themes of social redistribution, the abolition of class, and the return to productive labor as the source of all value. For Bani-Sadr, the rise of a world imperialism under the control of the United States had reduced resource-rich countries such as Iran to the status of parasitic rentier economies. Duped by the needs of the world's superpowers, the Iranian state had spent all its energies in the extraction of oil, reinvesting the profits in the maintenance of an oligarchy of rentiers, a bloated security state, and a frivolous service sector, to the detriment of the "real" industrial economy. In order to free itself from this dependence, Iran would need to abolish all foreign investment, reduce oil revenues, and reinvest in the productive industrial sector. Only then could the "positive equilibrium" of a society without class be established. Combining Quranic injunctions against unproductive interest (usury) with Marx's labor theory of value, Bani-Sadr demands that the excessive consumerism of Iran's foreign-dominated, service-led economy be replaced by the virtuous self-sufficiency of domestic, industrial production. In order to achieve the ideal of a "monotheistic economics," one is required "to produce according to one's capacities, to consume according to virtue [*taqwa*]."[40] Like other exponents of an Islamic economics, Bani Sadr understands this imperative in immediately sexual terms. The abolition of foreign investment signifies a return to the productive pursuit of pleasure within the confines of the domestic economy. For it is, above all, women's service labor outside the home, indicted by Bani-Sadr as a form of sexual transaction in and of itself, which fuels Iran's economy of luxury expenditure and unproductive consumption:

> The industrialist says "If we confine production to actual consumption and to actual human needs, it will not be long before the surplus of capital produces a crisis . . ." He considers which human instinct will never be satisfied. Sex . . . using sex you can force an addict to consume a product.[41]

While Iran invests its surplus petrodollars in the U.S. economy, the West floods the domestic markets of the world's dependent economies with a glut of commodified pleasures, transactional sex, and images of women. In this way, explains Bani-Sadr, it is not only the natural resources of the earth (oil) but the future reproductive body of the Iranian nation—the Iranian woman herself—whose pleasures are consumed without return in the rentier economy of pure expenditure. In the work of Bani-Sadr, as in the commentaries of Khomeini and Ayatollah Morteza Motahhari, the changes in gender relations brought about by the White Revolution, the Family Law Reform, and the rise of the service sector, are assumed to lead directly to the commodification of women. Women cannot escape from the law of the household, cannot in fact enter public space, without upsetting the virtuous household economy of limited exchange and properly (re)productive pleasure. Only the reimposition of divine law at the level of the household can reintroduce the just measure into the production of wealth and the consumption of pleasure.

The remarkable homology between modern Islamic conceptions of the economy (with their prohibition on usury, speculation, and excess pleasure) and Aristotelian–scholastic philosophy is no matter of chance. The scholastics, who transposed Aristotelian philosophy into the terms of medieval Christianity, were indebted to the translations and interpretations of classical Greek and Hellenistic literature carried out by twelfth-century Islamic scholars. The work of the Andalusian philosopher Ibn Rushd (Averroès, 1126–98), who wrote a commentary on the *Nicomachean Ethics*, was particularly important in shaping Thomist ideas around the *oikonomia* as the foundation of virtuous exchange. Following Aristotle, the medieval Islamic literature conceived of the management of political life (*tadbir al-madina*) on the model of the household economy (*tadbir al-manzil*), in which the transaction of money and pleasure is to be kept within the strict limits of the just mean.[42] As Louis Baeck notes:

> Individual (*krematistike*) as well as family (*oikos*) accumulation were subordinated to the solidarity of the social fabric. From this point of view, the economy was a political economy, subject to the norms of the ethic of the just mean. It was oikos–nomos.... Islam has borrowed this tradition of ancient thought, which arose out of a view of society that was both organicist and teleological. But Islam enriched the Greek ethic of natural order with the transcendental prescriptions of the Koran.[43]

When medieval Islamic philosophers reinterpreted the *oikonomia* of ancient Greek philosophy, they infused the concept of *nomos* with that of transcendent law—an interpretative move which they then bequeathed to the Christian scholastics. It is not altogether true then—as Foucault seems to suggest—that the sexual and civic ethics of Shi'ism eschews the absolute prohibitions to be found in a Christian morality of desire. As noted again by Louis Baeck, the transcendent interpretation of *oikonomia* as an absolute law of the household subsists in Islamic economics of the twentieth century and it is this peculiarity which distinguishes it from all other contemporary economics.[44] Like the medieval interpreters of Aristotle, modern Islamic economics refuses to distinguish between the logic of economic transaction and that of sexual transaction. Instead, Islamic economics proffers divine law as that which must regulate the circulation of both money and desire. Since the household stands at the intersection of economic and sexual exchange, it is above all here that divine law must stake its claim.

That the Islamic Republic understood the homology between sexual and economic transactions in the most literal of ways is confirmed by the sequence of legal reforms in the wake of the revolution. In the summer of 1979, the Provisional Revolutionary Government prohibited foreign investment in Iran, at the same time calling for the nationalization of private banks, insurance, and manufacturing companies.[45] Article 49 of the Constitution of the Islamic Republic confiscated all illicit sources of wealth including usury, theft, gambling, and the "operation of centres of corruption." These reforms coincided with the formal revocation of the Family Protection Law, which Khomeini declared "un-Islamic." In place of the Pahlavi-era reforms, a new Islamic Civil Code was promulgated, incorporating many elements of sharia law.[46] In 1981, a law codifying the provisions of the Quran set out more than one hundred punishable acts of sexual transgression, including prostitution, female adultery, and male and female homosexuality.[47] Women's ability to move in public space was policed through the strict delineation of male and female spaces; the imposition of the chador; and a ban on all expressions of a female "sexual aesthetics" in public, including the wearing of makeup, or dancing and singing. The relationship between these various measures must be understood as one of collusion. Through the imposition of laws governing the circulation of money and women in public space, through the limitation that is of unproductive (impure) surplus, the Islamic Republic sought to restrain the economy within the moral limits of domestic consumption. This it accomplished not through the literal return of women to the household but through the minute resegregation of public space, a delineation of borders that was played out on the bodies of women.

The Economic Theology of Oikonomia: Revolutionary Conservatism in the Household

In *Security, Territory, and Population*, the Collège de France lectures of 1977–78, Foucault outlines a history of political economy, tracing the moves through which the modern science of economics, in the course of the eighteenth century, begins to distinguish itself from the political theology of household administration or *oikonomia*. Pace Agamben, Foucault insists that these philosophies of power are irreducible to one another.[48] The distinctly "economic" processes of circulation, production, and consumption identified as targets of power by the new science of political economy cannot be understood as merely "secularized" translations of the political theological concept of *oikonomia*. Two very different arts of government are at work here. Political economy refutes the practical efficacy of sovereignty as a form of power capable of intervening in, managing, and controlling the turbulent processes of circulation in modern urban life. In this respect, it marks a radical break with the early modern tradition of political theology. "Economics is an atheistic discipline," notes Foucault, "economics is a discipline without God. . . . Economics is a discipline that begins to demonstrate not only the pointlessness, but also the impossibility of a sovereign point of view" (*BB*, 282). Henceforth, it must be assumed, political theology can only ever exist in resuscitated form, as an effort to revive and relegitimate the authority of the sovereign in the midst of its decline. The "modern" tradition of political theology, which in the twentieth century is most closely associated with the name of Carl Schmitt, must be understood as an essentially counterrevolutionary philosophy. As a political intervention, it must accommodate itself to the conditions of the new. It can only ever seek to reinvent a form of power on the grounds established by the modern state (which is not to underestimate the violence of its effects).

It is in terms of this problematic of impossible sovereignty, Foucault goes on to suggest, that we should interpret the various battles between liberalism and state centralization throughout the twentieth century:

> The absence or impossibility of an economic sovereign is a problem which will ultimately be raised throughout Europe, and throughout the modern world, by governmental practices, economic problems, socialism, planning, and welfare economics. All the returns and revivals of nineteenth and twentieth century liberal and neo-liberal thought are still a way of posing the problem of the impossibility of the existence of an economic sovereign. And with the appearance of planning, the state-controlled economy, socialism, and state-socialism the problem will be whether we may not overcome in some way this curse against the economic sovereign which was formulated by political economy at its foundation and which is also the very condition of existence of political economy: In spite of everything, may there not be a point through which we can define an economic sovereignty? (*BB*, 283)

The Keynesian welfare state, then, must be understood as an attempt to reestablish some kind of centralized political power over the economic process, to reassert, that is, the knowability of the future. This it achieved not only through the imposition of national economic controls on finance and labor but also through the intensive administration of "social reproduction"—the realm of sex, education, and health which Foucault studied under the rubric of the norm. The revival of neoliberal thought is associated with the return of the idea that the economic future is, in fact, unknowable. Neoliberalism renews the liberal critique of sovereign, patriarchal power, but does so on the very terrain opened up by the welfare state—the normative administration of everyday life in the household. The "new household economics" of Gary Becker offers the clearest illustration of this move.

Foucault responds to this new configuration of powers with what can only be described as a highly conservative maneuver. Relocating his analysis of power beyond the biopolitics of the welfare state, in the realm of the "new household economics," he seeks to fashion a new moral economy of pleasure and a new law of the household. In this, he comes close to the later Schmitt, who also looked to the *oikonomia* as a form of sovereignty more foundational even than that of the modern state. The "unity of *nomos* is only the unity of *oikos*," Schmitt wrote in the late 1950s, lamenting what he sees as the decline of patriarchal power brought about by the feminized household of the welfare state.[49] Schmitt, however, must be described as an ultraconservative—his philosophy consists in the simple reassertion of fundamental law in the mode of willful decision. In his texts on the Iranian Revolution, Foucault aligns himself more closely with the tradition of revolutionary conservatism, that tradition which from the later Heidegger to Alain Badiou, acknowledges the groundlessness of historical crisis (the event itself) only in order to refound absolute law in its place. For Foucault, it was the event of the Iranian Revolution that both confirmed the crisis of Western historical time and promised to restore the invisible law of truth to a future without redemption. It is a mark of Foucault's historical prescience and philosophical limits that he sought this invisible law in the household.

THREE

The Risks of Security: Liberalism, Biopolitics, and Fear

Thomas Lemke

In an interview published in 1983, Foucault presents his ideas about the problems and perspectives of the social security system. This text, which became known to an English-speaking audience under the title "The Risks of Security," is characterized by a certain ambivalence. At first sight, Foucault seems to subscribe to the neoliberal critique of the welfare state by identifying some "perverse effects" of the social security system, namely, the "growing rigidity of certain mechanisms and the creation of situations of dependency" (RS, 366). At the same time, he takes a critical stance towards the liberal opposition of state and civil society (RS, 371) and insists that he does not "advocate that savage liberalism that would lead to individual coverage for those who have the means to pay for it, and to a lack of coverage for the others" (RS, 379).

Foucault is obviously performing a double negation. He seeks to develop the idea of an autonomy that neither follows the rigidities of an authoritarian regime of social security by pre-designing "normal" ways of life nor subscribes to the neoliberal freedom of the market and consumer options. He envisions a system of social security that should "free us from dangers *and* from situations that tend to debase or to subjugate us" (RS, 366; emphasis mine). He puts forward a different idea of security: "a security that opens the way to richer, more numerous, more diverse, and more flexible relationships with ourselves and others, all the while assuring each of us real autonomy" (RS, 366).[1]

What kind of autonomy does Foucault have in mind, and how exactly does he conceive of the relation between security and autonomy? To answer this question I would like to go back to Foucault's lectures on governmentality delivered at the Collège de France in 1978 and 1979. I will first outline how Foucault introduces the notion of "technologies of security" in his analysis of liberalism and biopolitics. The next part investigates the relationship between security, freedom, and fear that Foucault sees as characteristic of liberal government. The third section develops further the notion of technologies of security as an analytical tool to account for current social and political transformations. The final section will advance the idea of critique as an uncertain and audacious enterprise that endangers the ontological status of individual and collective subjects, thereby rendering problematic the theoretical and political fixation on security.

Liberalism and the Birth of Biopolitics

The notion of "technologies of security" does not originate in Foucault's lectures on governmentality. It is already present in his previous work. Foucault uses it when he introduces the concept of biopolitics in his lectures at the Collège de France of 1976 and in the first volume of *The History of Sexuality*.[2] In these texts Foucault identifies a new form of power that is different from sovereign power. This "biopower" consists of two basic modes: the disciplining of the individual body and the regulatory control of the population (WK, 139). Foucault calls the latter a "technology of security" (*SMD*, 249). It aims at the mass phenomena characteristic of a population and its conditions of variation, seeking to prevent or compensate for dangers that result from its existence as a biological entity.[3]

Two years later, in his lectures at the Collège de France in 1978 and 1979, Foucault takes up the notion of "technologies of security." But he now discusses the topic of biopolitics in a different theoretical framework that goes beyond his initial interest in processes of disciplination and the regulation of bodies. Biopolitics now also refers to processes of subjectivation and state formation. Over the course of the lectures Foucault examines the "genesis of a political knowledge" (*STP*, 363) of directing humans, from the classical Greek and Roman periods via state reason and police science through to liberal and neoliberal theories. The notion of government, which Foucault uses in the "broad meaning of the word,"[4] is essential for this work. While the term has a purely political meaning today, Foucault is able to show that up until well into the eighteenth century the problem of government was placed in a more general context. "Government" was discussed not only in political tracts but also in philosophical, religious, medical, and pedagogic texts. In addition to management by the state or administration, government also addressed problems of self-control, guidance for the family and for children, management of the household, directing the soul, and other questions (SP, 341).

Within this analytics of government, "biopolitics" occupies an essential role. *The Birth of Biopolitics* (the title of the 1979 lecture series) is closely linked to the emergence of liberal forms of government. Foucault conceives of liberalism not as an economic theory or a political ideology but as a specific art of governing human beings. It has its target in the epistemic figure of population, and it relies on political economy as the principal form of knowledge. Liberalism introduces a rationality of government that differs both from medieval concepts of domination and from early modern state reason: the idea of a nature of society that constitutes the basis and the border of governmental practice. This concept of nature is not a traditional idea or something left over from premodern times; rather, it marks an important historical rupture in the history of political thought. In the Middle Ages good government was understood as part of the natural order created by God's will. State reason breaks with this idea of nature, which limited political action and embedded it in a cosmological continuum. Instead, state reason proposes the artificiality of a "Leviathan"—which provokes the charge of atheism. With the physiocrats and political economy, nature reappears as a point of reference for political action. However, this is a different nature that has nothing to do with a divine order of creation or cosmological principles. At the center of liberal reflection is a hitherto unknown nature, the historical result of radically transformed relations of living and producing: the "second nature" of the developing civil society (*STP*).

Political economy, which emerged as a distinctive form of knowledge in the eighteenth century, replaced the moralistic and rigid principles of mercantilist and cameralist economic regulation with the idea of spontaneous self-regulation of the market on the basis of "natural" prices. Authors like Adam Smith, David Hume, and Adam Ferguson assumed that there exists a nature that is peculiar to governmental practices, and that governments have to respect this nature in their operations. Thus, governmental practices should be in line with the laws of a nature that they themselves have constituted. For this reason the principle of government shifts from external congruence to internal regulation. The coordinates of governmental action are no longer legitimacy or illegitimacy, but success or failure; reflection focuses not on the abuse or arrogance of power but rather on ignorance concerning its use.

As Foucault points out, political economy introduces into the art of government for the first time the question of truth and the principle of self-limitation. As a consequence, it is no longer important to know whether the prince governs according to divine, natural, or moral laws; rather, it is necessary to investigate the "natural order of things" that defines both the foundations and the limits of governmental action. The new art of government, which became apparent in the middle of the eighteenth century, no longer seeks to maximize the powers of the state. Instead, it operates through an "economic government" that analyzes governmental action to find out whether it is necessary and useful or superfluous or even harmful. But this historical transformation is by no means accompanied by a reduction of state power. Paradoxically, the liberal recourse to nature makes it possible to leave nature behind, or more precisely to leave behind a certain concept of nature that conceives of it as eternal, holy, or unchangeable. For liberals, nature is not an autonomous domain in which intervention is impossible or forbidden as a matter of principle. Nature is not a material substratum to which governmental practices are applied, but rather their permanent correlate. It is true that there is a "natural" limit to state intervention, as it has to take into account the nature of the social facts.

However, this dividing line is not a negative borderline, since it is precisely the "nature" of the population that opens up a series of hitherto unknown possibilities of intervention. These do not necessarily take the form of direct interdictions or regulations: "laissez-faire," inciting, and stimulating become more important than dominating, prescribing, and decreeing.

In the 1978 and 1979 lectures, Foucault conceives of "liberalism as the general framework of biopolitics" (*BB*, 22). This account of liberalism signals a shift of emphasis in relation to his previous work. The theoretical displacement results from the self-critical insight that his earlier analysis of biopolitics was one-dimensional and reductive, in the sense that it primarily focused on the biological and physical life of a population and on the politics of the body. Introducing the notion of government helps to broaden the theoretical horizon, as it links the interest in a "political anatomy of the human body" with the investigation of subjectivation processes and moral or political forms of existence. From this perspective, biopolitics represents a particular and dynamic constellation that characterizes liberal government. With liberalism, but not before, the question arises of how subjects are to be governed if they are both legal persons and living beings.[5]

Technologies of Security

It is in this context that the question of security becomes acute. Foucault regards the establishment of "technologies," "apparatuses," or "mechanisms of security" (*STP*, 59; 108 and 7, respectively) as a distinctive feature of liberal forms of government. In the following, I would like to stress some important aspects of the relationship between freedom, security, and fear that Foucault sees as constitutive for liberalism.

To start with, we have to note that Foucault does not ground his analysis in the assumption that liberalism (in contrast to historically previous forms of government) seeks to enhance the freedom of individuals or to expand their rights. According to Foucault, freedom is neither an anthropological constant nor a historical universal that is limited or respected by different societies; freedom cannot be measured in quantitative means but denotes a social relation: "Freedom is never anything other . . . than an actual relation between governors and governed" (*BB*, 63).[6]

Liberalism is not limited to providing a simple guarantee of liberties (freedom of the market, of private property, of speech, etc.) that exist independently of governmental practice. Quite on the contrary: it organizes the conditions under which individuals could and should exercise these liberties. In this sense, freedom is not the counterpart of liberal government, but its necessary basis; it is not a natural resource but an artificially arranged product and instrument of governmental practices. In short: freedom is not the (negative) right of individuals to confront power, but the positive effect of governmental action. Liberal government does not expand the spaces of freedom, it is not limited to respect this or that freedom—it "consumes freedom" (*BB*, 63).[7]

But at this point things start to get complicated. In the very same process of the production of freedom, liberalism also endangers the freedom that it constitutes. It is precisely the "free play of forces" inside liberal forms of government that threatens these liberties and necessitates new interventions. Foucault illustrates this "paradox" (*BB*, 64) with the example of the freedom of trade. Freedom of trade can only be established if a whole series of preventive measures are taken that aim to avoid and counter tendencies of monopolization and concentration that would result in a limitation of freedom of trade:

> There must be free trade . . . but how can we practice free trade in fact if we do not control and limit a number of things, and if we do not organize a series of preventive measures to avoid the effects of one country's hegemony over others, which would be precisely the limitation and restriction of free trade? (*BB*, 64)

At the heart of liberalism there is a problematic and paradoxical relationship between the incessant production of freedom and the permanent danger of its destruction. Liberal freedom presupposes the establishment of limitations, controls, forms of constraint, and so forth. The problem of liberal government is to ensure that pursuit of individual or collective interests does not endanger the general interest. It follows that liberal freedom cannot be exercised in an unlimited way, but has to be regulated by a principle of calculation: apparatuses of security are the other side and the condition of existence of liberal government. The extension of control procedures and the deepening of mechanisms of constraint are the counterweight to the establishment of new freedoms.[8]

But the liberal relationship between freedom and security is even more complex. Liberalism does not only produce freedoms, which are permanently endangered (by their own conditions of production) and require mechanisms of security. Danger and insecurity (the threat of unemployment, poverty, social degradation, etc.) are not just unwanted consequences or negative side effects but essential conditions and positive elements of liberal freedom. In this sense, liberalism nurtures danger, it subjects danger to an economic calculus, weighing its advantages against its costs. Liberal government must never fix security, since the striving for security and the danger of insecurity are complementary aspects of liberal governmentality: "Everywhere you see this stimulation of the fear of danger which is, as it were, the condition, the internal psychological and cultural correlative of liberalism. There is no liberalism without a culture of danger" (BB, 66). This cultivation and stimulation of danger points to the moral dimension of liberal government. Individuals are expected to cope with social risks and insecurities, to measure and calculate them, taking precautions for themselves and their families. In this perspective it is entrepreneurial action, rational risk management, and individual responsibility that accounts for social success or failure.[9]

Over the course of the lectures Foucault also distinguishes analytically between legal regulations, disciplinary mechanisms, and technologies of security (STP, 55–63). This distinction between different power technologies is also of historical and political significance. At the beginning of the 1970s Foucault diagnosed an increasing disciplinarization of society. In the lectures on governmentality, he takes a different stance. He now states that in the "general economy of power" dominance has been displaced to security mechanisms. From this perspective, we are now living not in a legal state or in a disciplinary society but rather in a "security society" in which legal and disciplinary procedures and technologies have been increasingly colonized by apparatuses of security (STP, 11).[10]

This diagnosis was partially inspired by the political events of that time. Foucault's lectures of 1978 and 1979 took place at the climax of left-wing violence in Europe. The reactions of the different national states to so-called terrorism, the suspension of civil rights, and the establishment of a control and supervision apparatus could be seen as an involuntary confirmation of his thesis of a political dominance of security mechanisms. Foucault observed a relative devaluation of legal forms of regulation and the creeping development of an authoritarian security regime that operated against and beyond legal prescriptions and codes. The aim of political government is—according to Foucault—to stage a "fear game,"[11] to make clear that the legal arsenal is not sufficient to protect the population efficiently against existential dangers. He notes that the basis of security policy is not a social contract but rather a "security pact"[12] between state and population that explicitly transgresses the legally defined limits of state intervention.

In this context Foucault declared that the "fear of fear . . . is one of the preconditions of the working of a security state."[13] He stressed that the "misuses" of laws or the "infringement" of rights by the state are neither exceptional cases nor could they be reduced to the difference between ideal and reality; they are quite on the contrary the foundation and guarantee of the continuous and "normal" existence of a legal state. From this perspective legal uncertainties and threats constitute a permanent level of fear. The "state of fear [*État de peur*]" is thus, according to Foucault, the other side of the legal state.[14]

The Government of Fear

Foucault's account of the intimate relationship between liberal government, the rule of law, and the proliferation of fear is nearly forty years old, but it seems to be still useful to analyze contemporary political and social transformations. On the one hand, the proliferation and implementation of neoliberal forms of government has contributed to the production of insecurity and the cultivation of fear in ways that go well beyond the level Foucault observed during his lifetime. On the other hand, the relevance of the Foucaultian analysis is demonstrated by political reactions to terrorist attacks since 9/11. This includes the suspension of basic rights in the name of a general guarantee of security and also the reduction of politics to police measures and military actions.

More concretely, the concept of technologies of security presents a fruitful analytical tool for social theory and empirical investigations. First, the idea of security mechanisms emphasizes that the functioning of a capitalist economy necessitates a political and legal framework that not only provides the infrastructural means for market exchange but also employs mechanisms to regulate, compensate, or minimize social insecurities or risks like accidents, unemployment, illness, and so forth. This means that the often-cited separation of economy and politics, global capital and nation-state, is misleading since it is unable to account for their complex and dynamic interplay. Instead of the power of economy, the concept of apparatuses of security brings the "economy of power" (*BB*, 65) to the fore of analytical interest, thereby correcting the diagnosis of neoliberalism as an expansion of the economy into politics—a critical stance that too often takes for granted the liberal separation of state and market instead of regarding it as "a form of schematization peculiar to a particular technology of government" (*BB*, 319).[15]

Second, Foucault takes a critical distance from the tradition of political theory starting from Thomas Hobbes that claimed that security is the precondition or basis for freedom. Foucault problematizes this external and dualistic conception of freedom and security that is characteristic for the juridical discourse. For Foucault, security is a non-juridical concept that cannot be reduced to an authoritarian state or the rule of law but refers to social life. It relies on statistical facts, risk calculations, social routines, and so forth. The "game of liberalism . . . basically and fundamentally means acting so that reality develops, goes its way, and follows its own course according to the laws, principles, and mechanisms of reality itself" (*STP*, 48). There is no normative conflict between security and freedom; rather freedom is something that could be calculated and arranged. Foucault conceives of security and freedom not as opposing principles but as constitutive parts of liberal governmentality; they are both elements of a single technology of government.[16]

As a consequence, Foucault makes clear that the relationship between liberal freedom and mechanisms of security is more complex than a simple relation of complementation, compensation, or correction. Transience, instability, and incertitude are elementary ingredients of liberal government, in which freedom and fear refer to one another. The vision of an enterprising self promises manifold options and opportunities to consume, but it also necessitates the permanent calculation and estimation of risks, thus establishing a permanent fear of failure.[17] As Michael Hardt and Antonio

Negri note, contemporary societies produce "forms of desire and pleasure that are intimately wedded to fear."[18] Fear fulfills an important moral function in neoliberal government. The constant threat of unemployment and poverty, and anxiety about the future, induce foresight and prudence. Fear not only stimulates a consciousness of economic risks and uncertainties that accompany the socially expected entrepreneurship; it is also an important means in the medicalization and geneticization of society.[19] It transforms healthy individuals into asymptomatically ill people who are expected to take preventive measures, to go to regular medical checkups to supervise and control their bodily risks. Here, fear is instrumental to cultivate a sense of susceptibility and vulnerability.[20] In the context of neoliberal government, fear is the basis and motive for the constitution of the responsible, reliable, and rational self. It has a civilizing quality: barbarians lack fear—this is why they are so dangerous.

This brings us to another aspect: fear also has an important segregatory function. It divides society into distinctive homogenic groups, into communities of social, ethnic, religious, or economic equals that are governed by the assumption of non-dangerousness.[21] Here the difference between endangered and dangerous individuals comes into play—a line of demarcation that materializes spatially in gated communities and slums, but also visible in neighborhood watch programs. It is important to analyze this dynamic circle of production, regulation, and exploitation of fear. The government of populations and individuals operates by "technologies of fear"[22] that present society as an "exposed community," thus promoting an individual retreat to privacy. Coping with fear becomes a problem of individual psychology or a medical issue, while the material conditions and the strategic aims of the production of fear remain invisible.[23]

It is also necessary to investigate the contradictory norms that characterize the neoliberal government of insecurity. While individuals are on the one hand addressed as prudent and cautious subjects that choose a responsible and rational, which means risk-minimizing, lifestyle, they are on the other hand incited to entrepreneurial action as risk-taking is transformed into a public virtue. Pat O'Malley has diagnosed the hybrid of an "enterprising prudentialism":

> The prudent subject of neo-liberalism should practice and sustain their autonomy by assembling information, material and practices together into a

personalized strategy that identifies and minimizes their exposure to harm. Such risk management is frequently, and perhaps increasingly, associated with access to statistical or actuarial technologies and expert advice that render measurable the (probabilistic) calculation of future harms. . . . Enterprising subjects are imagined as innovators, who "reinvent" themselves and their environment. Here they appear as *entrepreneurs*, not as prudent *consumers* of risk. . . . For the subject as entrepreneur, the future that must be governed must also remain uncertain, as a condition of a specific but vital form of liberal freedom.[24]

There is a third reason to take up the notion of technologies of security for analytical and critical purposes. Mechanisms of security cannot be reduced to instruments and forms of regulation of a "security state" that employs top-down mechanisms of control and supervision. They cut across the difference between state and society or the distinction between private and public. While it is true that security is produced increasingly by private actors and less and less by state agencies, it would be misleading to simply confront state security on the one hand and mechanisms of civil society and capitalist economy on the other. What we observe is a pluralization and commodification of mechanisms of security that are more and more dissociated from the state monopoly of violence—without limiting or reducing centralized technologies of supervision and control.[25] Quite on the contrary: collective systems of security and state-led mechanisms of control are gaining more significance, to the extent that individuals no longer live according to continuous biographies of work or have to work in precarious labor conditions, as they are expected to act in an entrepreneurial mode and the risks of failure in professional life are principally attributed to them. The "privatization" of the production of security does not lead in any way to a demise of regulatory and steering competences of the state; rather, it has to be regarded as a reorganization or a restructuring of governmental technologies.

Furthermore, a reversal of the traditional relation between state and citizen is to be noted. Especially since 9/11, basic rights are no longer conceived as rights of defense against the state, but allow the state to intervene in realms that were formerly regarded as private spheres by referring to security as a "super right." Governments in many countries have established new surveillance and database technologies that sometimes even operate outside the established legal frameworks and juridical process. For example, the U.S. government has collected the domestic telephone and e-mail records of millions of businesses and households, thereby violating legal rights and federal laws. This precautionary risk management or "hyperprevention"[26] by state authorities has also created spaces that are exempt from ordinary legal procedures. It has resulted in the use of torture as a means in the so-called war on terror, and in indefinite detention of inmates in prisons around the world. In Guantánamo alone, nearly three hundred prisoners have never been charged with any crime and lack the right to challenge their imprisonment.[27]

The extension of the state's security apparatuses beyond or outside legal regulations and international law is complemented by another tendency which it seems to contradict: the extension of the market principle to the monopoly of violence in the form of private security agencies and service providers. This tendency leads to a new combination of class and risk society in which security has a price tag. The guarantee of security is not longer principally valid for everyone and to the same degree, but is subject to an economic calculus. Private enterprises offer security as a service, and the diagnosis and minimizing of socially produced risks is itself a profitable business.[28]

However, the security industry cannot be reduced to activities to eliminate or minimize "unwanted" insecurities. It not only includes private security contractors, the armaments industry, insurance companies, and developers of antivirus software, but also comprises agencies and providers that focus on those forms of desire that "dangerous" experiences of the self or "risky" leisure time activities provide. Beyond the aesthetic experience of controlled insecurity there is also an interest in the calculation of risk that is enjoyed as freedom in adventure holidays, rock climbing, drug experiences, and so forth. As Tom Holert notes, the consequences and the preconditions of such experiments with insecurity provide employment for medical doctors, psychologists, car repair workshops, and agencies specializing in the freeing of hostages.[29]

Finally, the notion of technologies of security is useful as a way of detecting historical transformations and displacements in the way security is conceptualized and arranged.[30] We can note a movement away from a defensive averting of danger or a retroactive compensation of social risks to the prevention of dangers and the active management of incidence rates of (unwanted) events. In more and more social fields we witness general diagnoses of risk that are disconnected from concrete determined and temporal limited dangers. These "preemptive strategies" evoke a permanent state of exception; they are not a provisional and limited institution but constitute a boundless and permanent social charge.[31]

Inside this political transformation two strategies exist in parallel. They seem to exclude each other, but in fact they complement each other. On the one hand, control is displaced from concrete persons to the supervision of spaces and abstract structures of opportunity. At the center of this strategy we find not individuals or groups, but rather situative contexts and possible actions. The control technologies no longer operate with moral categories like blame or responsibility, but rather aim at an economic–rational management of flows of mobility and information by regulating operational functions and admission schemes.[32]

On the other hand, it is also possible to detect a remoralization of political and social discourses giving rise to new forms of individual and collective responsibility concerning "dangerous" or "risky" forms of behavior. Also, remoralization plays a role in justifying political, military, or social interventions distinguishing between good and bad or friends and enemies. We may think of George Bush's religiously loaded rhetoric, which evokes a struggle between good and evil.[33]

These points offer some perspectives for ways in which one could take up Foucault's concept of "technologies of security." I have indicated how this analytical instrument could be used to critically investigate the triad of freedom, fear, and security that characterizes neoliberal government. In the remaining part of this essay, I would like to link up these considerations on security with some general thoughts on critique. Indeed, Foucault's lectures on liberal and neoliberal governmentality were not only contemporaneous with what might be called the first war on terrorism. In 1978, Foucault presented a paper to the French Society of Philosophy under the title "What Is Critique?" This text signaled the beginning of an interest in the relationship between Kant, Enlightenment, and critique that would last until his death. I will only focus on one aspect of Foucault's account of critique: the idea that critique materializes in a "fearless speech" by an individual or a group willing to expose their own ontological status.[34]

Critique as a Dangerous Enterprise

In the lecture "What Is Critique?" and in several other texts, Foucault stresses that the critical activity involves the risk to fall outside of the established norms of recognition.[35] The project of critique implies a "desubjectivation of the subject" (WC, 32). It seeks to make visible the limits of "what we are" (WE, 319) in order to transgress them. The objective of critique is to question the "government of individualization," claiming "the right to be different" while at the same time rejecting all strategies designed to isolate and separate individuals from "community life" (SP, 330). It follows from this focus on "desubjectivation" that Foucault is not so much interested in how individual and collective subjects act in accordance with established norms and how they could be brought to resist on the basis of shared ideas or convictions. Quite on the contrary, he wants to contribute to the constitution of new subjectivities and alternative norms that offer more space for autonomy and ethical self-formation:

> The problem is, precisely, to decide if it is actually suitable to place oneself within a "we" in order to assert the principles one recognizes and the values one accepts; or if it is not, rather, necessary to make the future formation of a "we" possible by elaborating the question. Because it seems to me that the "we" must not be previous to the question; it can only be the result—and the necessarily temporary result—of the question as it is posed in the new terms in which one formulates it.[36]

The questioning of established norms and the call for new subjectivities implies the will to expose oneself as a subject. It necessitates suspending and undermining one's own ontological status to engage in a process of self-distancing and self-questioning. As Judith Butler has pointed out in her comment on Foucault's lecture, the subject:

> is compelled to form itself, but to form itself within forms that are already more or less in operation and underway. . . . But if that self-forming is done in disobedience to the principles by which one is formed, then virtue becomes the practice by which the self forms itself in desubjugation, which is to say that it risks its deformation as a subject.[37]

In contrast to the juridical concept of critique, which is characterized by universality and necessity, critique as ethos, as the labor of the self-formation of an ethical subject, is marked by singularity and voluntariness. For Foucault, critique is "a voluntary choice made by certain people . . . a way, too, of acting and behaving that at one and the same time marks a relation of belonging and presents itself as a task" (WE, 309). This idea of critical activity as a relation of belonging and a task comes quite close to the notion of community put forward by the Italian philosopher Roberto Esposito. For Esposito, the central problem of Western political and social theory results from treating community as an identity or property. Against this line of interpretation, he reminds us of the etymological origin of the word *communitas* as *cum munus*. The Latin word *munus* means burden, obligation, duty, or charge. In this reading community is not defined by an essence or property; rather, community is realized by shared obligations and duties. It is not a territory or a conquest acquired in the past which has to be defended, but represents a future promise: a concern and a request. A community is not a given identity or an authentic collective, since there is no foundation or principle that guarantees identity or authenticity. Community in this sense exists only in the dispute over the common (that which does not exist yet, that which has to be produced), not as a substance but as a process, not as a foundation but as a project.[38]

While critical activity would be part of the construction of the community, assisting the invention of new cultural forms and lifestyles, *immunitas* seeks to defend an established identity and to define the borderlines that separate the community from strangers. *Immunitas*, which literally means the absence of duties, obligations, and burdens, relies on strategies of defense and securitization. It is a risk-minimizing activity characterized by the reduction of critique to a juridical procedure and a system of codes regulating proper belonging and legitimate access. As a result, the community is defended against strangers—hence exactly against what founds the community as an always unstable and shifting identity.[39]

Understood in this way, desubjectivation is not a negative procedure or a simple means to achieve a distant end. Rather, it represents an integral part and a visible sign of the ethical self-formation that is characterized by a peculiar symmetry of means and ends. As Foucault remarked concerning the *Solidarność* movement in Poland at the beginning of the 1980s, "People have not only struggled for freedom, democracy, and the exercise of basic rights but they have done so by exercising rights, freedom, and democracy."[40]

To conclude, and this is what I take to be one of the lessons we can learn from Foucault's engagement with the liberal triad of freedom, security, and fear: it is not sufficient to expose the risks of the liberal idea of security that operates by producing social segregation and anxiety. It is necessary to go one step beyond this, to invent a form of security that allows for difference and autonomy without creating fear. To pursue this objective will certainly be a risky enterprise, but hopefully one that will set limits to the dangerous imperative of preemption, prevention, and prediction that dreams of controlling the future by promising "happiness for a life to which nothing happens."[41]

PART TWO

Genealogies of Biopolitics

FOUR

A Genealogy of Biopolitics: The Notion of Life in Canguilhem and Foucault

Maria Muhle

Biopolitics: A Polemical Concept

In 1976, in the first volume of *The History of Sexuality*, Michel Foucault introduces what would become a polemical concept in his work as well as for his interpreters: the "bio-politics of the population" (with a hyphen which is dropped in the following years). This notion has since polarized the readings of Foucault's theory of power and maybe has played a much more important role then he ever intended. The most prominent and popular reading of biopolitics nowadays may very well be its "ethical" interpretation in terms of bio-ethics. Biopolitics would thus be the "political" administration of the changes and new possibilities of the life sciences, predominantly of biology and genetics.[1] This reading recovers another line of interpretation that, even though it considers biopower not in terms of governance but in politico-philosophical terms, gives way to a twofold misreading: either the analysis of biopower is structurally linked to an analysis of the regime of politics as a permanent state of exception, or it is subtended with a "positive" politics of life that thwarts the "negative" power over life. Roberto Esposito calls this polarity of the notion of biopolitics an "insurmountable oscillation" between a positive and productive reading of the relation between politics and life and another negative and tragic reading implied by Foucault's writing itself. While the latter interpretation awards life with an intrinsic power that resists biopower, such as Antonio Negri and Michael Hardt propose, the former, proposed by Giorgio Agamben, radicalizes the thanato-political aspect in the notion of "bare life."[2]

These varied interpretations of the notion of biopolitics are induced by an attempt to define the notion of life rather than the term "politics" or "power:" they give a "definition" of life (as biological life, as bare life, or as vital power) that Foucault himself, and for coherent reasons, has always omitted to give. This omission seems to have encouraged the ethical, productive, or tragic readings of Foucault's biopolitics. In order to propose a genealogical study of the term "biopolitics," it is thus important to take a closer look at the notion of life that may have inspired the Foucaultian analysis, and that does not correspond, as I would like to show in the following, to any of the three alternatives mentioned above.

The Birth of Biopolitics

As already mentioned, Foucault gives a somewhat "canonic" definition of biopolitics in *The Will to Knowledge* where he introduces "biopolitics" as *one side* or pole of a twofold power *over* life that he distinguishes from the right of death incarnated by sovereign power. The two principal forms, in which the power over life has developed, are not antithetical, but rather constitute the two poles of the changes that power undergoes around the seventeenth century and whose main role is "to ensure, sustain, and multiply life" (*WK*, 138). The first pole is constituted by the disciplines, "an anatomo-politics of the human body," that is, centered on "the body as a machine" (*WK*, 139) and to which Foucault has dedicated one of his main works, *Discipline and Punish* (1975) as well as his lecture series *Abnormal* at the Collège de France in 1974–75.[3] The second pole of the power over life—biopolitics—develops around the middle of the eighteenth century: it is a form of power centered on the "species body, the body imbued with the mechanics of life and serving as the basis of the biological processes" (*WK*, 139). This species body is governed (or "supervised") through an entire series of interventions and regulatory controls that Foucault calls "a biopolitics of the population" (*WK*, 139). And he concludes this first introduction of the notion of biopolitics as follows: "The setting up, in the course of the classical age, of this great bipolar technology—anatomic and biological, individualizing and specifying, directed toward the performances of the body, with attention to the process of life—characterized a power whose highest function was perhaps no longer to kill, but to invest life through and through" (*WK*, 139).

To resume, on the one hand, Foucault defines biopolitics through its reference to life *as its object* as opposed to the sovereign power whose object is the juridical subject, and to the disciplinary power, whose techniques are directed toward the individual. On the other hand, the specificity of the biopolitical techniques lies in the *positive* and not repressive relation to life and in the fact that such techniques are *intrinsic* and not exterior to its object. Biopolitical techniques increase, protect, and regulate life—in short, they "make live." And they do so by infiltrating the processes of life (instead of suppressing or submitting them) in order to govern or to rule them from the inside.

It is important to keep this twofold definition in mind, since it permits one to counteract the reduction of biopolitics to a simple politics *whose object is life* that has given way to the generalization of the notion in its (bio-)ethical version. While in the first occurrence in *The Will to Knowledge*, Foucault's focus lies with the fact that post-sovereign power is defined through a new object, the life of the population, in his lectures of the following years, namely *Security, Territory, Population* (1977–78) and *The Birth of Biopolitics* (1978–79), Foucault emphasizes the positive nature of the relationship between power and life. He therefore reformulates and amplifies the notion of biopower, referring to it by the name of governmentality. The introduction of this new name of power might be a reaction to a slightly too "narrow" notion of biopolitics that focuses mostly on the relation to its "new" object (life) and leaves aside the positivity of this relation. In any case, it allows him to refocus the analysis on the productivity of power that relies, as I would like to show, on the imitation of the vital dynamics of life. It is in the analysis of governmentality that the implications of biopolitics, as a positive and productive power over life, are completely unfolded.

Archeology of Life

The purpose of this essay is to analyze the sense of a "positive" relationship between power and life. Therefore, it is necessary to take a new look at the notion of life that is implicated in the term of "biopolitics" such as Foucault uses it. Foucault operates with a notion of life that he does not determine: life is a correlate of the techniques and strategies of power and knowledge. It lacks any ontological status and is itself "produced" by the power–knowledge constellation, or, to use the famous formula of *The Order of Things*, life *emerges* in the passage between natural history and biology, that is, in the epistemic break which occurs around 1800. This episteme emerges because of an archeological dislocation that introduces the notion of "organization" as fundamental to the study of the living and replaces the "tableau" of natural history by the constitutive opposition between the organic (the living) and the inorganic. This archeological dislocation permits to think of life as fundamentally dynamic: life is the polarity or tension between the two poles of the organic and the inorganic. It is here, Foucault explains, that a definition of life through death, that is, as "resistance to death"—such as the French anatomist and physiologist Xavier Bichat has proposed—becomes thinkable.[4] Life—one could say paraphrasing and transposing Canguilhem's definition of the normal—is a dynamic and thus a polemical notion,[5] since it is formed in the tension between these different poles; it is a polar movement between tendencies of self-preservation and tendencies of self-transgression.

Nevertheless it is crucial to understand that Foucault, unlike Bichat or Canguilhem, does not seek to analyze the vital dynamic in itself (i.e., at defining life as vital power); rather, Foucault analyzes the *epistemic fact* that life becomes *thinkable* as dynamic, vital, or living. It is this understanding of "life" (along with "labor" and "language") as a "quasi-transcendental,"[6] that is, the archeology of life that explains the indetermination of life in

Foucault's thought. This indetermination is thus not a lack or an omission in his thought, as Giorgio Agamben suggests, by making his own interpretation of life in terms of bare life come to fill this lack and complete the Foucaultian theory of power. On the contrary, this indetermination is a methodological point and ought to be taken seriously inasmuch as the sharpness of Foucault's reflections on biopolitics is due to the very indetermination understood as "normalizability" of life by power–knowledge strategies. Foucault's lack of a definition of life is neither an oversight nor an inexactness, but an intentional indetermination that is opposed, on the one hand, to an interpretation of life as force that would situate it beyond the power mechanisms, and, on the other hand, to an ontological reformulation of that same indetermination that considers life in its radical bareness.

The fact that Foucault himself gives no definition of "his" concept of life has been widely discussed, for instance by Agamben in his comparative analysis of the notion of life in the thought of Foucault and Deleuze titled "Absolute Immanence." Here, Agamben states that "a clear definition of 'life' seems to be lacking in both Foucault and Deleuze."[7] Even though his text centers on a reading of Deleuze's notion of life, he begins with a short reading of Foucault's "Life: Experience and Science," a reprinting of the English introduction to the translation of Canguilhem's *On the Normal and the Pathological*. Agamben sees in this text "a curious inversion of what had been Foucault's earlier understanding of the idea of life," when in *The Birth of the Clinic* he understood life, following Bichat's new vitalism, as "the set of functions that resist death."[8] Now, in his last text, he considers life, following Canguilhem, as the "proper domain of error." For Agamben, this "displacement" would be a further documentation of the crisis Foucault allegedly went through after the publication of the first volume of *The History of Sexuality*. But there is more to it, as Agamben follows up: "It is something like a new experience that necessitates a general reformulation of the relations between truth and the subject and that, nevertheless, concerns the specific area of Foucault's research. Tearing the subject from the terrain of the cogito and consciousness, this experience roots it in life."[9] A life that is essentially errancy. For Agamben, who follows Deleuze in this respect, this "dislocation of the theory of knowledge," that is, the connection of subjectivity to life (and not to consciousness), announces the "subjective turn" of the second and third volumes of *The History of Sexuality* and "coincides with the field of biopolitics, that could have furnished Foucault with the 'third axis, distinct from both knowledge and power' which Deleuze suggests he needed."[10]

Agamben thus raises two fundamental hypotheses: first, he claims that Foucault, at the end of his life, turned away from the "negative" notion of a life radically exposed to death toward a subjectivity understood from the position of a fundamentally dynamic notion of life. Second, he links the notion of life defined through death to the biopolitical paradigm, that is, to bare life, a life always already subjected to power, that constitutes the reference point of the biopolitical techniques. Whereas Agamben does not give any further comments on the question of a "subjectivity," which he calls a "form of life" that resists (bio)power, he extensively writes on the notion of *bare* life (*zoe*) that he considers to be the object of biopolitics.

Life as Biopolitical Substance

In *Homo Sacer: Sovereign Power and Bare Life* Agamben proposes his interpretation of the Foucaultian notion of biopolitics that relies on a structural identity between the biopolitical and the sovereign form of power. In the introduction, Agamben announces that his inquiry concerns precisely "this hidden point of intersection between the juridico-institutional and the biopolitical models of power."[11] The inclusion of bare life in the realm of the political constitutes the "original—if concealed—nucleus of sovereign power," whose *"original activity . . . is the production of a biopolitical body."*[12] The "biological life" that the modern state places at the center of his attention is therefore structurally the same life exposed to the sovereign right over life and death, and biopolitics and sovereign power therefore have the same origin.

The bare life produced by the sovereign states of exception is furthermore identified by Agamben in *Remnants of Auschwitz: The Witness and the Archive* as the "absolute biopolitical substance."[13] The affirmation of a necessary relationship between biopolitics and sovereign power culminates in the provocative and well-known conclusion that "today it is not the city [*polis*] but rather the camp that is the fundamental biopolitical paradigm of the West."[14] In the camp, populated by the *homines sacri*, who can be killed but not be sacrificed, the sovereign exception that has become the rule is unified with the biopolitical paradigm through the production of bare life. The biopolitical body produced by the sovereign power is identified with this bare life, *zoe*, that according to Aristotle is distinguished from qualified life, *bios*. Bare life, in Agamben's understanding, would then be the transcendental origin of modern politics and there would not be any structural difference (even though there are historical differences) between the functioning of sovereign power and the biopolitical techniques. Bare life is the negation of any qualification, and therefore it is a transhistorical notion, an ontological category. Instead of tracing the discontinuities in the succession of the forms of power and knowledge, Agamben pretends to reveal the hidden or invisible elements that determine *every* form of power latently.[15]

The fact that life is always exposed to power is also a basic statement in Foucault. Foucault also does not deny that there is an interaction between sovereign techniques of exception and the biopolitical techniques. In his lecture on March 17, 1976, at the Collège de France, Foucault gives the example of racism that permits to "justify" the killing of people, populations, and civilizations within modern societies that function in the biopower mode: "If the power of normalization wished to exercises the old sovereign right to kill, it must become racist" (*SMD*, 256). But for Foucault, this constellation is open to changes and can be situated historically, it is not a structural necessity, not the very "essence" of modern power. Agamben's intentional misreading of Foucault's notion of biopolitics becomes visible in his claim that Foucault was not aware of the *fundamental* nexus between biopolitics and sovereign power and that his "death kept him from showing how he would have developed the concept and study of biopolitics."[16] This may seem surprising since Foucault dedicated the lectures that followed the publication of the first volume of *The History of Sexuality* to the techniques and *dispositifs* of security (in *Security, Territory, Population*) and to *The Birth of Biopolitics*, where he developed the implications of the notion of biopolitics toward a theory of governmentality. Instead of approaching biopolitics from the notion of sovereign power, he examines the distance and differences between these two modalities of power. This distance crystallizes in an archeological understanding of life as a correlate to specific techniques of power and knowledge.

Polarity of Life

The articulation of power that governs the living thus supposes a knowledge of the living. In the epistemic conjuncture in which biopolitics emerges, this knowledge is articulated by medicine and biology at the beginning of the nineteenth century, both of which are related to a specific vitalist thought. Life is defined through its fundamental variability, through its possibility of deviation and error. And it is in this deviation or erring that life appears as fundamentally *living*, as bearing a vital dynamics. What is at play here is thus a *dynamic* notion of life that nevertheless is not subsumable under a mere teleology of the organic as Kant suggests in the modus of the "as if," nor a specific vitalist conception of the dynamics of life as an unitarian principle. At stake is the understanding of life as fundamentally dynamic *and* erratic, life as polarized between different dynamics of the living—the self-preservation of the organic and the self-creation of the vital that goes beyond the mere preservation of an organic equilibrium. The movement of self-creation is not to be disconnected from the self-preservative movement: life, as it becomes thematized around 1800, is neither pure transgression nor pure self-preservation, but defines itself in the tension between these two.

In his *Physiological Researches upon Life and Death* published originally in 1800, Bichat formulates a fundamental difference between the sciences of the living and the natural sciences. While the laws of nature are "unchangeable, invariable and constantly the same in any moment,"[17] the organic or vital laws are variable, irregular and unstable, since their object—life—is constantly submitted to variations, errors, deviations, and anomalies. In his *General Anatomy*, Bichat distinguishes:

> two things in the phenomena of life: firstly, the state of health; secondly, the state of illness; physiology is in charge of the phenomena of the first state, pathology has as its object the second state. The history of those phenomena in which the vital forces exhibit their natural type leads us to the history of those phenomena in which these forces are altered.[18]

Canguilhem reformulates this opposition in his major work *On the Normal and the Pathological* as a "fundamental epistemic fact."[19] While there can be (and there is) a biological pathology, a physical, chemical, or mechanical pathology cannot exist, because the physical forces cannot be altered in any way. While the physical phenomena are indifferent to their surroundings, there cannot be, as Canguilhem puts it, any "biological indifference":

> We, on the other hand, think that the fact that a living man reacts to a lesion, infection, functional anarchy by means of a disease, expresses the fundamental fact that life is not indifferent to the conditions in which it is possible, that life is polarity and thereby even an unconscious position of value; in short, life is in fact a normative activity. . . . Normative, in the fullest sense of the word, is that which establishes norms. And it is in this sense that we plan to talk about biological normativity.[20]

For Canguilhem, Bichat's major merit consists in having acknowledged the productivity of the irregularities, of the fallibilities of life, in short, of the "negative dimension"—the negative vital values such as anomaly, illness, death—*for* the living.[21] He speaks in this context of the "intelligence of anomaly" that retrieves the signs of a vital force (*pouvoir de vivre*) by turning these negative values of existence into "meaningful" elements that deploy the vital dynamics of life.[22] Canguilhem thus adopts at once from Bichat the epistemological thesis that the knowledge of life is based on the analysis of the morbid phenomena—life is only acknowledgeable through its errors, which refer every living being to its constitutive imperfection and incompleteness, and the determination of life as a dynamic that tends to a "natural type," to a norm.

The value of life, that is, life *as value*, life in its *inner normativity*, is thus founded on its own uncertainty or precariousness (*précarité*).[23] The normative dynamics of life unfold between the two poles: the preservation of the internal organic equilibrium (of the *milieu intérieur* in Claude Bernard's words), and the permanent challenge to this very equilibrium. Canguilhem thus differentiates two normative dimensions of life that stand in an intrinsic relationship to each other: a homeostatic, self-preservative dynamic that tends to organic normality, and a self-transgressive, genuinely normative dynamic that *creates* norms. While the former presupposes a holistic understanding of the organism and is thought by means of the global activity of regulation as the biological fact par excellence, the latter transgresses this organic equilibrium und creates new vital values. The achieved norms, or the normal situation, are constantly put at risk, because otherwise the living would immobilize itself in the artificial equilibrium of organ functions.

Vital normativity, for Canguilhem, is not assimilation or adaptation, but permanent challenge to the given. A living being behaves normatively if it does not adapt to a given milieu or norm—in that case, it would be pathological—but when it creates its own norms and its own milieu. Life is a twofold normative activity that, on the one hand, refers negatively or reactively to the threats of the internal and external milieu and its negative values, and, on the other, is a positive and creative activity that produces its own milieu and its vital norms. Only in its deviance from the norm can life be normative, that is, truly vital. Normativity consists in "breaking norms and establishing new ones [*faire craquer les normes*]."[24] An internal equilibrium is only possible on the background of such a creative force: normality is founded on normativity. The challenge of Canguilhem's notion of life lies in the fact that the organic normality is permanently exposed to the normative deviances, that is, that life does *not* stay in a state of equilibrium (such as, for example, the state produced in the laboratory artificially), but that it puts this state of equilibrium permanently in question in order to transgress it. If life is "only" organic, it would be pathological; instead it is a polarity and therefore organic and creative at once, that is, it is living in the emphatic sense of the word.[25] It is this notion of life in its active–reactive polarity that is illuminating in order to understand the specific modus operandi of the post-sovereign techniques of power that enfolds both the biopolitical and the governmental techniques.

Biopolitics as Life

Against this background, the main hypothesis of this article is that in order to govern life, the forms of biopower *imitate* or *mimetize* the proper dynamics of life, that is, its polarity between life and death, or between autotransgression and auto-conservation, between the normal (one should read normative) and the pathological. Life has thus to be understood in a double sense, as the *object* of post-sovereign techniques of power, and, in its dynamical dimension, as their *operational model*. Imitation has to be understood following the Aristotelian understanding of *mimesis* not as a simple copy (art as a copy of nature) but as the reproduction of the sense of a specific phenomenon or production. Hence the biopolitical–governmental techniques adopt the internal logic of life as the model of their proper dynamics and establish *a relation of internal exteriority* with the vital phenomena. The norms of biopower operate *as if* they were vital, that is, they adopt the vital functioning of the processes of life as their model and exteriorize them in the social norms. This hypothesis can be accounted for through two main notions that Foucault introduces in his biopolitical analysis: the "population" and the "milieu" that both have a specific constitution since they both operate at the intersection between the natural and the artificial, the organic (living) and the inorganic (physical), the vital and the social elements. It is in the production of a population and of a milieu as natural–artificial phenomena that life becomes governable.

For Foucault, biopolitics is a modality of power that in a precise historical moment overdetermines the other modalities of power. Therefore he proposes a *genealogy* of power that does not aspire at unveiling transhistorical or structural elements or at discovering the original and foundational scene of power in general, but at analyzing concrete constellations of power–knowledge as conditions of possibility of the constitution and imposition of specific forms of governmentality. Instead of speaking of power or politics of life, or of power over life, Foucault speaks of the "government of the living" in his lectures of the late 1970s, in order to highlight the insoluble relationship between power and life that however does not lead to the dissolution of life or of power, but to its necessary intrication. In this sense, even the formulation "power over life" that Foucault introduces in *The History of Sexuality: Volume I* may appear ambiguous since it supposes an exteriority between the processes of life and power. It is not until the lectures on governmentality that this ambiguity will be completely resolved in what I have been calling the amplified notion of biopolitics; that is, in a form of power that is always internally linked to life both as its object and its functional model: a government of life.

Adopting this amplified understanding of biopolitics, Foucault avoids what he calls in the lecture of March 7, 1979, a "reduction" of the different forms of power:

> For example, an analysis of social security and the administrative apparatus on which it rests ends up, via some slippages and thanks to some plays on words,

referring us to the analysis of concentration camps. And, in the move from the social security to concentration camps the requisite specificity of the analysis is diluted. (*BB*, 187)

In order to avoid this dissolution of the specificity of the analysis and the dilution of the differences that exist between the mechanisms of the welfare state and the concentration camps in a transhistorical and blurred notion of power, it is necessary to analyze the concrete phenomena that correspond to the different modalities of power.

When taking seriously the central hypothesis of the present text—that a reformulated and amplified notion of biopolitics is one whose techniques refer to life in two ways, taking it not only as its object, but also as its functional model[26]—we can state that the biopolitical norms not only *apply* to the phenomena of life but moreover that they *mimetize* its dynamics, that is, its normativity such as Canguilhem presents it. This hypothesis is confirmed by Foucault's reformulation of the biopolitical techniques under the name of "security techniques" in his lectures on governmentality that follow the same scheme, that of biological normativity. With the aim of regulating, controlling, and governing life *better*, the security techniques adopt the immanent dynamic of life that they exteriorize by *transposing* it to the social norms. This mechanism can be observed in the examples that Foucault gives of the operating mode of the security norms that "anticipate" the aleatoric processes of life in order to prevent major deregulations. For example, the empirical techniques of the inoculation campaigns against the smallpox (*la petite vérole*) are based on two strategies that are fundamental for the biopolitical modus operandi: first, they part from the phenomenon in its very reality (through quantitative methods/statistics); and second, they incorporate or imitate the dynamic of their object of reference.

The first strategy the techniques of variolization borrow from the biopolitical operations is its relation to the empirical reality of the phenomenon in question, in this case the epidemic, more specifically smallpox. The techniques of variolization are developed in a relation of double dependency to the statistic investigations that, first, indicate what groups of population are at higher risk, and, second, retain the success of the inoculation campaign by reflecting them in the mortality rate. Foucault calls this operation a process of *normalization* that he distinguishes in the lecture of January 25, 1978, from the disciplinary *normation*. Normation presupposes a purely prescriptive character of the norm that is at the base of the definition of the normal and the a(b)normal. The phenomena are submitted to the norm, they are *normed*. In contrast, normalization is a dynamic and variable process and its norm is "an interplay of differential normalities." The process of normalization covers life in its very reality, that is, in its vital multiplicity as a self-regulating and self-creative entity whose immanent dynamic results from the permanent deviations from the "normal" situations. In this sense, Foucault writes, "the normal comes first and the norm is deduced from it, or the norm is fixed and plays its operational role on the basis of this study of normalities." Or, as he adds in a note, "the operation of normalization consists in establishing an interplay between these different distributions of normality" (*STP*, 63).

The second strategy is the mimetization of the vital dynamics by the techniques of variolization. Since the efficiency of the security techniques is based on the very reality of the phenomenon, it is fundamental to take into account their dynamics. By doing so, the principle of the fight against smallpox through variolization is to assure the health of the population by producing the illness, and therefore by unchaining in the body its auto-immunization. Variolization, explains Foucault:

> did not try to prevent smallpox so much as provoke it in inoculated individuals, but under conditions such that nullification of the disease could take place at the same time as this vaccination, which thus did not result in a total and complete disease. With the support of this kind of first small, artificially inoculated disease, one could prevent other possible attacks of smallpox. We have here a typical mechanism of security with the same morphology as that seen in the case of scarcity. (*STP*, 59)

With respect to the treatment of scarcity, Foucault explains even more clearly, that:

> whereas the juridical–disciplinary regulations that reigned until the middle of the eighteenth century tried to prevent the phenomenon of scarcity, from the middle of the eighteenth century, with the physiocrats as well as many other economists, there was the attempt to find a point of support in the processes of scarcity themselves, in the kind of quantitative fluctuation that sometimes

produced abundance and sometimes scarcity: finding support in the reality of the phenomenon, and instead of trying to prevent it, making other elements of reality function in relation to it in such a way that the phenomenon is cancelled out, as it were. (*STP*, 59)

The techniques of the security *dispositif* thus correspond to an operational model that is not based on negation, but rather on grasping the dynamics of the vital phenomenon in its very reality that aims at reestablishing its internal equilibrium when it is threatened. Immunology as well as the physiocratic theory of scarcity are palpable examples of this mechanism that respond to the dynamics of a laissez-faire.

The Living Population and Its Milieu

The generalization of this operational mode of power goes along, as Foucault explains still in his lecture, with the emergence of what he calls "an absolutely new political personage" (*STP*, 67), the population, that is considered "as a set of processes to be managed at the level and on the basis of what is natural in these processes" (*STP*, 70). This population is not, then, a collection of juridical subjects in an individual or collective relationship with a sovereign will. It is a set of elements in which we can note constants and regularities even in accidents, in which we can identify the universal of desire regularly producing the benefit of all, and with regard to which we can identify a number of modifiable variables on which it depends. Taking the effects specific to population into consideration, making them pertinent if you like, is, I think, a very important phenomenon: the entry of a "nature" into the field of techniques of power, of a nature that is not something on which, above which, or against which the sovereign must impose just laws (*STP*, 74).

The nature that enters the realm of power relations through the population does not address the notion of sovereignty but what will be a new technique of power, the "government," which "is basically much more then sovereignty, much more then reigning or ruling" (*STP*, 76).

This new constellation of power, that refers to a "natural" object whose dynamics Foucault has spelled out in his lectures of the prior year, marks the central point of intersection between the vital and the social fundamental for the understanding of the amplified notion of biopolitics that imitates the vital dynamics of life exteriorizing it into social norms of security. Here, Foucault claims that population is an ensemble of natural and social elements which are both exposed to and produced by power relations. In this sense, the task of biopolitics is to introduce mechanisms of regulation into the natural–social phenomenon that is global population:

> Regulatory mechanisms must be established to establish an equilibrium, maintain an average, establish a sort of homeostasis, and compensate for variations within this general population and its aleatory field. In a word, security mechanisms have to be installed around the random element inherent in a population of living beings so as to optimize the state of life.... It is, in a word, a matter of taking control of life and the biological processes of man as species and of assuring that they are not disciplined, but regularized. (SMD, 246)

The *modus operandi* of the "new," post-sovereign techniques of power is to frame the hazardous play, the vital dynamics, the aleatory of life in the general population. They do so without repression or negation of the phenomena themselves, by allowing for an apparent freedom, that nevertheless needs to remain within specific limits that even though they can be very wide, are not to be exceeded: the post-sovereign techniques of power *pathologize* life's vital normativity in the way Canguilhem has defined it, by reducing it to normality.[27]

Thus, when the surplus of vital force creates a disorder in the forms of power, the vitality of life is to be dissolved in the internal (and quasi-natural) equilibrium (of the population), reducing the vital to the normal that therein becomes governable. Consequently, biopolitics and the forms of governmentality share a double relationship to the phenomena of life that they govern and whose dynamics they imitate and transpose to the norms of power that operate *as if they were vital*. The vital force is thus considered an organic element of biopolitics that,[28] by imitating the vital dynamics, imitates at once the polarized interplay between creation and conservation of the vital processes

The specific status of the population as natural–artificial hybrid is spelled out by Foucault through another central notion, the "milieu," in which the population becomes perfectly governable. The milieu is part of the biopolitical or governmental *dispositif* since it permits a non-direct—a disposing—access to the living. It is by intervening in the milieu that the population is regulated: "What one tries to reach through this milieu, is precisely the conjunction of a series of events produced by these individuals, populations, and groups, and quasi natural events which occur around them" (*STP*, 21). The living are not exposed directly to power mechanisms, but these get to the living through the milieu that is manipulated in order to secure the development of the population: post-sovereign power strategies create a milieu, in which the population can unfold its living dynamics, so that the means of self-conservation are held at the disposal of the living and life can regulate itself.

For Foucault, this milieu is paradigmatically represented by the "town," where the "naturalness" of human species emerges within an artificial milieu. This connection between the natural and living and the political and artificial is fundamental to biopolitics and presents Foucault's own "reformulation" or amplification of the mechanism of post-sovereign power techniques. It is not just a power that refers to life, but a power that creates a milieu where the interaction between the natural and the artificial follows the precepts of power itself. Through the milieu of the town, that is at once artificial and natural, the population can be reached, becomes permeable to power techniques. Referring to Moheau, whom he calls the first great theorist of biopolitics, and his *Recherches et considérations sur la population de la France*, Foucault explains that what has fundamentally changed in the relation to life and the naturalness of human species is its quality: "But what [before] then appeared above all in the form of need, insufficiency, or weakness, illness, now appears as the intersection between a multiplicity of living individuals working and coexisting with each other in a set of material elements that act on them and on which they act in turn" (*STP*, 22). Life is no longer perceived as fundamentally negative, insufficient, and needy, but as a positive dynamic that power mechanisms can adopt in order to govern the living more efficiently. It is not life itself that becomes the object of biopower, but the biological link of the living (the population) to the materiality within which it exists, that is, its hybrid constitution that oscillates between the biological, natural, living dimension and the permeability to an artificial, social, and material manipulation within the milieu, a manipulation through power that appears *as if* it was natural.

Power of Resistance

To conclude, it is thus possible to affirm, from an epistemic perspective, that the techniques of biopolitics participate in the very movement of redefinition of the notion of life. They do not "confront" themselves to a life that exists beyond its historical constellations of power–knowledge, but they "invade" a life that is saturated with these very techniques and constellations, a correlative life, that consequently lacks an ontological status, a life that is undetermined and open to determinations and normalizations from the outside: a hybrid, natural–artificial life. Consequently it is not only the conditions of possibility of a *biology* that appear around 1800, but also the conditions of possibility of a *biopolitics*.

From a political perspective it is important to take a careful look at the twofold processes of life and their relation to biopolitics, since the "amplified" notion of biopolitics, governmentality, stands out from the sovereign or disciplinary techniques of power inasmuch as the security *dispositif* encloses both the self-preserving aspect of vital processes as well as the transgressive aspect and inscribes it incessantly in the biopolitical efforts of the constitution of a "good" population through the interaction with a milieu. The problem that arises with this amplified reading of the notion of biopolitics is the question of a possible "way out" of this positive and omnipresent form of power. One might think, after the analysis of vital normativity as a fundamental element of the post-sovereign strategies of power, that this is where a possible resistance to the forms of power lies, in a "form of life" that transcends its inscription into a power mechanism. But it is crucial to understand that the normativity of life, even taken as the model of the modus operandi of post-sovereign power, is not exterior to these strategies of power and thus cannot propose an "outside of power" as some of the recent interpretations of Foucault's notion of biopolitics suggest.

Foucault himself does not treat explicitly the problem of resistance in relation to biopower beyond the unveiling of their quasi-organic entanglement. In the first part of *The History of Sexuality* he thus presents the identification of a simple affirmation of sexuality to resistance against power as an illusion created by power itself. The so-called sexual revolution does not mean the liberation of a dominated subject but its major inscription into the sexual *dispositif*:[29]

> We must not think that by saying yes to sex, one says no to power; on the contrary one tracks along the course laid out by the general deployment of sexuality. It is the agency of sex that we must break away from, if we aim— through a tactical reversal of the various mechanisms of sexuality—to counter the grips of power with the claims of bodies, pleasures, and knowledges, in their multiplicity and their possibility of resistance. The rallying point of the counterattack against the deployment of sexuality ought not to be sex–desire, but bodies and pleasures. (*WK*, 157)

This somehow imprecise affirmation does not give many leads to understand what resistance to power might be, but it has given way to various "positive" readings of the "last" Foucault. These readings link the apparent rupture in the theory of power (between biopolitics and governmentality) to the third "theoretical shift"[30] that following Foucault had become necessary in order to analyze "what is termed 'the subject'" (*UP*, 6).

Instead of following this path that links the subjective turn to a reformulation of the theory of power (that allegedly has ended in a "dilemma") and the possibility of a space beyond power that seems not fully coherent with Foucault's thinking,[31] I would like to focus on an alternative way of approaching the phenomena of resistance by taking a brief look at what Foucault himself introduces under the term of "counter-conducts" or "counter-discourses." In his reading of Foucault's work, Deleuze describes the question of resistance within biopower as follows:

> When power becomes bio-power, resistance becomes the power of life, a vital power that cannot be confined within a species, environment or the paths of a particular diagram. Is not the force that comes from outside a certain idea of life, a certain vitalism in which Foucault's thought culminates?[32]

Deleuze explicitly affirms the existence of a vital force that is fundamentally resistant and escapes the biopolitical techniques: "a force that comes from the outside." He thus realizes two operations that according to my understanding of biopolitics would be inadmissible: he identifies life as the ontological support for a resisting force, and he localizes this resistance in an "outside" of power. By doing so, he misses two crucial points in the Foucaultian analytics of power. Deleuze is unable to think the dynamics of power as the (social) imitation or reenactment of the vital dynamics (since this operation would put the vital resistance in a dangerous proximity to power). But he also misses the ubiquity of post-sovereign power which is one of its main features and does not represent a "dilemma."

Nevertheless the vital force, or the specific vitalism, that Deleuze understands as the third axis needed by Foucault in the crisis after the publication of *The History of Sexuality: Volume I*, as Agamben has recalled, might seem homogeneous to the vital dynamics Canguilhem introduces. However, life as understood by Canguilhem is a normative concept, defined in the polarity between two tendencies, self-regulation and self-transgression. Life is the normative tension between these two poles and it is fundamentally related to vital negative values such as anomaly, illness, and death. For Canguilhem, there is no self-regulation without self-transgression and vice-versa. The homeostasis of the organism is produced through the deviations of the organism, deviations that are not reducible to their organic function, but that permanently transgress the cycle of equilibrium of the organism in order to be fully vital, that is, normative. The notion of life is fundamentally determined by this polarity. The power *over* life refers to life insofar as it is polar, that is, it encompasses both, the organic and the vital, dimensions of life. Therefore the force of life is not an alternative to power, but rather a structural moment (an organic element) of power. Thus, for Foucault, the tactical production of deviation is to be understood as a step further toward the inscription of life in the paradigm of post-sovereign power. In fact this form of power adopts the features of an immunitarian democracy, that is, the features of a form of power that tends to immunize life in its totality, so that the production of differences (under the global motto of multiculturalism) may be considered nothing else than the last spin of this same power.[33]

Precisely the modus operandi of biopower that imitates the dynamics of life makes this affirmation more transparent. The governmental operation of biopower consists in reducing the normative potential of life to its normal equilibrium from the moment on when this dynamic–normative potential tends to transgress the admissible limits for the good operation of government, or, to follow up on the biological metaphor, when the creative force of life and its tendency to self-transgression tends to exceed the self-regulating and self-conservative (homeostatic) tendencies of life. Biopolitics in this amplified sense is characterized by confronting this twofold dynamics. Consequently it is impossible to speak of a power *of* life that imposes on or exceeds the power *over* life. Biopolitics admits the free play of creative tendencies of life as long as they can be integrated in the global equilibrium of the population. If they exceed the limits of integration and threat to become *ungovernable*, their normativity ought to be reduced to their normality, because *society must be defended*.

As regarding the second point of Deleuze's analysis, it is useful to take seriously Foucault's affirmation that there is no outside to power. More than in his books, it is in his "minor" writings where Deleuze once called the other side of Foucault's thought, where lines of actualization can be traced, that Foucault adopts what he himself would later call a "critical posture." In an interview that Jacques Rancière held with Foucault for the newly founded magazine *Les Révoltes Logiques* in 1977, a year after the publication of *The History of Sexuality: Volume I*, he puts it as follows:

> There are no relations of power without resistances; the latter are all the more real and effective because they are formed right at the point where relations of power are exercised; resistance to power does not have to come from elsewhere to be real, nor is it inexorably frustrated through being the compatriot of power. It exists all the more by being in the same place as power; hence, like power, resistance is multiple and can be integrated in global strategies.[34]

The question of resistance cannot be asked outside the analytics of power; and resistance ought to be formulated as "counter-conducts" or "counter-discourses." There is no exteriority to power in the Foucaultian theory of power, and resistance is intrinsically linked to the very dynamics of power and thus initiates the interminable spiral of power and counter-power. Resistance to power does not derive from a theory of social exclusion, but it is itself a "theory" in the Foucaultian sense: a "non-totalizing, local and regional practice," a "prise de parole" of those exposed to power relations. These "words [*paroles*]" understood as counter-discourses and counter-conducts can destabilize the sensible conditions of visibility and sayability, or rather the determination and restriction of these conditions, that is, the partition of the sensible, to speak with Rancière. And they will thus reenact a stage of the political where the supposed naturalness of the constellations of power and knowledge are exposed and possibly deconstructed.

FIVE

Power over Life, Politics of Death: Forms of Resistance to Biopower in Foucault

Francesco Paolo Adorno

Biopower as the Marriage of Medicine and Economics

As Foucault was working on his analysis of the transformation of power from the Renaissance to the contemporary world, he wrote a number of essays, for the most part in the form of conferences, on the relationship between economics, medicine, and biology.[1] In these texts, Foucault describes various changes pertaining to the role of medicine. At the turn of the eighteenth century under the pressures of a significant modification in Europe's economic geography, the health and physical well-being of the population became targets for political power. From this moment on, power will be concerned with the population understood as a living body that is itself composed of other living bodies.[2] Medicine will become a major part of this device (*dispositif*) of biopower, since medicine is precisely what must guarantee the health of both individuals and of the population in general. But the insertion of medicine into this new device requires that medicine change its nature: to its "classical" occupation with individual healing is added a social medicine, that is, a generalized hygenicism achieved through a set of social measures that prevents any weakening of the population's body.[3] The population becomes the object of a "nosopolitics," a politics of health which is simultaneously an administration or management of the body. Modernity is haunted by the will to know the body so as to manipulate, alter, and modify it, and finally so as to make it immortal: in this will to modify the body one sees the elements of a "somatocracy" that, according to Foucault, takes the place of a "theocracy."[4]

The premise of this project can be found in Bacon, accompanying, more or less explicitly, all scientific or technical progress that has been made since the seventeenth century.[5] But the mutual arrangement between medicine and an economics that plugs itself into the body gains enormously in importance by the mid-twentieth century, as exemplified by the Beveridge Report which enacted, in the middle of World War II, the institutionalization of this relationship between medicine and economics, bringing health "into the field of macroeconomics." In modernity, power is not only concerned with life and rooted in subjects as living bodies and in the population as a body of living subjects, but power also works toward specific ends that have been dictated by economics. If biopower is power that takes life as its chief object, then the care for life is a form of life administration that seeks to preserve life.[6] As power takes life under its wing, this very act enables a rational management of the forces of power, leading to their expansion. The individual is endowed with a "human capital" in its physical strength, which ought to be used toward the best possible results, for both its own good and for the good of society (*BB*, 215–37; *STP*, 311–32).

In *The History of Sexuality: Volume I*, Foucault describes the way in which life irrupts into the realm of politics and the resultant formalization of the economy as an instrument of the rationalization of politics. Foucault starts from the definition of the sovereign's power, symbolized by the sword, a power which has the right to put to death and allow to live. This sovereign power is essentially a power to take, to appropriate things: "Power in this instance was essentially a right of seizure: of things, time, bodies, and ultimately life itself; it culminated in the privilege to seize hold of life in order to suppress it" (*WK*, 136). In sovereign power, the relationship between politics and economics is quite simply the idea that the richer one is, the more power one has; that the more things one possesses, the more powerful one is. The right to seize defined sovereign power to such an extent that this right could even become the right to eliminate what others possessed: the death sentence that the sovereign could pass was the legitimate, legal consequence of the proprietary right he had to things and persons.

Foucault observes that, beginning in the early modern period, the way in which power was exercised changes. The relationships between politics and economics were no longer reduced to the relationship between wealth and poverty:

> "Deduction" has tended to be no longer the major form of power but merely one element among others, working to incite, reinforce, control, monitor, optimize, and organize the forces under it: a power bent on generating forces, making them grow, and ordering them, rather than one dedicated to impeding them, making them submit, or destroying them. (*WK*, 136)

In this new art of government, law cedes to economics its previous role as a check to the sovereign's appetites. From now on, the sovereign or the governing bodies will look to economics for the validation and legitimation of their actions, and the economy will henceforth become the limiting principle of sovereign power (*BB*, 44).

The immediate consequence of this change will be a total redefinition of the relationships between economics, politics, and law:

> On the basis of the new governmental reason—and this is the point of separation between the old and the new, between raison d'État and reason of the least state—government must no longer intervene, and it no longer has a direct hold on things and people; it can only exert a hold, it is only legitimate, founded in law and reason, to intervene, insofar as interest, or interests, the interplay of interests, make a particular individual, thing, good, wealth, or process of interest for individuals, or for the set of individuals, or for the interest of a given individual faced with the interest of all. (*BB*, 45)

With modernity the situation changes drastically on the basis of a theoretical phenomenon: the "entry of life into history" (*WK*, 141). Power no longer deals with "legal subjects over whom the ultimate dominion was death, but with living beings, and the mastery it would be able to exercise over them would have to be applied at the level of life itself; it was the taking charge of life, more than the threat of death, that gave power its access even to the body" (*WK*, 143). With this decline in the force of law comes a progressive increase in the importance of the norm—insured by its economic value (*WK*, 144). The direct consequence of the entry of life into the political scene will be the substitution of the dyad economy–norm in place of the dyad right–law (*WK*, 145). In reality, biology grafts itself onto this new art of government which was already beginning to give way to economics: "The essential issue of government will be the introduction of economy into political practice. And if this is true in the sixteenth century, it is still the case in the eighteenth century" (*STP*, 95).

Economics of Police Power

From the beginning of the seventeenth to the first half of the eighteenth century, governmental reason, that is, the system of veridiction that validates governmental practices (*BB*, 16–38), is constituted by mercantilism and reason of state, two doctrines that sought to achieve the same goals. Foremost among them is the preservation of sovereign power (*STP*, 102), which can and must be realized only through the use of a specific knowledge that is not entirely law and is not yet political economy. All definitions of reason of state, starting with the one given by Giovanni Botero ("*Raison d'État* . . . is the knowledge of the appropriate means for founding, preserving, and expanding such a domination" [*STP*, 238]) contain a reference to this new knowledge. So as best to define the characteristics of the new art of government, Foucault's analysis centers on three questions: the question of salvation, the problem of truth, and the legitimation of obedience, which is our chief interest here.

Foucault discusses an essay by Francis Bacon, "Of Seditions and Troubles," to reveal a set of problems concerning the way to avoid crises about the king's legitimacy, a subject which Machiavelli had already brought to light but which Bacon takes up in an entirely new manner. The English chancellor argues that it is possible to guarantee tranquility to a government by eliminating all material causes of revolution, meaning the destitute state of the people and the discontent of the aristocracy (*STP*, 268).

While for Machiavelli the source of sedition is always to be found among the aristocracy, for Bacon the people are far more dangerous. Extreme poverty poses the most serious problem for the stability of the state and must be eliminated or at least reduced. The methods to be employed in this pursuit are economic and statistical: to allow everyone to have a standard of living that is above poverty, Bacon writes, action must be taken regarding commerce, the circulation of men and merchandise, eliminating slothfulness, putting everyone to work, promoting commerce, reducing the most dramatic differences between the rich and the poor, and so forth. At a basic level, the state guarantees its preservation through an essentially *economic* calculation. In this way, the state is able to manage the population by assuring a satisfactory standard of living. The state must calculate all of its strengths so that it may preserve that same strength in all of its parts. But the state must also calculate its strengths so as not to find itself in a position of inferiority in relationship to the strength of other states. The conservation of power is achieved through the careful maintenance of a homeostatic relationship between interior and exterior, so that the pressure exercised from the outside does not crush the state and the pressure exercised from the interior does not become explosive. For this art of government, it is no longer a question of:

> conforming to, approaching, or remaining true to the essence of a perfect government. Henceforth the art of government will not consist in restoring an essence or in remaining faithful to it, but in manipulating, maintaining, distributing, and re-establishing relations of force within a space of competition that entails competitive growths. (*STP*, 312)

In this theoretical configuration, the police play a crucial role. *Police* "begins to refer to the set of means by which the state's forces can be increased while preserving the state in good order" (*STP*, 313). The police as well as the knowledges it employs in the exercise of its functions will allow the state to maintain the same strength as that of the other states. In a sort of implicit continuity, the concrete functioning of the police, as it is described in the eighteenth century, takes up and applies the imperatives proclaimed by Bacon.

In his work *La monarchie aristodémocratique*, Turquet de Mayerne indicates that the conserver and the general reformer of the police manages four offices: the Police Bureau, concerned with the instruction and occupations of the young; the Charity Bureau, concerned with the poor, the ill, the disabled, thus "public health in times of epidemic and contagion, and also at other times"; a third bureau, concerned with merchants and all questions linked to commerce and production; and, lastly, the Bureau of the Territory, concerned with questions of property and property ownership (*STP*, 320). Fundamentally, the object of the police are individuals in their biological life and existence: their health, the conditions of their physical and moral development, the labor conditions they experience and that will allow them, once again, to look after themselves properly.

Theorists of the science of police declare, more often than they suspect, that the goal of politics or government is the happiness of individuals and of the population, and this is indicative of the point at which politics anchors itself in subjectivity (OES, 320). For what does happiness mean to these theoreticians, from Machiavelli to von Justi? Quite simply, what matters to these thinkers is the capacity to guarantee everyone the necessities of life, happiness being a full belly. As Foucault presents von Justi's theory:

> The police, he [von Justi] says, is what enables the state to increase its power and exert its strength to the full. On the other hand, the police has to keep the citizens happy—happiness being understood as survival, life, and improved living. He perfectly defines what I feel to be the aim of the modern art of government, or state rationality, namely, to develop those elements constitutive of individuals' lives in such a way that their development also fosters the strength of the state. (OES, 322)

All in all, one is completely justified in thinking that the art of government which holds valid from the beginning of the seventeenth century to the first half of the eighteenth century is articulated around the economic management of individuals' lives so as to maximize their strength (*STP*, 319). In other words, human life is the most precious of the state's goods: by acting on the well-being of individuals, the existence of the state itself, as well as the power of the sovereign, is reinforced.

Foucault's next Course, *The Birth of Biopolitics*, carries forth this genealogy of governmentality: he examines physiocracy and both German and American economic liberalism in succession. As always, he will tease out a complex series of similarities and differences between these doctrines which are arts of government more than economic theories. But beyond these differences, beyond the changes in the points at which power becomes connected with individuals and the population, beyond an economic reasoning that rests on an anthropology and an ethics which are continuously changing, the juncture between economy and biology, as well as the reasons for this marriage between them, will always remain constant in the different arts of government. From the start of the seventeenth century and up to and including the present day, the practice of government will be an art in which what is at stake is the life of the individual and of the population. And if the ways in which power "deals with" life change, its goal remains always the same: to guarantee the preservation of power and the stability of the political framework, or, to borrow Foucault's words, to freeze power relations into relations of domination through the economic maximization of the life of individuals.

This is indeed what Foucault sets out to demonstrate in *The History of Sexuality: Volume I* through his study of sexuality. Power found in sexuality a particularly favorable anchoring point, since it is *the* essential biological phenomenon from the perspective of both the individual and the population. But sexuality is also of central importance because it is the phenomenon whose mastery permits the control and management of the lives of individuals by means of its maximization and optimization. It is not enough to emphasize that biopower is a power over life; it is also necessary to add that biopower takes up once more, for its own ends, the modality of the enactment of economics so as to ensure its grip on subjects: in other words, biopower guarantees itself their subjection by taking the subject's well-being into account.

From Biopolitics to a Politics of Death

The flipside of the coin of this new art of government is represented by the change in the status of death: if sovereign power is a "right to let live and put to death," modernity's governmental art is a "right to make live and let die." More precisely, Foucault asserts that "the ancient right to *take* life or *let* live was replaced by a power to *foster* life or *disallow* it to the point of death" (*WK*, 138). In a broad sense it is the relationship between life and power, the description and the analysis of the modification power undergoes as it passes from one epoch to another, which has drawn the attention of Foucault's readers. All the same, besides this transformation of a right to let live into a right to make live, there is also the transformation of a putting to death—a seizing of life—into a letting die or casting into death. Not much importance has been attributed to this second transformation, and it has been viewed as only one modality of the power over life. This is how Foucault's formula "massacres have become vital" (*WK*, 137) has been understood: insofar as the life of populations must be guaranteed, it can become necessary to sacrifice one group of individuals so that another group may continue to live. Thus biopolitics is also, in this sense, a thanatopolitics—a politics which operates through a politicization of death;[7] a politics which, inasmuch as it must manage, optimize, and guarantee the health of life, cannot afford to ignore the necessity of sacrificing some part of the population. This is an old topos of Catholic literature which is reactualized in an entirely new context: it is possible to cut off a part of the mystical body of the Church to guarantee its *health* which is nothing other than its *salvation*, even if this intervention takes place on a moral and spiritual level. From the very moment in which the goal of the state becomes the management of the body, and government becomes a "somatocracy," the amputation of sick parts takes on a new meaning in accordance with the new goals of government, for amputation is about eliminating what endangers the health of the body. Medicine and politics go hand in hand. They produce techniques of social hygiene to eliminate or restrict the detrimental effects of diseases, poor nutrition, or dilapidated housing. But they can also cooperate, still working for the same goals, in the extermination of one part of the population that biologically endangers society's existence.[8] These two disciplinary methods are so complementary that, as Roberto Esposito argues, in Nazism's biomedical vision curing and assassinating were two faces of the same coin.[9]

Nevertheless, analyzing the biopolitical apparatus in this way may lead one to ignore the most important aspect of Foucault's critical discourse: the way in which politics grafts itself onto life to satisfy imperatives of an economic order, and the fact that death is also taken into this economic circle. Biology is a knowledge with strong ties to economics, or, better, the developments of biology obey imperatives of an economic order—not only in the trivial sense that biological discoveries are subject to economic exploitation, but also in the sense that the economy directs biology to take up the ends of the economy. How to interpret in light of this idea of biology the fact that death turns into a vital question? To say that death is a possibility that life provides for itself to maximize itself, to enlarge its power, is doubtless true but also partial. It is true that biopower immediately seizes on life as a biological fact, but this captivation is only realized inasmuch as life, the brute biological fact, is the substrate of a certain number of statistical events, demographics that are fundamental for economics since the very first attempts to formalize a political economy. Furthermore, Foucault is not discussing death but rather mortality (*SMD*, 248).

On the other hand, insofar as the threat to put entire populations to death is mobilized, individual death—the individual's own power to throw himself into the abyss of nonbeing—is seen as scandalous and relegated to the margins of society and politics. Individuals are cast off into death, but death itself is also cast off—these two gestures are in some way synchronous. The dying man from now on occupies an asocial position that enables the repression of death on the individual as well as on the societal level. Of course, funerals, practices of mourning, and rites pertaining to the dead have not entirely disappeared, but their lack of meaning is more and more evident. Nevertheless, the care that is taken to avoid dying is, according to Foucault, "linked less to a new anxiety which makes death unbearable for our societies than to the fact that the procedures of power have not ceased to turn away from death" (*WK*, 138). It is thus no longer a moral question, but instead a particular political choice: power over life never manages to get hold of death, and because of this power over life chooses to ignore and repress death, even while dispensing death on an industrial scale, as was the case in Nazism.

But is this all one can say about death? Are there only two options to choose from in speaking of death? The first of these would be to approach this event from the perspective of a biopolitics of the population, thus by relating it to questions about the hygiene of states in the broad sense, always tackling death as a generality and representing only its large-scale events, that is, those with some political value. The second would be to enter into mourning for the death of mourning, to return to the anatomopolitics of the individual and protest the normalization of death, to dissect the reasoning that relegates death and the dying to the political and social fringes of society. One seems to be caught in the jaws of a political machine that deals with all aspects of human life, including death, whenever it suits the goals of the machine to do so, and that can alternately repress any of these aspects, removing them from the social realm, when it cannot draw any further advantages from them. But this standpoint leads back to saying that, in one way or another, death is incorporated into life and into the processes of maximization, optimization, and augmentation to which life itself submits. If biopolitics is an art of government that takes the living being as living into account, that manages the living, in the pursuit of economic ends (augmentation, maximization, optimization), that grafts itself onto the body so as to draw out of it all its strength, then it would certainly seem that death also has entered into this economic cycle. Perhaps by returning to the context in which these analyses of governmental devices take place one would be able to find an alternative to this situation which appears to be completely saturated by the relations between economics, biology, and medicine.

Death as Resistance to Biopower

We know that biopolitics is, in fact, a politics that centers on the management of the passage from the zero degree of life, what the Greeks called *zoe*, to *bios*, a life which possesses form. The power–knowledge device used in mercantilism and reason of state, and later in physiocracy and liberalism, takes charge of biological life so as to subjectivize life in accordance with its own ends—with one important difference. Whereas *zoe* and *thanatos* are mutually exclusive, since biological life and biological death correspond to each other in such a way that where the one is the other has ceased to be, *bios* and *thanatos* are not exclusive, and even may not be able to exclude each other since *bios* includes *thanatos* among its moments: "To a characteristic life belongs a characteristic death. This life is indeed characterized by the manner of its ceasing to be."[10] In other words, if one can say that for *zoe*, death is an incomprehensible paradox because when death takes place *zoe* has ineluctably reached its end, then for *bios* death is a constitutive and integral element. On the other hand, if *bios* is entirely a production of power, it must follow that the forms of death are themselves modalities allowing power to fix itself in individuals. The modalities of dying are themselves productions of power: power produces a form-of-life but also a form-of-death. But, as I have discussed above, biopower exerts itself mainly by maximizing the *zoe* that is inside *bios* itself, to the point where this maximization itself becomes a *bios*. Hence one can say that biopower functions on the individual level by appropriating for itself, through the maximization of *zoe*, the processes that form life as *bios* and channeling them into directions that optimize the probability that this *bios* will be preserved. Since death is an integral part of *bios*, it too is caught up in the net cast by power to entrap human life.[11]

Power holds the social realm hostage; and what's more, it has infiltrated all the domains of human existence, even its biological life, to a point where the search for some possible space of freedom, which would be situated outside of the devices of power, seems doomed. It is true that to the individual there remains the (entirely theoretical) possibility of folding otherwise the lines of force that subjectivize him or her from the outside. By establishing genealogies of her present position, the subject can attempt to desubjectivize herself. But perhaps there may be another form of resistance to power that could take root in the definition of some other relationship between *bios* and *thanatos*. Indeed, the opposition to power's appropriation of death, to the inclusion of death in the economic cycle, could open up some movement that removes individuals from the governing mode of production of forms of life. Would not the definition of the forms of death that represent the apogee of *bios* also count as a mode of resisting biopower, since these would steal back human existence from the economic reduction of life to its purely biological form?

Given that the fundamental element of biopower is its dangerous liaison with economics, this way of dying should structure itself so that in the end the biological body, bare life, would be removed from its infinite productivity which corresponds to the goal of power as it exerts itself on the living. Perhaps Foucault's words on suicide—which in no way constitute an apologia—are significant here. Suicide became a privileged object of analysis for nineteenth-century sociology precisely because it demonstrated the limits of biopower, in that it "testified to the individual and private right to die, at the borders and in the interstices of power that was exercised over life" (*WK*, 139).¹² The condemnation of suicide, draping itself in a cloak of theological and moral argumentation, is in fact motivated by economic and political considerations. A power that is dedicated to the biological optimization of the living finds it immensely difficult to comprehend the will to put oneself to death. Indeed, suicide, "this determination to die, strange and yet so persistent and constant in its manifestations, and consequently so difficult to explain as being due to particular circumstances or individual accidents, was one of the first astonishments of a society in which political power had assigned itself the task of administering life" (*WK*, 139; see also *SMD*, 238–63). This is why suicide is scandalous, indeed why suicide is *the* absolute political scandal in contemporary societies. If society is traversed by an infinite web of power relations that constantly encounter resistances whose strength is, for the most part, merely relative, what better resistance could be encountered by biopower than the removal of its very object? If one views suicide as a political, rather than a moral, question, one understands better the immensely violent reactions that accompany any attempt to manage one's own death by oneself. Clearly, one cannot underestimate the fact that these reactions may also spring from some explicit or implicit reiteration of the Christian interdiction that teaches that God alone can take away what He has given. What becomes more and more evident is the role that medicine is beginning to play in this interdiction. Suicide, or the individual and autonomous will to direct one's own disappearance, is a stumbling block for the therapeutic imperative that demands that medicine take control of the individual moment of death, to keep it in suspension or, even worse, to push it back indefinitely if necessary. A therapeutic imperative appears to coincide perfectly with the theoretical configuration of biopower, in which bare life can and must be managed in all of its manifestations, optimized to the point of its final exhaustion, before being ultimately removed from the political and social realms when it can no longer produce anything.

It would thus appear completely legitimate to ask if one form of resisting the biopolitical invasion could consist in opposing the gradual loss of meaning in death as well as the indefinite optimization of the event of death. Perhaps it would be precisely in the definition of a thanatopolitics, articulated around anti-economical, non-productive, powerless phenomena associated with death, rather than in political analyses of the biopolitical governmentality, that one could construct a form of resistance to the hegemony of political economy. This reappropriation of death would have two moments. First, death ought to correspond to life as *bios*: just as to a biological life there corresponds a biological death, so to a formed life should correspond a formed death. Second, when death is understood in this way, it must also be able to give some kind of non-productivity back to the body, to make the body useless as a body, to annihilate it, to preclude its introduction in the economic cycle of biopolitics as a living body, and thus—and above all—as a dead body.[13]

The history of philosophy and of anthropology furnishes examples of both of these moments. The Platonic tradition of the *melethe thanatou* (learning how to die) has always symbolized the possibility of a philosophy organized around death rather than life, a philosophy of decline and diminution rather than improvement and accumulation, of disappearance rather than production. For Plato the *melethe thanatou* had a very precise meaning: as stated in the *Phaedo*, "true philosophers do practice dying, and death is to them of all men least terrible."[14] It is true that this "practice" is based in training oneself to "separate the soul from the body," to return the soul to its true life that can begin once more after this separation, but what needs to be retained here is the idea that learning to die transforms "the level and tone of one's inner life." The value of this asceticism, a value which is not only ethical and individual but political and social, has been neatly summarized by Montaigne, who writes that "he who hath learned to die, hath unlearned to serve."[15] The echoes of this phrase resonate beyond the sixteenth century, passing through the master–slave dialectic of Hegel and reaching up to Heidegger's being-toward-death.[16]

At the crossroads of the anatomo-politics of the individual and the biopolitics of populations, the reflection on death forms the central moment of a way of taking responsibility for one's own existence that can even lead the subject toward conversion. This entire tradition of thought, articulated around a memento mori that is irreducible to a Christian attitude of resignation and contrition, or to a Platonic will to know truth at last, but that may possibly open onto specific patterns of political and social conduct, has been entirely dissolved under the pressure of the increasing medicalization of the physical and social body, operating more and more in the service of economic constraints.[17] It would seem that the West has lost not only all its forms of mourning or ritualizing death, which makes it difficult to die with dignity, but also the value accorded to death by wisdom, death's capacity to give shape to existence, and thus its political value.

As has been justly remarked, "the hubris and ambition of biomedical science is largely responsible for the dangerous and damaging denial of death within contemporary society."[18] Nevertheless medicine has not taken the upper hand in the management of the terminal moment of existence for purely scientific reasons. The entire theoretical configuration of modern thought, at least since Descartes, has moved in this direction, inasmuch as it considers death to be merely a physical event. The consequences of viewing death in this way are visible every day. But without getting held up in ethical questions, one can still take note of the fact that this conception of death and this reduction of the body to its mechanisms is the result of a connection between biology and economics. To oppose this scientific and theoretical tradition, one might evoke the way archaic cultures deal with the corpse. The corpse is not a thing among other things, but remains a body in possession of qualities that differ fundamentally from those of other things. It is the bearer of forces that transcend material reality, and as such it cannot be touched without obeying the multiple necessary precautions. The cost of such an error would be the destruction of the subjectivity of the one who has improperly handled the corpse.[19] Indeed, any relationship to the corpse is highly regimented. Archaic thought is completely shot through with a thanatology that "is not reducible to the set of rituals around death. It is a *Weltanschauung* and it is *weltanschaulich*, 'ideology.'"[20] For these archaic societies, death is not an object of reflection or the occasion for a particularly meaningful ritual; rather, and more profoundly, it is the center of life, of production, of rites, of society, because "when thought makes the meaning of the whole subordinate to the process of death, even the eclipse or rise of major stars will be affected by it."[21]

SIX

Identity, Nature, Life: Three Biopolitical Deconstructions

Judith Revel

In these past few years, the term "biopolitics" has enjoyed great success: in philosophy as well as in history, and more generally in the social and human sciences, a great number of scholars have helped themselves to the Foucaultian tool kit and used the term as an integral part of their analyses. In this essay I attempt to "deconstruct" three discursive employments of "biopolitics." Giorgio Agamben maintains that deconstruction represents a thwarted form of messianism. If one were to reverse this formula so as to understand messianism as an incomplete form of deconstruction, then the deconstruction that I would like to put to work in this essay could be understood as the necessary prologue to the construction of a way of thinking that would be simultaneously critical and affirmative—what some of us are calling "affirmative biopolitics." When extended by an affirmative reconstruction that checks its negative impulses and is simultaneously immersed in history, sifted through the mesh of a historicization that arrests its turn to metaphysics, deconstruction can become a powerful tool to think, in the wake of Foucault, about our own relationship to the present.

In Foucault, the activity of critique is inseparable from the work of construction (of experiences and problematizations, of fields of inquiry and conceptual tools): this is what he calls "genealogy." But this practice of genealogy in turn needs to be historically situated: whenever we talk, think, and act, we always do so in a given time and place, and thus we never escape the determinations of our own history. It is important to recall this rather obvious point because in the past twenty years an evident dehistoricization of several concepts has occurred, giving way to their metamorphosis into universal keys for the comprehension of reality. The concept of biopolitics has not escaped this trend: its applications are now as wide-ranging as they are vague, as if one and the same idea of biopolitics were at stake in Weimar Germany and in late Hellenistic antiquity, in the Middle Ages as in the Holocaust or in 1968—as if a single standard could be used to size up a history that had been reduced to a unity.

Contrary to this trend, I attempt to show that certain Foucaultian readings of biopolitics produce the exact inverse of what Foucault attempted to do. Even worse, these readings are undergirded by a series of presuppositions that Foucault tried to radically criticize by all means available to him. These readings mainly draw on ideas of "identity," "nature," and "life" which frequently turn up in Foucaultian biopolitical analyses. I could have taken up other terms like "norm," "governmentality," "individuals," or "populations," but I have chosen these three ideas because deconstruction is particularly important, if one is to forestall or avoid "sliding effects" or other potentially disastrous blunders.

The Critique of Identity and Biopolitics

Foucault's critique of identity is far earlier than his coinage of biopolitics. This critique first appears in the analysis of the great division between reason and madness at the center of *Madness and Civilization*. Here, Foucault systematically associates identity with the power of the *same*. Self-identity is what the *episteme* of the early modern age requires of us: because what appears as a figure of alterity—what the self cannot recognize as belonging to ipseity—is defined here, despite everything, as a variation, a derivation, a gap in relation of the self to itself. Consequently, all alterity would appear to be held prisoner to an identification linking it to what it is not (through the forms of the negative, the inverted double, exteriority). This dialectical stratagem that captivates what ought to be different, non-identical, and non-identifiable is explicitly a gesture of power (*pouvoir*), an act of violence. Modern rationality functions through a practice of "inclusive exclusion," which counts identification as one of its essential instruments. Foucault seeks to understand the epistemological mechanisms through which this identity can be fixed, organized, hierarchized, and controlled both from the perspective of knowledge and from that of power relations, both in the order of discourse and in the strategies for managing social and political order. To be identified is to be doubly objectivized: as the object of discourse and as the object of practices. Self-identity is the paradoxical construction of an objectivized subject of knowledges and powers, discourses and practices.

Since the 1960s, Foucault's radical critique of identity refers to a first analytic of powers which presents itself chiefly as an analytic of knowledges; but there is also in Foucault, on the other side of this analytic, an early investigation of those modes of subjectivization (*subjectivation*) that attempt to escape from the objective order of knowledge and attempt to present themselves as non-identifiable subjectivities. This identity critique "watermark" can already be discerned, although only with difficulty, in *Madness and Civilization* itself and in *The Order of Things*. However, it is entirely explicit in the majority of the texts on literature that Foucault was concurrently writing in the wake of the analyses produced around the work of Raymond Roussel.[1] The problem in these texts was: how can a subjective expression escape being immediately identified, objectivized, and subjectified within the system of knowledge–power in which it is inscribed? Only much later, in 1982, Foucault remarks, "This form of power that applies itself to immediate everyday life categorizes the individual, marks him by his own individuality, attaches him to his own identity, imposes a law of truth on him that he must recognize and others have to recognize in him" (SP, 331).

I believe that Foucault poses the same problem from within the framework of his work on biopolitics, although it is now present in a divided and doubled form, which does not make matters any easier. Starting in the 1970s,

Identity, Nature, Life 115

Foucault develops a double analysis of the way in which men and women are simultaneously "objectivized" in knowledges and practices, in discourses and strategies, which is to say everywhere and by all possible means assigned to an identity that proves their inclusion in the system. This double analysis focuses, on one side, on the governing of singularities through the production of the "individual," and, on the other side, on the government of masses of such "individuals" through the production of equally objectivized and identitary "homogeneous populations." Beginning with *Discipline and Punish*, this analytic division of labor is evident—I refer, for example, to the extraordinary pages dedicated to the functioning of the maritime hospital, or more generally to the rule of "productive placement" (*emplacement productif*). Still, in *Discipline and Punish* the discourse on "populations" is not pursued to its ultimate conclusion because it is missing a concept that would be able to account for both the production and the identification of a population as well as for its political management. Foucault is still lacking the concept of the norm as a new instrument of governmental technology which only makes its appearance with his formulation of biopolitics. This idea of norm no longer corresponds to the old juridical rule as the expression of a sovereign will, but to a natural rule (or one presumed to be natural) applied to homogenous groups, which are in turn defined on the basis of several common traits that are presented as "natural," and on the basis of which it is possible to construct a *social clinic*. From this point onward, subjectivization must avoid a trifecta of pitfalls: identification, individualization, and naturalization.

For Foucault, this theoretical and historical insight finds confirmation in an event which emerges in an entirely different context (passing from the birth of political economy in eighteenth-century Europe to the United States in the 1970s), and yet presents exactly the same problem—and, above all, calls for an answer that avoids the three pitfalls of identification, individualization, and naturalization. This event is the formation of the gay rights movement. On this occasion Foucault writes, "Although on a tactical level it's important to be able to say 'I am homosexual,' in my opinion, in the long term and in view of a greater strategy, one should avoid continuing to raise questions about *sexual identity*. In this case, what is most important is not confirming one's sexual identity, but *refusing the injunction to identify with sexuality, with the different forms of sexuality*."[2] For Foucault there is a sharp distinction to be made between what power relations construct in the form of an identity (as an objectivized, reified subjectivity, reduced to a set of defined characters, which will become the object of specific practices and knowledges) and the way in which subjectivity itself fashions its own relation to itself. In the first case, we are dealing with a subjectivation (*assujettissement*) that fixes identities on the basis of a set of determinations meant to "reveal the truth about the subject." This is the case with sexuality, which is transformed into a "symptom" or code of what the individual is objectively reduced to. In the second case, Foucault's rejection of the reduction of subjectivities to identities pushes him to theorize another kind of relation to the self and to others—even in sexual practices—by introducing a notion which will become essential in numerous texts from his last years, the notion of a "way of life [*mode de vie*]": "This notion of a way of life seems important to me. . . . A way of life can be shared among individuals of different age, status, and social activity. It can yield intense relations not resembling those that are institutionalized. It seems to me that a way of life can yield a culture and an ethics. To be 'gay,' I think, is not to identify with the psychological traits and the visible masks of the homosexual, but to try to define and develop a way of life."[3]

For Foucault, a way of life excludes neither age difference, nor social or status differences, but he does not reduce these multiple differences which run through us and make us into who we are to something which would be of the order of the identical or the same. These differences, *as* differences, subsist in a *way of life*. A way of life makes common these differences *as* differences; it constructs the common on this differential base. This is the mirror opposite of all those theories of the relation to the other that call for a fundamental decentering of the self toward the other, that postulate oneself as an other. American gay rights movements in the early 1980s were trying to experiment, according to Foucault's interpretation, with living in a relation to the other without these differences (self, other) ever being reified (objectivized) or reduced to some kind of "greatest common denominator" (forced universalization, reduction to the same) or even considered as something one needs to get rid of in order to have access to one's neighbor (oneself as an other).

A way of life, Foucault tells us, is an ethics—a way of living together. It is *stricto sensu* a gesture which constitutes a shared space in an entirely new way: this *constitution*, so far removed from the *institutions* that Foucault casts in a negative light in the citation I have just commented on, is for that reason the experimental enactment of a *polis*, and thus of a *politics*. This political character of ethics goes counter to those interpretations that see in Foucault's texts of the 1980s a retreat from politics and its replacement by an "ethics" understood as some kind of return to morality or to the reassuring order of values. Ethics in Foucault is neither a "moral" nor an "individualist" or "egoist" retreat. Ethics means the problematicization of the common which is constructed on the basis of differences and puts these differences to work in a new way of leading one's life. And the conduct of one's existence here always includes a relation to others—apprenticeship, reciprocal construction and subjectivization, pleasure—that rejects not only a return to individualism (as if Foucault's analyses of ethics authorizes constructing the individual as a free entrepreneur of itself, in the neoliberal manner) but also rejects the naturalization, substantialization, and essentialization of this self that is put into play in the shared elaboration of ways of life.

When I speak of an ethics or a politics of "ways of life," that is, a program that makes subjectivization—or the always renewed construction of the common on the basis of differences—into the *barycentre* of resistance to the objectivization, ordering, hierarchizing, and controlling of who we are, I am speaking of a life that, precisely because it implies irreducible singularities, exists as a *qualified*, situated, specified life. Each singularity is irreducible to the others—in this sense it is *different*—because it emerges and *becomes* in a determined context, inside a web of relations and contacts which include, to be sure, not only other subjectivities with which that singularity will attempt to develop and work out previously unknown ways of life, but also power relations and *dispositifs* that always run through any singularity, no matter what the latter may do. I do not need to recall how chimerical Foucault considers the dream of being "outside" of power: resistance takes place from the inside of a complex network that links resistance to powers, links subjectivization to the process of objectivization, links the opening of freedoms to the reins of norms, and lastly links the logic of becoming to the strategies that substantialize being. On the other hand, nothing can transform the very motor of resistance—subjectivization—into an impersonal power, a "third person," or into the "absence of qualities" of singularities. Recent readings of Foucault, in particular the ones coming out of Italy, are pursuing this path, and in my opinion are getting lost because of it. For Foucault, subjectivization must necessarily proceed by becoming more complex because becoming is a subjectivization that does not merely integrate something of the new difference to its own initial difference, but proceeds by augmenting its predicates: ontological power (*puissance*) is at work here, a transition toward a "surplus of being [*plus d'être*]." In so doing, subjectivation builds the common on the basis of the laying out of these differences, which not only remain such as they are (irreducibly "different") but also, because they become, enter into a differential relationship with their own singularity: one is not singular; it is only because one becomes that one gains access to singularity. In Italian readings of Foucault such as one finds in the writings of Giorgio Agamben, Roberto Esposito, or Paolo Virno the transition through a state of being without qualities (*le quelconque*), through the impersonal, or through the pre-individual, obeys nothing but a logical necessity, which in turn rests on a mistake. This logic runs as follows: by de-subjectivizing singularity, one believes that one is able to return to the common which is taken as the basis of all shared resistance. The common, in the three configurations I have just mentioned, is what precedes, or, better, what is obtained once the surface of the singular existences of men and women is scraped away. I believe that such a "return" to the common pays the price of transforming a political thought—that of the powerful (*puissante*) subjectivization of differences, of their becoming and of their resistance—into a new postmodern metaphysics. But the common is not the reassuring basis from which to think political production: to the contrary, the common is its result. Once singularities are eliminated, one eliminates what allows for resistance in the first place: the articulation of difference as becoming and of subjectivization as the power (*puissance*) to invent shared ways of life, as the invention of the common. The common lies ahead of us and it can only be predicated of differences.

The Concept of Nature in Biopolitics

I now come to the second central notion in the elaboration of biopolitical thought. Here again, Foucault did not wait until his Courses at the Collège de France in the late 1970s to formulate what I take to be the foundation of his virulent anti-naturalism. Foucault began by associating nature to the origin and to the universal; later, he associates nature to the political strategy of biologizing life that will be interpreted as one of the characteristics of biopolitics from the nineteenth century on. In the first two cases, nature is denounced as the basis of Western metaphysics, which is embodied first in the idea of a foundation or of an origin, and then in the idea of a transcendent and unquestionable universal. Nature is what must be dissolved so as to escape from the metaphysical illusion. The Nietzschean (i.e., historicizing) tone of Foucault's critique is clear:

> History becomes "effective" to the degree that it introduces discontinuity into our very being—as it divides our emotions, dramatizes our instincts, multiplies our body and sets it against itself. "Effective" history leaves nothing around the self, deprives the self of the reassuring stability of life and nature.[4]

Nature stands for everything that is opposed to discontinuity and to difference: it is what restrains becoming.[5]

In the famous 1974 debate with Noam Chomsky about human nature, Foucault once more affirmed his critique of each and every form of universality, of the unconditioned, and of nonhistorical givens (represented in this case by Chomsky's notion of nature, considered as a set of invariants), as well as his distrust of the more general idea that there exist "regularities" in the actions and productions of men which exceed their own history. The historicization of regularities (and thus also the historicization of their identification, measurement, and classification) is for Foucault an essential methodological element, one he had already developed in *Madness and Civilization*, and even more so in *The Order of Things*, in which the slow transformation of the principles and objects of classification in the natural sciences—and in particular in the transition from Linnaeus to Geoffroy Saint-Hilaire—is of fundamental importance:

> To say that these regularities are connected, as conditions of existence, to the human mind or its nature is difficult for me to accept: it seems to me that one must, before reaching that point ... replace it in the field of other human practices, such as economics, technology, politics, sociology, which can serve them as conditions of formation, of models, of place, of apparition, etc. I would like to know whether one cannot discover the system of regularity, of constraint,

which makes science possible, somewhere else, even outside the human mind, in social forms, in the relations of production, in the class struggles, etc.[6]

It is this same attempt at historicization that one finds at work in the texts dedicated to the birth of biopolitics: if indeed biopolitics posits and employs a new kind of rule—the norm—that rests upon the idea of a "biological" naturalness of life, which social medicine preserves and protects by implanting into life new techniques of managing both individuals and populations, then this means that power relations in the nineteenth century constructed a new reference to naturalness so as to transform it into a novel instrument of control. It is not that nature in itself does not exist, but, in his investigation of the nineteenth century, Foucault discovers the emergence of a new political use for this reference to the natural, which is in itself absolutely nonnatural and whose genealogy must be established. In sum, "Everything in our knowledge which is suggested to us as being universally valid must be tested and analyzed."[7] The vitalism that appears to have established biopolitics consequently needs to be considered as a historical product, and not as the condition of possibility for all knowledge about human beings: "History draws these sets before erasing them; we must not look here for brute, definitive biological facts that would impose themselves on history from out of the depths of 'nature.'"[8]

For Foucault, life is not exclusively biological life. One sees this in his discussion of the notion of "ways of life" as strategies of resistance in the writings on subjectivity and ethics of the 1980s. But this is already true much earlier on: to say that one must always set the inquiries back into the context of "economics, technology, politics, sociology, which can serve them as conditions of formation, of models," that is, in "social forms, in the relations of production, in the class struggles,"[9] does that not put the emphasis on life as a historical construction, as an existence rather than as a biological and physiological process? I do not mean to suggest that biological life does not exist—quite simply, it is one of a multiplicity of elements that are given the task of characterizing the lives of men and women, but not the only element. The power over life—"biopower"—is not exclusively a biological power but is also composed of devices (*dispositifs*) of subjection and exploitation, of captivation and regulation, of control and ordering of life in general—that is, of existence writ large. Of course, the recent development of biotechnologies and of genetic engineering calls for vigilance: the Orwellian descriptions are in all of our minds. But it is not preordained that all this new research on living beings must exclusively be the omen of evil, just as it is obvious that this research is only one of the various faces of the power over life that confronts us daily. Undoubtedly the mystification of biopower works in order to mask all these *other* aspects behind the smokescreen of an excessive biologization.

Lastly, it seems that today, paradoxically, this "biologization" of life is found in even the most sophisticated Italian readings of Foucault. The problem of the paradigm of immunity in Esposito, or (in another register) the paradigm of bare life in Agamben, is precisely that they maintain an ambiguity with respect to whether Foucault's understanding of life is reducible to biological life. Although both authors take care to distinguish *bios* from *zoe*, their analyses seem to ensure right away that what makes biopolitical power special is precisely its capacity to blur this distinction. One would like to reply to both: the paradigm of immunity, or, if one prefers, the definition of the political as a body, is it really separable from a political thought peculiar to modernity, starting with Hobbes's Leviathan? As for bare life, the concept seems to allude to something on which life understood as a historico-social construction would be founded, some sort of primal nucleus or primordial stratum, which Agamben defines exactly as the reduction of *bios* to *zoe*? Yet, even the way in which one attempts to think biology—or "nature" in general—does not escape history, that is, a cultural construction. It is sufficient to recall Foucault's work on the natural sciences in the 1960s, for instance in *The Order of Things*, or to more recent analyses of the way in which the opposition between nature and culture, so fundamental in anthropology, is in fact ripe for an *anthropological* deconstruction. In short, the idea of "biological life" is no more able than the idea of "nature" to save us the trouble of a spatial, temporal, and cultural contextualization.[10]

Life and Creativity

This brings me to the third deconstruction I assigned myself, that of the idea of "life." Foucault approaches the theme of life from three main directions. The first of these, which is linked to the notion of the archive, consists in reading, for the most part out of the records of the Hôpital Général and the Bastille from the seventeenth and eighteenth centuries, the fragmentary accounts of the lives of anonymous men as so many traces of what Foucault calls "power's takeover of life's ordinariness."[11] Foucault is struck by the strength of these shreds of anonymous existence, whose violence and poetic character, extreme theatricality and savagery were later to be flattened by administrative procedures into a nomenclature that contented itself only to register their essential data and sift them through its own categories. Foucault planned to devote an anthology to them; the project would in the end become a series of publications at Gallimard, titled *Parallel Lives*. The memoir of Herculine Barbin and *Le cercle amoureux d'Henri Legrand* were both published in this collection. To interest oneself in the "lives of infamous men" (the title of one of Foucault's most beautiful texts) is to devote oneself to understanding how strategies of power are intertwined with the setting into discourse of minute details and why "these things that constitute the ordinary, the unimportant detail, obscurity, days without glory, communal life, can and must be said—and, even better, written."[12]

The second approach is that of biopolitics and biopowers—in their strictest sense: powers over life, which in fact represents a continuation of this setting of life into discourse, but also adds a new dimension to discourse—the emergence of new kinds of knowledge (police knowledge, the knowledge of the penal institution, psychiatric knowledge, etc.). From the beginning of the nineteenth century, life becomes simultaneously the object of power relations and also what is at stake in power relations. In the economic, demographic, and political genealogy of this new way of governing men, Foucault underscores the manner in which life in its most intimate aspects becomes an object of investment so as to maximize production and minimize costs: sexuality and nutrition, demography and health brusquely become the matter for public policy. Finally, in the 1980s Foucault seems to turn the definition of biopowers (powers over life) over to the space of a possible resistance. Where life falls prey to procedures of management and control, exploitation and captivation, it can also affirm that which no power (*pouvoir*) will ever possess: its own capacity (*puissance*) of creation. This is life as a capacity of subjectivization, the working out of this long and differential becoming of singular differences, and thus also, as we have seen, the constantly renewed construction of the common as the powerful (*puissant*) interweaving of differences.

As stated at the beginning of this chapter, deconstruction is only useful inasmuch as it escapes the temptation of the negative and avoids getting bogged down in a philosophy of loss or lack. Deconstruction should make possible a reconstruction—or, more precisely, a *construction* that repeats nothing: a production, an innovation. These three Foucaultian deconstructions allow one to think biopolitics as an affirmation (i.e., a working out, a creation) of being, as a radical positivity. Just as one must not reduce life to biology, it would be a mistake to understand my argument as a reintroduction of some transcendent perspective. Being is always caught up in a network of historical determinations, and in this sense it is absolutely immanent. However, this fact does not exclude either the invention of forms of being ("ways of life," "relations to oneself and others") or the idea that this invention expresses a capacity that is, in its very immanence, excessive in relation to the devices (*dispositifs*) of power. The dissymmetry between the powers (*pouvoirs*) over life and the inventive capacity (*puissance*) of life appears in the form of an "ontology"—a term which Foucault increasingly deploys in his final years—which should be understood literally as an immanent production of new being. Now, this ontology is, for Foucault, both an "ontology of the present" and an "ontology of ourselves." Consequently, one must simultaneously think the determinations that make us be what we are *and* our possibility to rid ourselves of what we are. Or, better, one must simultaneously think determination *and* freedom, the knowledges/powers of objectivization of singularities *and* the paradoxical capacity these singularities have to subjectivize themselves. Foucault's texts, with their constant reference to creation and invention, testify to an opposition between *pouvoir* and *puissance* as terms for "power." This opposition is never stated directly in Foucault but can be found in Deleuze's works from the same period. Where power administers life, life, for its part, innovates; where power subjects life, life resists by introducing a simultaneously ontological and political strategy of resistance: a creation, an augmentation of being. This explains why one of the recurrent themes in Foucault's final texts is precisely the possibility to "make one's life into a work of art," to establish a relationship to oneself and one's own existence that would highlight "the creation of new forms of life, of relations, of friendship, in society, art, and culture ... that would establish themselves through our sexual, ethical, and political choices."[13] And Foucault concludes, "We must not only defend ourselves, but affirm ourselves, and affirm ourselves not only as identities, but as creative forces."[14]

The concept of "creative force" is not an alibi for a postmodern return to Bergson's vitalism; nor does it signify a resurgence of Nietzschean "vital forces" and of the transmutation of values. Foucault, in reality, borrows from Nietzsche only his radical anti-Hegelianism and a particular conception of history which is quickly grafted on to borrowings from post-Annales historiography and Canguilhem's history of science. These references takes Foucault's thought far from a revival of *Zarathustra*. For him, "creative force" must be a capacity of subjectivization. These yet-to-come forms of subjectivization are what give biopolitics its true meaning; they "pose a problem to politics":

> But it is also necessary to determine what "posing a problem" to politics really means. Richard Rorty points out that in these analyses I do not appeal to any "we"—to any of those "we's" whose consensus, whose values, whose traditions constitute the framework for a thought and define the conditions in which it can be validated. But the problem is, precisely, to decide if it is actually suitable to place oneself within a "we" in order to assert the principles one recognizes and the values one accepts; or if it is not, rather, necessary to make the future formation of a "we" possible by elaborating the question. Because it seems to me that "we" must not be previous to the question; it can only be the result—and the necessary temporary result—of the question as it is posed in the new terms in which one formulates it.[15]

The "we" must be preceded by the effort of problematizing our own present; it must be produced by the creative power of men and women; it must articulate singularities in a new common without this common ever seeking to erase either these differences or the possible future. An affirmative and positive thinking of biopolitics would thus be a thinking of the yet-to-come forms of the becoming differential of singularities, that is, the slow invention of a new common as the incessantly (re)worked-out space of subjectivization and of resistant ways of life.

PART THREE

Liberalism between Legality and Governmentality

SEVEN

From Reason of State to Liberalism:
The Coup d'État as Form of Government

Roberto Nigro

A few years ago Foucault's readers had still to grope in the dark to reconstruct the theoretical itinerary of his last production. In fact, after the publication of the first volume of *The History of Sexuality* in 1976, for eight long years Foucault did not add any further volume to the series he announced with *The Will to Knowledge*. When *The Use of Pleasure* and *The Care of the Self*, respectively the second and third volumes of the series, appeared in 1984, only a few weeks before his death, it became evident that the initial project had undergone such important changes that its original inspiration could hardly be recognizable. Foucault wrote:

> This series of studies is being published later than I had anticipated, and in a form that is altogether different. I will explain why. It was intended to be neither a history of sexual behaviors nor a history of representations, but a history of "sexuality." . . . It was a matter of seeing how an "experience" came to be constituted in modern Western societies, an experience that caused individuals to recognize themselves as subjects of a "sexuality." . . . What I

planned, therefore, was a history of the experience of sexuality, where experience is understood as the correlation between fields of knowledge, types of normativity, and forms of subjectivity in a particular culture. (*UP*, 3)

So, not only had Foucault reorganized his whole research around the question concerning the formation of a hermeneutics of the self, but he had also traced back his analyses from modern times through Christianity to antiquity in order to study the modes of subjectification of human beings.[1]

Today, we are in a better position to understand the peculiarity of his last production, since the recent publication of his courses delivered at the Collège de France between 1976 and 1984. The edition of the *Dits et écrits*, which appeared in 1994, had already provided almost the entirety of articles, interviews, and conferences Foucault wrote and pronounced throughout his whole life. These posthumous publications shed a new light on Foucault's work and call our attention to new issues at stake in his work. They have fueled interest in concepts such as biopolitics, governmentality, and (neo)liberal practices of government that are now at the forefront of political debates. They help to uncover an important part of Foucault's work, which would have otherwise remained hidden, and to answer a question that has never ceased to haunt Foucault's researchers: "What happened during the fairly long silence following *The History of Sexuality*?"[2] The following pages are intended to form part of the answer to this question.

In a recent article on Foucault, Alessandro Fontana develops important critical remarks about the way of reading his work today. He suggests that one should never dissociate Foucault's courses from his books, interventions, and conferences; in a word, one should always keep an eye on the meaning of his political and philosophical activity. If one forgets the context in which different texts (be they articles, books, interviews, and conferences) emerged, one neutralizes the critical impact of Foucault's work. One should never forget the *Kampfplatz* in which Foucault argued, what urged him to elaborate some concepts, what were the lines of actualization of his intellectual activity.[3]

Foucault's final work developed in a context characterized by important events.[4] His attentiveness to discourses stemming from French leftism can be considered a constant of his work during the 1970s. However, in the second half of the 1970s his dialogue with radical leftist groups intensified and no doubt played an important role in shaping his last thought. Foucault raised important objections against discourses that could be interpreted as "Marxists." His confrontation with Marx, with different Marxist currents, and with discourses that pretended to be part of a Marxist constellation, probably reached its zenith in this period. In this regard, *The History of Sexuality: Volume 1* is all the more important since it mingles the critique of some Marxist discourses with the critique of Freudianism. Foucault recognized common issues in Freudianism and Marxism, in particular concerning the use of the notion of repression. His attempt to dismantle the repressive hypothesis constitutes one of the main targets of his critique in the first volume of *The History of Sexuality*.[5]

This critique goes hand in hand with another major issue emerging in the same period: the discussion about forms of violence and the increasing role they were playing in the political activities of many radical groups. This involved questioning the practice of armed struggle, to which an important number of political movements in France, Germany, and Italy were resorting.[6] At the core of these debates was the role and function of the state. The elaboration of a theory of the state has always been a central issue in a number of Marxist theories. For instance, Althusser had begun work on this issue through a reflection on ideological state apparatuses, which is not unrelated to Foucault's analytics of power.[7] Foucault's elaboration of the notions of government and governmentality, which emerged in 1978, should be interpreted in connection with such issues. His remarks on that topic are all the more important since they call for a different approach to the problem of the state:

> We know the fascination that the love or horror of the state exercises today.... I think this overvaluation of the problem of state is basically found in two forms. An immediate, affective, and tragic form is the lyricism of the cold monster, confronting us. But there is a second way of overvaluing the problem of the state that is paradoxical because apparently reductive. This analysis consists in reducing the state to a number of functions like, for example, the development of the productive forces and the reproduction of the relations of production.... But the state, doubtless no more today than in the past, does not have this unity, individuality, and rigorous functionality.... After all, maybe the state is only a composite reality and a mythicized abstraction whose importance is much less than we think. Maybe. What is important for our

modernity, that is to say for our present, is not then the state's takeover [*étatisation*] of society, so much as what I would call the "governmentalization" of the state. (*STP*, 144)

And later, he adds:

What if the state were nothing more than a way of governing? What if the state were nothing more than a type of governmentality? What if all these relations of power that gradually take shape on the basis of multiple and very diverse processes which gradually coagulate and form an effect, what if these practices of government were precisely the basis on which the state was constituted? (*STP*, 325)

If, on the one side, the introduction of the notions of government and governmentality in 1978 meant his engagement in current political debates, then, on the other side, it involved a profound reorientation of Foucault's own theoretical work. The ground on which he had built his previous analyses was being shaken. Foucault was calling into question concepts on which his analytics of power rested. He was questioning his interpretation of the power relations as a warlike clash between forces. Such a shift included important consequences and ruptures, as I will discuss in what follows.

After 1976 Foucault suggests abandoning some cornerstones of his previous analyses. In so doing, he was also getting rid of some forms of revolutionary struggle. He was calling into question the effectiveness of a kind of revolutionary utopianism and the efficacy of some political experiences. It could be tempting to see a link between this critical attitude and his interest in the question of liberalism, clearly displayed at the end of the seventies. We should not, however, give in to this temptation too easily, or these ideas took unforeseen directions and resonated with one another in different ways. It would be highly misleading to suggest that Foucault's reading of liberalism was *liberal*. One should ask, rather, what place the question of liberalism occupies in Foucault's intellectual itinerary. How does it relate to other issues at work in his theoretical production?

To the question of liberalism and neoliberalism Foucault devoted his course *The Birth of Biopolitics*. This was his sole incursion into the field of contemporary history throughout his teaching at the Collège de France.[8] After some initial lectures on the specific features of liberalism as an art of government emerged in the eighteenth century, Foucault examined the

German neoliberalism (in its Ordoliberal form), its diffusion in France, and finally the American neoliberalism, born in 1934 with the Chicago School. Some references are also made to the Austrian School (von Mises and Hayek), which, on Foucault's account, played an important role as a bridge between the German Ordoliberals and the American neoliberals.

By suggesting that liberalism is the general framework of biopolitics (*BB*, 22), Foucault connects his course to the previous one. In fact, in *Security, Territory, Population* he had begun work on the notion of biopolitics and had simultaneously put forward an important thesis on liberalism: instead of interpreting it as an ideology, he saw in it a way of governing (*STP*, 48). But why should liberalism be the general framework of biopolitics? In Foucault's view, liberalism needs to keep elements under control in order to ensure their free movement. Being avid for freedom, liberalism consumes what it tries to produce. Foucault points out:

> [This governmental practice] is a consumer of freedom inasmuch as it can only function insofar as a number of freedoms actually exist: freedom of the market, freedom to buy and sell, the free exercise of property rights, freedom of discussion, possible freedom of expression, and so on. The new governmental reason needs freedom therefore, the new art of government consumes freedom. It consumes freedom, which means that it must produce it. It must produce it, it must organize it.... And so, if this liberalism is not so much the imperative of freedom as the management and organization of the conditions in which one can be free, it is clear that at the heart of this liberal practice is an always different and mobile problematic relationship between the production of freedom and that which in the production of freedom risks limiting and destroying it. (*BB*, 63)

Liberalism is this new type of rationality in the art of government consisting in "the self-limitation of governmental reason" (*BB*, 20).[9] Liberalism is both the radical critique of the excess of government and what allows politics to take charge of life. On one side, liberalism is in search of techniques that govern and administer life (which constantly escapes them [*WK*, 16]); on the other, such encompassing administration turns against itself, since the best government is the one governing the least. The coexistence of these two aspects of liberalism is all the more paradoxical for it leads to recurrent crises of governmentality. This is what Foucault investigates as he explores both the relationship between reason of state and liberal reason in

Security, Territory, Population, and the ruptures and continuities between classical liberalism and neoliberalism in *The Birth of Biopolitics*.

The long detour through the problem of government in the sixteenth century, the spiritual direction in the Christian pastorate, reason of state, and police, is not a departure from the question of biopolitics in its relation to the problem of liberalism.[10] It functions, rather, as preparation for the discussion of neoliberal practices of government. In fact, at the beginning of *The Birth of Biopolitics* Foucault can suggest that liberalism becomes the critique of the excess of government, the promotion of a critical governmentality, "the solution that consists in the maximum limitation of the forms and domains of government action" (*BB*, 21) inasmuch as it developed as a critique of authoritarian and juridical practices of government.[11] Foucault also remarks that "this self-limitation of governmental reason characteristic of 'liberalism' has a strange relationship with the regime of *raison d'État*" (*BB*, 21). It behooves us to pay more attention to the issues involved in this crucial passage.

Foucault's account of reason of state starts with critical remarks on Machiavelli's work.[12] However, he rapidly moves on in order to talk about what is understood by *raison d'État*. By examining, among other texts, the works of Giovanni Botero and Antonio Palazzo (who first defined reason of state)[13] Foucault can hint at a kind of split emerging within the debate on *raison d'État* around the end of the seventeenth and the beginning of eighteenth centuries. The way was paved by Botero, inasmuch as he did not object to Machiavelli on the basis of moral or ethical assumptions, as many of his contemporaries did. He shifted, rather, the debate on reason of state from the ethical ground to the economic terrain. So, Botero's work accounts for the emergence of an art of government centered on the common good. In his wake, governmental reason comes to orbit the problem of the satisfaction of interests. Botero's discourse not only contributes to deepening a different form of anti-Machiavellism, but also delineates the pathway for the emergence of economics, as a form of political rationality. His project tends to maximize and rationalize the techniques of government and the forms of command. Against the violent and uncertain experience of the French absolute and impersonal monarchy, Botero opposes a different project resting on the idea of prudential reason of state.[14] On Botero's account, reason of state is reason of interests. A prudential government pursues an organization of social life centered on the acknowledgement of specific interests. The cement of political discipline and civil obedience resides in the defense of particular interests.[15]

Setting out from mercantilist theories, Botero paved the way for the emergence of economics as political discourse that will function as the self-limitation of governmental reason. The emergence of political economy goes hand in hand with the formation of modern liberalism. In this connection, the reference to Botero is all the more important for it sketches the birth of economics from inside the field of debates on reason of state.[16] However, this is only one of the pathways Foucault followed in his discussion of reason of state. In fact, he not only referred to Italian authors, but also explored political thought under Richelieu. In this connection, he devoted a few pages to the question of the coup d'état with reference to the work of Gabriel Naudé.[17] Is this reference not astonishing?

If one pays attention to the fact that through his analytics of power Foucault was getting rid of the notion of sovereignty, his reference to a political act embodying the stigmata of the highest form of decisional sovereignty might appear surprising. Apparently, this could never match the idea of the governmentalization of the state. But the peculiarity of Foucault's interpretation of the coup d'état resides precisely in the fact that he does not give an account of it in terms of decisional power of the sovereign. Foucault examines the coup d'état as an art of government, entirely inscribed in the rationality of government. The coup d'état in the sixteenth century is part of the process of governmentalization of the state; it is a practice that constitutes its own object: the state. This fits in with Foucault's outline of the state not as a cold monster extending its powers on civil society, but rather like a praxis, the result of governmental practices, the general effect of overall practices of government, a type of governmentality.

By exploring the difference between the classical and the modern coup d'état, Jens Bartelson submits important remarks about the relationship between the regular and the exceptional in political theory. By setting out from the study of Naudé's work, he provides an interpretation of the regular as the result of the exceptional.[18] By way of an analysis of classical works, he discusses problems that are at the forefront of political debates today. Without making any mention of Foucault, his analysis sheds light nevertheless on issues involved in Foucault's approach. Let's consider them briefly.

What is striking in Naudé's work is his definition of the coup d'état as an extraordinary act that princes are forced to undertake in difficult and hopeless matters, contrary to common law and regardless of any justice.[19] The prince has to suspend laws and to repeal them, if necessary. What comes out from this definition of the coup d'état is the idea of a violent act, of an important decision, that is carried out from the *inside*. In fact, the important difference between the classical coup d'état and the modern one, is that the coup d'état in the sixteenth century was intended as an extraordinary act staged *from inside* the locus of legitimate authority: it is the act of the prince or the government aiming at the salvation of the state. That's the reason why the coup d'état is far from opposing the logic of the reason of state; on the contrary, it represents its intrinsic logic of functioning. The coup d'état is the manifestation of the functioning of the reason of state. The classical coup d'état presents the paradox of being an act carried out from the inside and directed outward, toward the social body and for the benefit of the common good. As such, it does not bring along the stigmata of illegitimacy or usurpation that will be attributed to it later.[20]

The classical coup d'état is carried out by a prince who acts against the backdrop of perceived emergency and necessity. As such, this definition of the coup d'état presupposes that the prince remains identical with himself during and after the coup. It is a quite different situation compared with the modern definition of the coup d'état that postulates a change of persons, but not of the forms and rules of the government. The modern coup d'état does not affect the identity of political institutions. This means that the object of the coup—the state—is a *fact*, an institution with a life of its own. The state remains essentially the same even after the coup has been successfully accomplished. The state continues functioning even after the coup, since its existence is independent of rulers as well as the ruled. The modern concept of coup d'état presupposes the existence of an abstract machine, called state. The coup d'état is the political act, which will substitute a particular interest—that of an individual or a group—to a general one and, as such, it carries the stigma of illegitimacy.

On the contrary, in the classical coup d'état, the act of the prince looks more like a means to constitute its object—the state. The action of the prince shapes the state, tends to constitute it. The classical coup d'état seems more like a practice, a practice of government, which tends to constitute its object—the state—instead of presupposing its existence as a fact. The classical coup d'état remains an exceptional act that bursts into the night like a flash of lightning. However, in the early seventeenth century it has not yet acquired the meaning of an anomalous deviation from regularities. On the contrary, the coup d'état is considered as the essence of reason of state and as such exemplifies the functioning of power. To use the words of Louis Marin, the coup d'état is "the apocalypse of the origin," inasmuch as it reveals "as a flash of lightning into the night" the basis on which power resides.[21] Such basis is the exception, in Bartelson's view.

But how should the exceptional be understood? If one gives in to the thesis that the exceptional is a new key for understanding the regular and the normal, one is led to interpretations of the coup d'état in decisionist terms. The prince is competent for such an act.[22] The prince has the ultimate decision of the coup d'état. Hence, the question of exception is coupled with the problem of sovereignty: the following question "under what circumstances can the prince take his decision" goes along with the problem that the prince has the ultimate power to decide on the state of exception. This is what makes him a sovereign, on Carl Schmitt's account.

Schmitt remarks that the ultimate condition of sovereignty is visible neither in everyday political practice nor in the normative order of the constitution, but only in the exception. According to him, the exception is more interesting than the rule, since "in the exception the power of real life breaks through the crust of a mechanism that has become torpid by repetition."[23] His remarks focus on the unstable relationship between sovereignty and exception and call into question the original relation of the political. Nevertheless, Schmitt's decisionist sovereignty can embody indifferently the power of applying or suspending laws, inasmuch as it rests on the "transcendence of the sovereign towards the state."[24]

Foucault's account of the coup d'état in the seventeenth century implies rather different issues, since it in no way leads to the privilege of transcendent sovereignty. Foucault studies reason of state as an art of governing. In this connection, he discusses the necessarily theatrical character of the coup d'état: "Just as in politics *raison d'État* manifests itself in a kind of theatricality, so theater is organized around the representation of this *raison d'État* in its dramatic, intense, and violent form . . . theater represents the state itself" (*STP*, 265). Foucault hints here at a crucial question concerning the relationship between exercise of power and forms of representation that has recently attracted the attention of many commentators. The issues it involves could doubtless be deepened, if they were put in connection with the analyses developed by Louis Marin, who insists on the structural role that representation plays in the exercise of power. Marin explains that power and representation are inextricably intertwined, since they share the same nature. Power makes force visible and is, at the same time, an effect of representation; representation makes the functioning of power possible. In his influential work, Marin examines the function of symbols, rituals, signs on which power resides, with regard to the classical age. His research on the coup d'état as baroque essence of political action sheds light on the mechanisms of legitimization of power in modern societies.[25] However, Foucault did not take the path of the analysis of representation. The trajectory of his analysis was driven by other theoretical urgencies. By referring to the arts of government Foucault engaged in a process of rethinking politics that shook the ground of his own theoretical assumptions. What modifications did it imply? Let me consider this last aspect before concluding my remarks in these pages.

The beginning of the course *Security, Territory, Population* expands on the project developed in the previous years. After one sabbatical year Foucault restarts his lectures at the Collège de France from the same point left behind in the last lecture delivered in 1976. What is at stake in both analyses is the genealogy of power over life. Foucault interpreted the emergence of biopolitics as one of the most important changes in the history of human societies. In his course *Society Must Be Defended* he shows that during the second half of the eighteenth century emerged a new technology of power, which works closely with discipline.[26] It is not a disciplinary technology and it does not eliminate the power of discipline. The new technology focused on what Foucault names the "species body," the body imbued with the mechanics of life and serving as the basis of biological processes: propagation, births and mortality, the level of health, life expectancy and longevity, with all the conditions that can cause these to vary.

If during the seventeenth and eighteenth century discipline emerged like a technology centered on the body as a machine, which ensured the optimization of its capabilities, its integration into systems of efficient and economic control, then this new technology takes the body of the population as object of its intervention. To some extent, the analyses of disciplinary technologies and biopolitics interlock and draw an excellent picture of the genealogy of modern capitalism. In *Discipline and Punish* Foucault explains that if the economic takeoff of the West began with the techniques that made possible the accumulation of capital, it might perhaps be said that the methods for administering the accumulation of men made possible a political takeoff in relation to the traditional, ritual, costly, violent forms of power, which soon fell into disuse and were superseded by a subtle, calculated technology of subjection. By referring to Marx, he shows that the two processes—the accumulation of men and the accumulation of capital—cannot be separated; the techniques that made the cumulative multiplicity of men useful also accelerated the accumulation of capital. Each makes the other possible and necessary; each provides a model for the other.[27]

Foucault also highlights that biopower was without question an indispensable element in the development of capitalism, too. The latter would not have been possible without the controlled insertion of bodies into the machinery of production and the adjustment of the phenomena of population to economic processes. The adjustment of the accumulation of men to that of capital, the joining of the growth of human groups to the expansion of productive forces, and the differential allocation of profit were made possible in part by the exercise of biopower in its many forms and modes of application (*WK*, 140). When the division of labor created a need for people with different aptitudes, when the new rising capitalist order was threatened by popular movements of resistance or of revolt, a specific surveillance of all individuals was necessary. There was a time when it was necessary for everybody to be perceived by the eye of power. The first "simple" measure was to exclude or to control dangerous individuals.[28]

Such a reconstruction draws a picture of Foucault's analytics of power in terms of juxtaposition of different strategies and technologies that overlap and interlock with one another. It undeniably calls our attention to the genealogy of modern powers and helps to understand how we have been trapped in our own history.[29] Antonio Negri and Michael Hardt have doubtless expanded on this track the most, by going beyond a philological analysis of Foucault's texts. From *Empire* to *Commonwealth* their reading not only identifies biopolitics with the localized productive powers of life, but also affirms it as the creation of new subjectivities. In this connection, they exploit the potential of Marxist analyses of the real subsumption, as sketched out in the *Grundrisse*, on a new level. In fact, on their account, biopolitics involves the production of affects and languages through social cooperation and the interaction of bodies and desires.[30]

Their analyses match Foucault's remarks on life as the issue of political struggle. In fact, in *The History of Sexuality: Volume 1* Foucault writes:

> Since the last century, the great struggles that have challenged the general system of power were not guided by the belief in a return to former rights . . . what was demanded and what served as an objective was life. . . . Whether or not it was Utopia that was wanted is of little importance; what we have seen has been a very real process of struggle; life as a political object was in a sense taken at face value and turned back against the system that was bent on controlling it. It was life more than the law that became the issue of political struggles, even if the latter were formulated through affirmations concerning rights. (*WK*, 144)

This account, nevertheless, does not account for important ruptures and changes that occurred in Foucault's thought. If one reads the beginning of the course *Security, Territory, Population*, it seems that these analyses are intimately connected with what Foucault did in previous years. And to some extent they are. But the emergence of the notions of government and of governmentality in 1978 marks a turning point that signals the abandonment of the paradigm of war on which Foucault's previous analyses rested.[31]

Society Must Be Defended might be seen as a real critical point in Foucault's itinerary, since it calls into question the efficacy of two great systems for analyzing power:

> Two grand hypotheses—Foucault says—; according to one, the mechanism of power is repression—for the sake of convenience, I will call this Reich's hypothesis, if you like—and according to the second, the basis of the power—relationship lies in a warlike clash between forces—for the sake of convenience, I will call this Nietzsche's hypothesis. (*SMD*, 16)

So, Foucault wonders if "what is rumbling away and what is at work beneath political power is essentially and above all a warlike relation" (*SMD*, 17). During the first half of the 1970s the interpretation of power relationships as a warlike clash between forces played an important role in Foucault's analyses. He explains that this model should in no way be confused with the idea of war found in Hobbes. In his course *La société punitive*, Foucault clearly remarks that civil war is the form power relations assume in our societies. If, on the one hand, Foucault is getting rid of some notions such as transgression and exclusion (notions that recall the model of struggle and repression), he makes extensive use of the idea of war.[32]

What happens in 1976? Foucault asks:

> I would like to try to see the extent to which the binary schema of war and struggle, of the clash between forces, can really be identified as the basis of civil society, as both the principle and motor of the exercise of political power. Are we really talking about war when we analyze the workings of power? Are the notions of "tactics," "strategy," and "relations of force" valid? (*SMD*, 18)

Foucault wonders if oppressions, class struggles, and conflicts emerging in a specific society and characterizing it can be really deciphered as a sort of war.[33] He asks:

> Is the relation between forces in the order of politics a warlike one? I don't personally feel prepared to answer this with a definite yes or no. It just seems to me that the affirmation, pure and simple, of a "struggle" can't act as the beginning and end of all explanations in the analysis of power-relations. This theme of struggle only really becomes operative if one establishes concretely—in each particular case—who is engaged in struggle, what the struggle is about, and how, where, by what means and according to what rationality it evolves.[34]

By getting rid of the hypothesis of a warlike relation, Foucault is not only casting doubt on the validity of a paradigm for analyzing power; he is also deeply questioning forms of political activism. One should interpret his last effort to go through an analysis of the Christian hermeneutics of the subject and the Hellenistic culture of the self as the attempt to figure out new political practices for the creation of a new subject and a new politics. Foucault's last courses at the Collège de France may be interpreted from this perspective.[35]

We are now in a better position to understand that the question of liberalism and biopolitics, apart from playing a pivotal role in Foucault's analyses, also functions as a real turning point in his pathway. In fact, if on the one hand, it allows for the expanding of his analyses of mechanisms of power to the whole society, on the other, it calls attention to the peculiarity of the notion of freedom that is at issue in liberal governmental practices. Thus, if the analysis focusing on the interconnection between liberalism and biopolitics also leads to a better understanding of new forms of exploitation, since life is affected by power mechanisms in each single moment of its production and reproduction, on the other hand, this new attentiveness to the problem of freedom makes possible the transition toward the question of the technologies of the self, which is at the core of Foucault's last investigation during the eighties. To be sure: freedom is neither a realm of purity and authenticity nor a lost paradise that the subject tries to regain. Far from being associated with an idea of originality, freedom is the space where the action of the subject takes place. It is the interval where movement occurs and change becomes possible. Freedom is the free room which enables the subject to transform itself and the others through its action. As such, the question of freedom intersects the question of revolution, which was at issue in political practices and discussions in particular throughout the seventies. Michel Foucault speaks of a second phase of revolution, within which the revolution is no longer interpreted as a political project, but rather as a rearrangement of modes of existence. He speaks of a form of activism attested by life in the form of a way of life, that necessarily represents a break with the conventions, habits, and values of society. He says that this form of activism "must manifest directly, by its visible form, its constant practice, and its immediate existence, the concrete possibility and the evident value of another life, which is true life" (*CT*, 184). For Foucault, it is by no means a figure of the authentic that is evident in this "different," "true" life, which is also supposed to be a good life and a beautiful life. The aesthetics of existence is specifically not given by nature, but rather develops first through intensive techniques of self-formation. It is something that must be practiced for a long time as care for the self and for others.[36]

EIGHT

Foucault and Rawls: Government and Public Reason

Paul Patton

Foucault and Rawls represent very different approaches to political philosophy. Whereas the former pursues a resolutely descriptive approach to the techniques, strategies, and forms of rationality of power, the latter is explicitly normative in setting out and arguing for principles of justice that should inform the government of society conceived as a fair system of cooperation. I propose to show that the distance between them is less extreme than might be supposed and that differences between them are instructive. They converge on the analysis of particular conceptions of the proper business of government and the institutions and policies it should embrace. While Rawls is explicitly concerned with ideal theory rather than actual societies, he recognizes that a theory of justice will have implications for the way that society should be governed and that these should be spelled out and examined in order to test the theory. By contrast, Foucault is explicitly concerned with actual historical conceptions of government rather than normative considerations about the most reasonable form of government.

The comparison with Rawls serves to highlight the fact that normative questions are an inescapable dimension of any genealogy of liberal or neoliberal government that aspires to be critical. Conversely, Foucault's analysis of neoliberal "governmentality" shows up the influence of neoliberal thought on Rawls's conception of the nature and functions of government and his preferred economic regime of "property-owning democracy." This unlikely combination of egalitarian and genealogical approaches adds historical depth to our understanding of the public political culture of liberal capitalist democracies.

Descriptive and Prescriptive Approaches to Power in Foucault

Foucault's approach to political philosophy consistently avoids questions of legitimation and justification in favor of a focus on the question of how power is exercised. As he says in "The Subject and Power," "'How' not in the sense of 'How does it manifest itself?' but 'How is it exercised?'" (SP, 337). Although *Discipline and Punish* dealt primarily although not exclusively with the exercise of power over individual bodies, *The History of Sexuality: Volume 1* suggested that the management of an entire society could also be studied in normatively neutral terms as the exercise of power over populations. In his *Security, Territory, Population* lectures (1977–78), Foucault took up the concept of government in order to provide a rubric for the study of different ways in which the conduct of individuals and groups could be "conducted" (*STP*, 193). At the outset of his 1978–79 Course, *The Birth of Biopolitics*, the study of government is presented as a means of showing that this kind of analysis of power "is not confined by definition to a precise domain determined by a sector of the scale, but should be considered simply as a point of view, a method of decipherment which may be valid for the whole scale, whatever its size" (*BB*, 186). *The Birth of Biopolitics* begins with a series of methodological comments designed to distinguish his approach to political government from the normative concerns of traditional political philosophy. He renounces universals such as "the sovereign, sovereignty, the people, subjects, the state and civil society" (*BB*, 2) and instead proposes to begin with the ways in which the practice of government has been theorized and described, in short, with the study of governmentality.

Foucault explains at the outset that the focus of his 1978–79 lectures will be the liberal governmentality that emerged in Europe over the course of the eighteenth century. His initial lectures canvass some of the features that differentiated this liberal art of government from the *raison d'État* that it replaced. These include the emergence of a principle of limitation of state power that was not extrinsic to the practice of government, in the way that law was in the seventeenth century, but intrinsic to it: "an internal regulation of governmental rationality" (*BB*, 10). The basis of this new kind of evaluation and limitation of government was the naturalistic conception of the market that developed in tandem with the emerging science of political economy, while the concept of interest connected market exchange with the utility of government. A distinguishing feature of liberal governmental reason was the manner in which it involved the interplay of individual and collective interests. The actions of government were justified only to the extent that they touch on the interests of each or of all, so much so that government "is now to be exercised over what we could call the phenomenal republic of interests" (*BB*, 46). A further distinguishing feature of liberal government was the way in which it functioned as both consumer and producer of freedom. It required for its successful operation various kinds of market freedom: the free exercise of property rights, freedom to buy and sell, freedom of information and expression, and so on (*BB*, 63). However, at the same time, it regulated the activities of individuals and markets in order to produce those very freedoms.

The paradox implicit in the liberal management of freedom provides the pretext, at the end of the third lecture, for Foucault's abrupt transition to a discussion of the crisis in liberal government that emerged during the 1920s and 1930s. This crisis was provoked by the fear that the very forms of economic and political intervention introduced to ward off the threat of communism amounted to a surreptitious introduction of measures that had precisely the effect of what was feared, namely, the limitation of individual and market freedom:

> This is precisely the present crisis of liberalism. All of those mechanisms which since the years from 1925 to 1930 have tried to offer economic and political formulae to secure states against communism, socialism, National Socialism, and fascism, all these mechanisms and guarantees of freedom which have been implemented in order to produce this additional freedom or, at any rate, to react to threats to this freedom, have taken the form of economic

> interventions, that is to say, shackling economic practice, or anyway, of coercive interventions in the domain of economic practice.... But is it not the case that these mechanisms of economic intervention surreptitiously introduce types of intervention and modes of action which are as harmful to freedom as the visible and manifest political forms one wants to avoid? (*BB*, 69)

The next five lectures are devoted to the analysis of German neoliberalism associated with the Freiburg School and the following two to the American libertarian neoliberalism associated with the Chicago School. Foucault argues that, whereas the problem of classical liberalism in the eighteenth century was how to limit the activities of an existing state to make room for the market and the economic freedoms it required, the issue for neoliberals was in a sense the opposite: how to take the free market as the "organizing and regulating principle of the state" (*BB*, 116). He presents the postwar West German state and the political consensus that sustained it as exemplifying this inversion in the relation between economy and state. This was a "radically economic" state in which "the economy, economic development and economic growth, produces sovereignty" (*BB*, 84). It was also a state whose principal architects and early advisers included key figures from the Freiburg School such as Walter Eucken, who in 1936 founded the journal *Ordo*, which gave its name to this group that became known as the "Ordoliberals." Other influential members included Alfred Müller-Armack, Wilhelm Röpke, and Alexander Rüstow, while a more distant influence was Friedrich von Hayek, who founded the Mont-Pelerin Society in Switzerland in 1947 to promote neoliberal ideas.[1] Other members of this society besides Eucken, Müller-Armack, and Röpke included Karl Popper, Ludwig von Mises, and Milton Friedman.

Foucault sought to show that neoliberalism amounted to a reinvention of liberal governmentality rather than simply a reprise of classical liberalism. The differences between them are evident in elements of the Ordoliberal conception of the appropriate economic functions and methods of government, such as the concern to establish that monopolies are not a natural or inevitable consequence of free markets and that measures must be taken to ensure that they cannot form and be allowed to distort the pricing mechanism. The Ordoliberals distinguished permissible kinds of market regulation from impermissible kinds of intervention associated with economic planning. They identified the kinds of regulation of the social framework that would be necessary if markets were to be able to function, along with the appropriate means to provide for the welfare of those who, for whatever reason, were unable to provide for themselves. The general principle of their social policy was that the socialization of consumption goods and direct transfers of income were to be avoided wherever possible. Instead, government should ensure that individuals have sufficient resources to insure against economic and other risks. In these and other ways, Ordoliberalism promised to overcome not only the crisis of liberalism referred to above but also the historical and institutional constraints of capitalism itself. From this perspective, Foucault suggests, the problem of the Ordoliberals "was to demonstrate that capitalism was still possible and could survive if a new form was invented for it" (*BB*, 165).

Foucault's descriptive approach to the exercise of state power does not mean that normative concerns play no role in his analyses. One of the justifications he gives for studying neoliberal governmentality is what he calls "a reason of critical morality" that relates to his own intellectual and political milieu (*BB*, 186). These lectures on neoliberal governmentality are presented as an explicit challenge to a certain kind of "state phobia," common among his colleagues in the French extra-parliamentary left during this period, that regarded state power as a phenomenon with its own essential characteristics and dynamics. He points out that state phobia is not confined to the left and that the versions current in his intellectual milieu overlook the long tradition of suspicion of the state from within twentieth-century liberalism. His analysis of the origins and emergence of German neoliberalism seeks to show how this kind of critique of the state and its "intrinsic and irrepressible dynamism" was already formulated during the period from 1930 to 1945, in the context of efforts to criticize the whole range of interventionist policies from Keynesianism to National Socialism and Soviet state planning (*BB*, 189). He argues that the influence of anti-state liberalism in the postwar period meant that all those on the left who participate in this state phobia are "following the direction of the wind and that in fact, for years and years, an effective reduction of the state has been on the way" (*BB*, 191).

At the heart of this state phobia is an essentialist conception of the state such that administrative, welfare, bureaucratic, fascist, and totalitarian forms of state may all be regarded as expressions of the same underlying form: "there is a kinship, a sort of genetic continuity or evolutionary implication between different forms of state" (*BB*, 187). Foucault objects that this essentialist conception of the state allows its protagonists to deduce a political analysis from first principles and avoid altogether the need for more realistic empirical and historical knowledge of contemporary political reality. In contrast, he is explicit that part of his reason for undertaking these historical analyses is the role of the German political and economic model in the immediate political context: "The German model which is being diffused, debated and forms part of our actuality, structuring it and carving out its real shape, is the model of a possible neoliberal governmentality" (*BB*, 192). He outlines the historical specificity of neoliberal government partly in order to disqualify the kind of political analysis that simply applies preexisting historical molds. In this respect, his partial genealogy of neoliberal government serves the objective pursued in all his historical studies, namely, "to let knowledge of the past work on the experience of the present" (*BB*, 130).

Foucault's efforts over the course of these lectures to distance himself from state phobia imply that he has no fundamental objection to government or to the institutions and policies that this implies. He is not an anarchist.[2] On the contrary, he had been a willing observer of efforts to rethink the political orientation and strategies of the French left with a view to its anticipated electoral victory in 1978. Recent commentators have made much of his association with elements of the "Second Left," a minority current within the Socialist Party with links to the CFDT (French Democratic Confederation of Labor).[3] The antistatist "self-management" (*autogestion*) approach of this current shared some of the concerns of neoliberals about the role of the state in governing social and economic life. It may well be an exaggeration to suggest that Foucault's 1979 lectures "should be read as a strategic endorsement of economic liberalism."[4] However, these debates and the electoral failure of the French left in 1978 provide the context in which he raised a question about the nature of socialist governmentality at the end of the fourth lecture: "What would really be the governmentality appropriate to socialism? Is there a governmentality appropriate to socialism?" (*BB*, 94). His answer was that if there is such a thing as socialist governmentality, it remained to be invented.

It is worth dwelling for a moment on this question—what would be the governmentality *appropriate* to socialism?—since it implicitly raises issues of the kind addressed by normative political theorists. Socialism here can only refer to an ideal conception of society. How could this question be answered without reference to the normative principles that would characterize a socialist society? These might include the absence or at least the diminution of class divisions in relation to wealth, opportunity, or the value of civil and political liberties. More positively, they might include principles that seek to give effect to the equality of all citizens, such as equal opportunity for those similarly endowed and motivated, or the kind of presumption of equality that underlies Rawls's difference principle whereby departures from equal access to primary social goods are allowed only on the condition that they benefit the least well-off. Foucault does not address these questions, either on his own behalf or in relation to the policy prescriptions of neoliberal governmentality. However, as I will show, some of these questions have been taken up by political theorists, including Rawls, and by political practitioners who were receptive to elements of neoliberal thinking.

Public Reason and Public Policy According to Rawls

In contrast to Foucault's resolutely descriptive approach to the nature of government, Rawls is unashamedly utopian in setting out the normative principles that should inform the government of a just and democratic society. He seeks to describe "how things might be, taking people as a just and well-ordered society would encourage them to be."[5] A well-ordered society is one in which three conditions are met: first, "an enduring majority" of citizens accept, and know that others accept, one or other of a family of reasonable liberal conceptions of justice;[6] second, the basic structure of the society is known to be effectively regulated by one or more of this family of reasonable liberal conceptions; and third, citizens have an effective sense of justice and so comply with the basic institutions which they regard as reasonable. These conditions are intended to spell out the political unity available to citizens of a modern liberal democracy, where it is assumed that they do not share the same moral commitments and beliefs. This is less than the kind of unity sought by communitarian conceptions of political society, but more than the purely contractual forms of association defended by libertarians. It is the collective unity of citizens who, equally and deliberatively, exercise coercive political power over one another.

Central to Rawls's conception of legitimate democratic government is a concept of public reason, by which he means the reasoning of the citizens about matters of basic justice and public good. This reasoning is governed by an ideal of respectful and reciprocal relations between citizens:

> As reasonable and rational, and knowing that they affirm a diversity of reasonable religious and philosophical doctrines, they should be ready to explain the basis of their actions to one another in terms each could reasonably expect that others might endorse as consistent with their freedom and equality. Trying to meet this condition is one of the tasks that this ideal of democratic politics asks of us. Understanding how to conduct oneself as a democratic citizen includes understanding an ideal of public reason.[7]

This ideal of public reason specifies the manner in which citizens should determine their collective will in drawing up and amending a constitution, in enacting laws relating to the basic structure of the society, and in addressing fundamental questions of justice.[8] It implies relatively stringent restrictions on the kinds of reasons that citizens can put forward in arguing a point of view on essential constitutional issues or matters of basic justice. The discursive framework within which citizens and public officials can argue in ways that are not beholden to their particular moral, philosophical, or religious views is provided by the publicly acceptable conception or conceptions of justice that can be objects of overlapping consensus.

Rawls's political liberalism provides a clear answer to the question under what conditions the exercise of such coercive political power is legitimate, namely, when it is exercised in accordance with a constitution the essentials of which all citizens as free and equal may reasonably be expected to endorse in the light of principles and ideals acceptable to their common human reason.[9] However, it might be supposed that he does not pay much attention to the ways in which political power can be exercised. In Foucault's terms, this would amount to saying that Rawls does not concern himself with the "how" of power.[10] This is a mistake. His remarks about the "special subject matter" of public reason make it clear that large swathes of public policy will fall within the scope of public reason. For example, he notes that the principle of legitimacy requires that "on matters of constitutional essentials and basic justice, the basic structure *and its public policies* are to be justifiable to all citizens."[11] It is clear that such key elements of the basic structure as the system of property and the policies that regulate the ownership, transfer, and derivation of income from property fall within the sphere of public reason. Further examples of fundamental questions that will be subject to the limits imposed by public reason include the extent and conditions of the political franchise, the list of religions that are to be tolerated, and who is to be assured fair equality of opportunity.[12] He notes that "many if not most political questions do not concern fundamental matters," although sometimes they will and, as a result, a "full account of public reason" would explain in more detail than he offers in *Political Liberalism* which matters are subject to the restrictions of public reason and to what degree.[13]

Within the framework of political liberalism, the institutional and policy details of the basic structure will be determined by the outcome of public political reasoning on the basis of the political conceptions of justice available in a given society at a given time. In consequence, it is to these liberal conceptions of justice that we must turn in order to see how far and in what ways political liberalism implies a form of what Foucault would describe as governmental discourse or rather, in view of the plurality of reasonable liberal conceptions of justice, as a family of governmental discourses. The two principles of justice as fairness that Rawls argues would be chosen by rational and reasonable parties behind a veil of ignorance both have substantial implications for economic institutions and policies. Even though they are proposed as consequences of an ideal theory that addresses a simplified model of society, the institutional and policy requirements of justice as fairness amount to elements of governmentality.

The first principle requires that any legitimate government will have to maintain a secure and stable system of basic civil and political liberties, and ensure a fair value of those liberties for all citizens. By "fair value," Rawls means approximate equality in the capacities and resources available to all citizens to make use of the formally equal civil and political liberties. While the political process might be insulated from the effects of large concentrations of wealth and capital by the public financing of elections and free public discussion on matters of basic justice, it is unlikely that such policies alone would be sufficient to preserve fair value of basic liberties in the absence of additional measures to ensure "the elimination of at least the most severe underlying economic and social inequalities."[14] Rawls's preferred strategy for preserving the fair value of political liberties is to ensure more widely dispersed ownership of capital, along with the provision of public education to ensure the widespread acquisition of skills and capacities.

The second principle of justice as fairness requires that government will ensure fair equality of opportunity and that inequalities in the distribution of primary social goods work to the advantage of the least well-off. In *Theory of Justice*, Rawls simplified the model of society to which his principles of justice applied by assuming the absence of disease or disability: one of the ways in which his principles were restricted to ideal theory was that citizens were assumed to be fully functional over their normal life span. Daniels argues that we can bring the theory closer to real-world conditions by abandoning this assumption and supposing that fair equality of opportunity requires the provision of health care broadly defined to include public health policies and environmental protection as well as access to personal medical services.[15] Fair equality of opportunity requires, in addition to the absence of overt discrimination against any particular caste, class, sex, or religious affiliation, genuinely equal prospects of achievement for everyone endowed with similar abilities and motivation. This implies the need for policies that aim to counteract negative effects on opportunity produced by socioeconomic inequalities or the legacies of historical injustice. These might include the provision of public education, effective health care, and other "opportunity-improving early childhood interventions."[16] Such measures may well go some way toward achieving fair equality of opportunity. However, complete equality will not be achieved so long as the family remains the primary institution for child care. Here, as in the case of measures to insulate the political process against the corrosive effects of large inequalities of wealth, there is a limit to the degree to which such measures will be effective. For this reason, Rawls takes the second principle of justice as well as the first to require measures to ensure the dispersal of ownership of capital, both in the form of productive assets and human capital.[17]

Both principles of justice therefore call for further measures to ensure the dispersal of property ownership, such as inheritance laws, progressive taxes and incentives, or other measures to encourage saving among the less well-off. These are precisely the kinds of measures proposed by the British economist James Meade and other so-called revisionist Labour politicians and advisers during the 1940s and 1950s. A significant current of British Labour thought at this time sought to dramatically reduce social and economic inequality by directly addressing "the underlying *ex ante* distribution of property and marketable skills rather than simply accepting these as given and undertaking only *ex post* income redistribution through the welfare system."[18] It was of course from Meade that Rawls adopted the term "property-owning democracy."[19]

Rawls's principles of justice are often supposed, wrongly, to provide some form of apologia for social democratic capitalism.[20] In fact, his preference was for property-owning democracy. In *Justice as Fairness* he acknowledged that the distinction between this economic system and welfare-state capitalism was not made sufficiently clear in *Theory of Justice*. He clarified the differences between them and the fact that he always regarded property-owning democracy "as an alternative to capitalism."[21] He objects to welfare-state capitalism on the grounds that it would not preserve fair value of political liberties: it allows large inequalities in the ownership of productive property "so that the control of the economy and much of political life rests in few hands."[22] The same is true for laissez-faire capitalism, but this system is also ruled out on the additional grounds that it would allow differential incomes on the basis of economic efficiency alone, thereby violating the difference principle. In contrast to welfare-state capitalism, the institutions of property-owning democracy are designed to disperse wealth and the ownership of capital, thereby preventing the control of economic and political life by a small part of the population. A second major difference is that, whereas welfare-state capitalism redistributes income to those at the lower end of the scale, property-owning democracy seeks to ensure widespread ownership of productive assets along with access to the education and training that equips individuals with human capital, thereby enabling them to "manage their own affairs" on the basis of relative social and economic equality.[23]

Rawls's opposition to laissez-faire and welfare-state capitalism does not imply opposition to all forms of market economy. On the contrary, he takes the principles of equal liberties and fair equality of opportunity to require a market-based system in which citizens have a free choice of careers and occupations and in which there is no central direction of labor.[24] On this point, he agrees with Hayek who also defended the importance of free choice of occupation and its association with a market economy.[25] In contrast to Hayek and other proponents of minimal government, however, Rawls distinguished between the allocative and distributive functions of markets. While he denies that the distribution of wealth and other primary social goods should be left to markets, he does insist on their role in the efficient allocation of resources.[26] State socialism is thus eliminated as a potential means of achieving just economic government. This leaves two regimes of political economic institutions and policies potentially compatible with the requirements of justice as fairness: liberal or market socialism and the "property-owning democracy" that Rawls adopts from Meade.[27] The choice between them is not determined by the principles of justice alone but must be made in the light of the political traditions, social forces, and particular historical circumstances within a given country.[28]

Neoliberalism and Egalitarianism

The emphasis on individual autonomy in Rawls's preferred economic model provides one indication of the impact of neoliberal ideas on his thought. The influence of neoliberal conceptions of the nature and function of government was already apparent in *Theory of Justice*, where he characterized the role of government as providing for public goods that could not otherwise be provided by market mechanisms, correcting failures and imperfections in market processes such as those resulting from the emergence of monopolies, lack of information or external diseconomies, and generally ensuring that a market economy would function in accordance with the requirements of justice as fairness. This implied, among other things, that government should work to ensure equality of opportunity by maintaining effective public education for all and by "policing the conduct of firms and private associations and by preventing the establishment of monopolistic restrictions and barriers to the more desirable positions."[29] Finally, he suggested, government should guarantee "a social minimum either by family allowances and special payments for sickness and employment, or more systematically by such devices as a graded income supplement (a so-called negative income tax)."[30]

This idea of a negative income tax had a long history in postwar neoliberal thought. Milton Friedman put forward an early version of the proposal at the first meeting of the Mont-Pelerin Society in 1947.[31] He later popularized the idea in his *Capitalism and Freedom* (1962). It was explored as a policy option in the United States under the Nixon administration (1969–74), before being discussed by the French government under Giscard D'Estaing in 1974–75. Foucault recounts how French economic ministers and advisers during this period considered the abandonment of the postwar policies of full employment and a social security system that relied on the wartime principle of national solidarity to deal with the risks faced by individuals. Instead, they proposed a neoliberal system of social security that would avoid imposing additional costs and constraints on the operation of a market economy. The introduction of a negative tax that would replace various forms of welfare assistance with monetary payments to those whose income fell below the taxable threshold was one of the policies considered (*BB*, 203–7). Although it was not adopted in France at the time, and has never been implemented in its pure form, variants of the proposal have been adopted in the United States and elsewhere in the form of earned income tax credits for low-income earners.

The adoption of policy proposals such as negative income tax in the context of Rawls's proposed alternative to capitalism was not simply an instance of what Foucault once referred to as the "tactical polyvalence of discourses" (*WK*, 100). The early phases of neoliberal thought shared a number of commitments with progressive liberals and even socialists, such as equality of opportunity, social justice, and economic security. Hayek and Popper even discussed the possibility that the Mont-Pelerin Society should be open to liberal socialists as well as neoliberals and Hayek made it clear in his opening paper in 1947 that efforts to promote greater economic security and equality were compatible with his conception of a free society.[32] Jackson argues that, at this early stage, neoliberal criticism was not directed at leftist political ideals but rather at the methods advocated to achieve those goals.[33] He provides evidence to show that the primary target of neoliberalism during the 1930s and 1940s was fascist and communist state planning rather than Keynesian macroeconomic policies or the emerging welfare state. Some Ordoliberal members of the group, such as Rüstow and Röpke, even argued that a genuinely free and competitive economic order would require intervention to ensure a wider diffusion of private property, along the lines suggested by Meade and the revisionist British socialists: "their 'ordo-liberalism' envisaged the creation of a decentralized economy composed of smaller population centres and enterprises and characterized by a more equal spread of individual property holdings."[34] Others accepted that taxes on capital, especially inheritance tax, could be legitimate means to promote equal opportunity. While there were some such as von Mises who rejected all forms of state intervention above the night watchman state, others were prepared to support particular forms of state regulation, such as legislation to break up monopolies and large corporations, and even redistribution in the interests of a social minimum wage and equality of opportunity. Jackson suggests that during the early phase of neoliberal policy discussion there was "a broad acceptance of the need for a state-sponsored minimum income, and of a legitimate role for fiscal policy in narrowing inequalities of opportunity. The early neoliberals were not advocates of a completely unpatterned distribution of income and wealth, nor of constructing a market economy without a safety net."[35] Strategies to promote more widespread ownership of property and productive capital, as developed by Meade and others during the 1940s, have continued to influence liberal egalitarian policy proposals.[36] This tradition represents another potential source of answers to Foucault's question about the nature of socialist governmentality, one that a more comprehensive genealogy of twentieth-century liberalism would need to consider alongside German and American varieties of neoliberalism.

The Changing Content of Public Reason

As noted above, Rawls's ideal of public reason implies relatively stringent restrictions on the kinds of argument that citizens can put forward in defending a point of view in relation to constitutional essentials and matters of basic justice. In their public deliberation, citizens in a well-ordered society must respect a duty of civility and offer reasons to one another in terms that all can reasonably be expected to endorse. They should appeal only to "beliefs, grounds and political values it is reasonable for others to also acknowledge."[37] Not all of the discussions in which citizens may engage will be subject to the restrictions of public reason. Rawls specifies that these limits

> do not apply to our personal deliberations and reflections about political questions, or to the reasoning about them by members of associations such as churches and universities, all of which is a vital part of background culture.[38]

Within the sphere of background culture, citizens may argue about all kinds of things related to the political and the public good, including theories of justice and the nature and business of government. Here, citizens engage in forms of nonpublic reasoning in which they are free to argue from the perspective of their respective comprehensive beliefs and commitments. Background culture includes all of the kinds of nonpublic reasoning found in churches, universities, scientific societies, and professional groups.[39] It includes the philosophical theories in terms of which philosophers might theorize about politics and the political domain. It also includes the philosophical and historical theories that inform certain kinds of political parties and that, according to Foucault, are one of the ways in which government has been diverted into forms of "non-state governmentality" over the course of the twentieth century (*BB*, 191).

Rawls's broad contrast between public and nonpublic reason seems intuitively straightforward, although the precise limits of each are far from certain and the borders between them somewhat porous. Uncertainty arises, first, because of the way that the restrictions imposed by the ideal of public reason have been weakened by Rawls's successively more inclusive versions of the "proviso" that allows nonpublic reasons to be invoked in public forums, so long as properly political reasons that support whatever it was that the nonpublic reasons were supposed to support can be provided in due course.[40] Second, the constraints imposed by the ideal of public reason are weakened by Rawls's acknowledgment that the content of public reason is not specified by any one political conception of justice but rather by the family of reasonable political conceptions.[41] At any given moment, what can properly be said within the sphere of public reason will be constrained by the norms of the existing family of reasonable liberal conceptions of justice. The ideal of public reason no longer requires that any one liberal conception of justice provide the terms of public debate, but only that:

citizens are to conduct their fundamental discussions within the framework of what each regards as a political conception of justice based on values that others can reasonably be expected to endorse and each is, in good faith, prepared to defend that conception so understood.[42]

As well as distinguishing between background culture and public reason, Rawls occasionally refers to the "public political culture" of democratic societies, where this includes their political institutions and the public traditions of their interpretation.[43] It is clear that he means this public political culture to include the range of fundamental ideas that inform the family of liberal conceptions of justice, such as the idea of citizens as free and equal and the idea of society as a fair system of cooperation. Public reason proper is the core of this public political culture, while at the heart of public reason are the political values derived from the ideal of free and equal citizens engaged in democratic deliberation over constitutional essentials, matters of basic justice and the public good. These political values are not simply drawn from the values shared within a given society, which might include moral or religious values, but from the overtly normative ideal of the person as democratic citizen. At the same time, however, these political values are not completely isolated from the nonpolitical values held within the society.

Rawls notes that political conceptions of justice may be revised as a result of their interactions with one another and as a result of the emergence of new social groups and hitherto unrecognized political problems.[44] He points out that the family of liberal political conceptions of justice may vary over time, as new variations may be proposed to existing conceptions in response to new or newly perceived problems, just as older conceptions may no longer be represented: "It is important that this be so, otherwise the claims of groups or interests arising from social change might be repressed and fail to gain their appropriate political voice."[45] In the introduction to the paperback edition of *Political Liberalism*, he notes that the principles, ideals, and standards of argument that make up the content of public reason are those of "a family of reasonable political conceptions of justice *and this family changes over time.*"[46]

In addition to political values, public reason includes the range of norms of reasoning and standards of argument and evidence that govern properly democratic deliberation. As Rawls's own theory of justice as fairness shows, the political values that define a given liberal concept of justice must be supplemented by a range of economic, sociological, and psychological ideas in order to be fully developed into a conception of the basic structure and institutions of a just society. No more than the political values, these are not simply derived from the scientific and other theories actually held within a given society. If this were the case, Samuel Freeman points out, reliance on neo-Darwinian theories of natural selection would carry little weight in societies where religious views predominate.[47] As in the case of political values, here too the criterion of what properly belongs to public reason derives from the democratic ideal of rational and reasonable citizens. As far as possible, Rawls suggests, the forms of knowledge and ways of reasoning appealed to in applying principles of justice to constitutional essentials and matters of basic justice should involve only "plain truths now widely accepted, or available, to citizens generally."[48] This implies that the content of this evidentiary and argumentative component of public reason also will change over time. Reasonableness may dictate that scientific views about climate change that are widely accepted by a majority of specialists in the relevant fields should form part of public reason, but this might not apply when such views were first proposed or as long as they remain controversial.[49]

It follows that public reason is a historical phenomenon, not unlike the manner in which, for Foucault, a discursive formation is a historical object: that is, a more or less systematic body of statements (*énoncés*) that is identifiable within a culture at a given time. Discursive formations are quasi-empirical objects in the sense that they are expressed in but not reducible to things said in the relevant domain. So too with public reason. In a given society, its content at any time will be determined by the available political conceptions of justice, which in turn will depend on the settled convictions of the society along with the background culture which sustains efforts to systematize and theorize such judgments.[50] Different political traditions and cultures may formulate liberal principles of justice differently. The content of the evidential and argumentative values of public reason may vary along with changes to the content of "plain truths widely accepted." Rawls reminds us that political liberalism can take different forms depending on the principles of justice employed and the acceptable standards of evidence and argument: "These forms have in common substantive principles of justice that are liberal and an idea of public reason. Content and idea may vary within these limits."[51]

Institutional Contexts of Public Reason

The makeup of the public political culture may also be approached from the point of view of the institutional contexts subject to the restrictions of public reason. Rawls insists that these restrictions apply primarily to citizens, officials, holders of public office, and aspirants when they are engaged in discussions that will determine the exercise of political power. The restrictions of public reason therefore apply in the first instance to officers of the government, including legislators and members of the executive branch. They apply "in a special way" to the judiciary and above all to members of the supreme court, which is in many ways the exemplary institutional embodiment of public reason.[52] They apply to citizens "when they engage in political advocacy in the public forum" and, as a result, to candidates for public office, political parties, and other groups who support them.[53] However, the concept of background culture presupposes that citizens may also engage in nonpublic reasoning among themselves or in situations that do not involve political advocacy or that do not take place in the public forum. Larmore suggests, and Rawls agrees, that we should distinguish between open discussion and decision making and allow that citizens may openly discuss issues of public concern in the light of their comprehensive moral views.[54] It follows that the limits of public reason apply only in those contexts that bear directly on the exercise of political power. Yet how are we to draw the boundaries of such contexts? There is clearly a continuum between the nonpublic discussion of public policy in universities, private think tanks, and the policy development committees of political parties. The views emanating from these forums may contribute to open discussion on matters of basic justice and, over time, change the terms of public reasoning about particular issues.

By way of an example, consider the history of the concept of property-owning democracy that Rawls employs in his characterization of a just basic social structure. The term was coined during the 1920s by an English conservative who supported more widespread property ownership, especially in the form of small rural holdings, cooperatives, and profit sharing, as a means of encouraging individual self-reliance. It was used by progressive conservatives during the 1930s and 1940s, before being accepted by Conservative Party leaders and incorporated into party policy in 1946. While it provided an ideological riposte to socialist attacks on the idea of private property, in policy terms it soon came to mean little more on the Conservative side of politics than home ownership for all.[55] However, toward the end of the 1940s, the term was taken up by so-called revisionist socialist Labour politicians and advisers, chief among them James Meade, who used it to recommend policies aimed at reducing the vast inequality in the ownership of property in Britain at that time:

> The revisionists . . . aimed to develop a new egalitarian policy agenda that took account of the changed fiscal constitution of the 1950s, that responded to the striking evidence about wealth inequality, and that could match the seductive political appeal of [Anthony] Eden's evocation of the virtues of private property.[56]

While this was in part a response to a political environment in which calls for nationalization were unlikely to attract sufficient public support, it was not simply opportunism but a considered policy response that drew on longstanding social democratic ambitions to reduce inequality by dispersing ownership of property.

Discussion of this policy agenda took place in a variety of private forums in and around the policy-making apparatus of the Labour Party, such as the XYZ Club, an important dining group that brought together politicians, academic economists and business leaders, the Fabian Group on Taxation, and conferences organized by the Socialist Union and the Fabian Society. Less private but not yet public forums in Rawls's sense of the term included the formal policy-making committees of the Labour Party, its research department, along with various academic and semi-academic publications, journals, and books.[57] Meade produced an early statement of the property-owning democracy agenda in a memorandum prepared for the Labour Party Research Department in 1948, in which he advocated policy measures aimed at producing a citizenry that would be "both worker and property owner at the same time."[58] The following year, in papers presented to the XYZ Club, he argued that widespread small-property ownership should be regarded as the basis of a social democratic or, as he preferred to call it, a liberal socialist community.[59] Subsequent discussion of policy mechanisms to implement this ideal focused on various forms of taxation, such as a capital levy, capital gains tax, wealth tax, and a tax on inherited wealth as well as gifts *inter vivos*, but also on measures to encourage saving, promote home ownership and increase access to education on the part of those less well-off. While some of these policies eventually found their way into legislation, such as the capital gains tax introduced into UK law in 1965, others did not progress beyond proposals put forward by the Labour Party in or out of office. They have continued to contribute to the public political culture of liberal democracies, not least through their impact on the political economy advocated by Rawls and other left-wing critics of existing capitalism.

Conclusion

Ideas about the proper functions of government, such as reducing inequality or ensuring fair value of political liberties for all, along with the policies by which they might be achieved, clearly fall within the wide view of public political culture. So too do the views about the appropriate purposes, functions, and techniques of government that Foucault considers under the rubric of governmentality. In the terms of Rawls's distinction between public and nonpublic reasoning, Foucault's analyses clearly belong to the background culture of politics. This is where Rawls situates his own political philosophy and that of other normative theorists such as Habermas.[60] Foucault's lectures on neoliberal governmentality, along with his critical remarks about state phobia prevalent in his own intellectual milieu, are offered from the position of citizen within civil or political society. Nonetheless, they bear directly on our understanding of the changing content of public reason in liberal capitalist democracies. They draw attention to a kind of discourse about the nature and function of government that, while it may not form part of public reason proper, is capable of inspiring a range of contributions to public reason on matters of basic justice.

The proposal to introduce a form of negative tax as a way of ensuring a basic level of access to health and other goods and services provides an example of the manner in which neoliberal political economy could affect the content of public reason as Rawls defines it. In direct contrast to welfare state policies that aim at equalizing access to social goods, neoliberal social policy is subject to the overriding economic goal of price stability, which is obtained through the market and the game of differentiation that occurs with any form of competition. In consequence, "social policy cannot have equality as its objective. On the contrary, it must let inequality function" (*BB*, 143). Foucault suggests that negative taxation amounted to an implementation of the "rule" that no one be excluded from the economic game. This rule is a consequence of the neoliberal idea that social policy should be neutral with respect to the operation of the labor market and that assistance should be provided to those unable to participate in the economic game only in order to ensure the maintenance of an enterprise society (*BB*, 206). The discussion of American neoliberalism also shows how rational choice approaches to "human capital" and criminality lead to policies grounded in economic rationality alone. At the point where they become sufficiently acceptable to be put forward as appropriate mechanisms of government, these policies fall within the sphere of public reason as Rawls defines it.

The founding texts of neoliberal governmentality that Foucault discusses do not fall within the sphere of public reason narrowly defined, but they do have consequences for the kinds of policies put forward and the kinds of reason that might be offered in their support. As such, these texts do not fall solely within the sphere of the background political culture. They occupy an ambivalent place in between background culture and public reason, forming a kind of historically moveable border region between them. To the extent that neoliberal ideas have emerged from the pages of academic journals such as *Ordo* and private forums such as the Mont-Pelerin Society to become the guiding principles of government throughout the capitalist world, they have progressed from background culture to public reason proper. In directing our attention to ideas such as these, Foucault's analyses of neoliberal governmentality draw attention to changes in the implicit rules governing what can and cannot be said in the sphere of public reason. They show us how the content of public reason has shifted by virtue of changes in the background political culture and its impact on policy considerations. They point to one important vector of change in the content of public reason during the twentieth century.

By retracing the emergence of some of the terms in which contemporary debates about public policy took shape in the postwar period, Foucault enlarges our understanding of the discursive frameworks within which state power is effectively exercised in liberal capitalist democracies. At the same time, as the examples of Meade, Rawls, and other proponents of property-owning democracy show, the evaluation of elements of public political culture cannot avoid consideration of the normative principles these are intended to serve. The search for an answer to Foucault's question about the governmentality appropriate to socialism would benefit from a detailed elaboration of this ideal, but also from knowledge of the history of liberal egalitarian public policy.

NINE

Foucault and Hayek: Republican Law and Liberal Civil Society

Miguel Vatter

Neoliberalism as Framework of Biopolitics

In *The Birth of Biopolitics* Foucault refers to Hayek's thought as the clearest illustration of what he calls the "neoliberal project: to introduce the principles of rule of law into the economic order" (*BB*,159). As Foucault argues, in the Hayekian and German Ordoliberal versions of neoliberalism, what makes possible the coordination of expectations and valuations achieved by the free market is the fact that the "natural order" of the market has become radically impregnated and molded by a "certain legal order" whereby it is impossible to separate abstractly the economic from the legal dimensions of the relations of production. Foucault terms this crucial innovation in neoliberalism the constitution of an "economic rule of law [*État de droit économique*]." At the same time, he argues that neoliberalism ought to be understood as offering the "general framework" of biopolitics (*BB*, 22 [32]). One of the most striking theses put forward by Foucault as an illustration of the biopolitical core of neoliberalism is the idea that the neoliberal "economic rule of law" introduces a new form of individuation that requires of everyone to become an "entrepreneur" of their own biological lives (*BB*, 144–50, 172–77). This chapter attempts to account for this simultaneous juridification and biologization of the political world, which Foucault was the first to identify as the salient feature of the neoliberal normative order.

In order to achieve this aim, I shall focus on Hayek's legal and economical thought because, following my hypothesis, both the juridical and the biological dimensions of "normative order" are found in what Hayek calls the "liberal social order." In fact, they constitute its very heart. Hayek's discovery is the dependence of "spontaneous" social orders, exemplified by the free market, on certain legal rules: the coordination of expectations of individuals having very different knowledge is only possible thanks to the assumption that they all are following abstract rules of law. Hence, it is Hayek's neoliberalism that spearheads the juridification of economics and, ultimately, of politics in the age of neoliberal hegemony. Likewise, the biological understanding of normative order is also found in Hayek. I do not refer here merely to his evolutionary conception of the growth of knowledge,[1] but more precisely to his claim that only spontaneous social orders generate their own kind of normative subjectivity: a free market works thanks to the freedom, creativity, and responsibility of the individuals, not despite these normative characteristics.[2] For Hayek, this freedom and responsibility is itself normative, that is, creative of new norms: the name for such a normative individual, the free subject of economics, is the entrepreneur. The entrepreneur's conduct of life is biopolitically normative because the entrepreneur is constantly placed in a situation of having to decide where to invest his or her energies and capital and where not to, what to select, help live, and strengthen, and what to ignore, cast aside, and let die.

The juridification of the economy as well as the rise of biological normativity found in neoliberalism leads to an unparalleled growth of new legalities and normative orders, most of which escape the horizon of the sovereign state: this is what we have come to know as the rise of a "civil" and now a "world" society. Surprisingly, Foucault believes that neoliberalism is an age of "juridical regression."

> We should not be deceived by all the Constitutions framed throughout the world since the French Revolution ... a whole, continual and clamorous legislative activity: these were the forms that made an essentially normalizing power acceptable. (*WK*, 144)

This comment is surprising because we have been taught that Foucault is no friend of the law. In this essay I shall attempt to dispel this picture of Foucault as an enemy of legality. To the contrary, I put forward the thesis that his judgment of neoliberalism as a "juridical regression" is due to his belief that the dependency of order on law in neoliberalism masks another reality, namely, the hijacking of a republican conception of (constitutional) law by neoliberal political economy in order to depoliticize civil society. Additionally, I show that Foucault holds on to this republican conception of law in order to criticize biopolitical governmentality and uncovers the republican idea of the rule of law as a source of resistance to neoliberalism.

Foucault and the Antinomy of Law and Order

There is a commonly held opinion that Foucault wrote about power but neglected law.[3] I think this is misleading. In one of his last essays, Foucault claims that modern political rationality, that is, modern governmentality, is caught within "the *antinomy of law and order*. Law, by definition, is always referred to a juridical system, and order is referred to an administrative system, to a state's specific order."[4] This claim, which takes for granted a principled separation between law and state, may sound surprising because, as everyone knows, Foucault is famous for having advanced an "analytics of power that no longer takes law as a model and a code" (*WK*, 90). In *The History of Sexuality* he says that instead of the representation of "power-as-law," modernity is witness to the emergence of a new kind of power, the "power over life" (*WK*, 139), whose two forms are disciplinary power and biopower. This new representation of power works through "norms" instead of "laws": norms both generate an order and grow out of order (*WK*, 144).[5] And yet the very fact that Foucault speaks of an "antinomy of law and order" suggests that for him power-as-law is never simply a model that has been or could be completely surpassed by the new technologies of disciplinary power and biopower.[6]

If one takes seriously this "antinomy" between order and law, three theses with respect to Foucault's view of law suggest themselves. First, neoliberalism as a rationalization of biopower functions by integrating the sphere of law into that of order. Neoliberalism is a form of political rationality which attempts what Foucault calls "the reconciliation between law and order."[7] A neoliberal order is impossible without a juridical foundation, but, at the same time, the neoliberal conception of law is deeply corrosive to the rule of law in its republican sense by turning the constitutional aspect of law into an epiphenomenon of normative orders (in the dual sense of the term discussed above) and their normalizing effects. This is the basis for Foucault's negative or critical view of "civil society" as it has emerged in liberalism and neoliberalism.

My second thesis is that Foucault rejects all attempts at reconciling law with order: this project, he says, "has been the dream [of liberals], [and] must remain a dream. It is impossible to reconcile law and order because when you try to do so it is only in the form of an integration of law into the state's order."[8] Foucault here appears as an advocate of the autonomy of law with respect to the sovereign state, a position that is often associated with republican, even Kantian constitutionalism. In fact, there is an internal link between Foucault's work on liberal governmentality and his return to the Kantian idea of critique as a sort of response to this governmentality. Here Foucault turns to the autonomy of law in order to defend a positive conception of "civil society," but a conception that is contrary to neoliberalism, in ways that I shall detail below. The neoliberal rationalization of politics, by way of contrast, oversteps the limits imposed by the antinomy of law and order, and that is what makes neoliberal rationalization profoundly irrational. Foucault's critique of neoliberalism thus follows a Kantian structure: to engage in a critique of a form of rationality means to reveal its antinomies. Irrationality is not determined by the presence of antinomy, but rather by the ignorance of its inevitability.

My third thesis is that Foucault never does away entirely with the representation of power-as-law because there is no alternative understanding of legitimacy.[9] Biopower, as he says, is only "acceptable," that is, legitimate, because it claims to have a juridical framework. Within his genealogies of liberal governmentality Foucault always tries to develop an alternative conception of power-as-law, one that subverts modern biopower because he wishes to reestablish the antinomy of law and order as the unsurpassable horizon of all government. Some commentators have claimed that Foucault lacks a legal philosophy of his own.[10] Others have argued that if biopower still depends on the law for its acceptability, then maybe biopower is only the last mask adopted by sovereign power, and does not constitute a real break with sovereignty.[11] Still others have seen in his later writings on liberal governmentality a rapprochement of Foucault to liberal ideals and an advocacy for new rights of individuals in the age of biopower, what is nowadays called "biological citizenship."[12]

In my opinion, none of these readings quite hits the mark: for the late Foucault, the law is not originally an expression of sovereign power, but belongs to an ideal of self-mastery, that is, of political independence which in the Western tradition corresponds to the republican idea that a free individual is someone endowed (by nature) with a *sui iuris* status, that is, someone "capable" of (making) law because they are capable of judgment or capable of forming their own opinion on matters of concern to all.[13] In his last Courses, dedicated to *The Government of Self and Others*, Foucault became interested in the genealogy of this connection between self-mastery, the capacity for (making) law, and the freedom of opinion formation, or what the Greeks called *parrhesia* (free or frank speech). Foucault's genealogy of the capacity for law (the *sui iuris* status) opens up another possible reading of his growing appreciation for the discourse of rights and his support for *Solidarność* and other movements of dissidence in Eastern Europe, namely, it suggests a sophisticated attempt at saving the discourse of republicanism against liberalism and neoliberalism. For him, only a republican conception of law and power remains true to the antinomy between law and order, and therefore resists the reduction of politics (*Politik*) to a matter of governmentality or police (*Polizei*).[14] To sum up my position: Foucault understands that only a conception of the law which is independent with respect to technologies of power can reestablish the antinomy between law and order as the unsurpassable horizon of any and all forms of governmentality. In this sense, the return to the law offers Foucault a surprising source of resistance to the subjectivations of biopower (SP, 331).

In order for there to be an antinomy between law and order, one would expect these to have distinct origins. This is in fact what one finds in Foucault's genealogy of modern governmentality. In *The History of Sexuality* he offers one of his most complete characterization of power-as-law. It is a form of power which only says "no," whose power resides in "the function of the legislator" (*WK*, 83); this power can be either obeyed or disobeyed by a subject that remains free to choose whether to follow the law or not. The origins of this juridical representation of power are said to be medieval, when law became the crucial instrument in the hands of the development of both sovereignty and the state. Power-as-law emerges with the formation of the new monarchies who looked for "a principle of right that transcended all the heterogeneous claims, manifesting the triple distinction of forming a unitary regime, of identifying its will with the law, and of acting through mechanisms of interdiction and sanction" (*WK*, 87). In this text of 1976, which recapitulates an idea of law found throughout Foucault's early work, he claims that even later condemnations of monarchy employ the very same juridical thinking that accompanied the development of monarchy: "The representation of power has remained under the spell of monarchy. In political thought and analysis, we still have not cut off the head of the king" (*WK*, 88).

Foucault opposes to this "juridical monarchy" two new technologies of power. He calls these the governmentality of discipline and the governmentality of security (OES). In these forms of governmentality, power does not adopt the form of the law, but that of the norm. Foucault's conception of the norm derives from the work of Canguilhem, the French philosopher of science and one of Foucault's teachers, who argued that the phenomenon of life had to be understood from out of the polarity normal–pathological because every living thing is an ensemble of parts that functions according to its internal norms. In addition, Canguilhem also showed that every living thing is itself "normative" because it is capable of creating new norms for itself on which depends its state of being "healthy."[15]

Canguilhem distinguishes between two kinds of normativity: a biological and a social normativity.[16] Whereas normativity in a living system is an internal regulation between the parts of an organism which is "lived without problems,"[17] social normativity imposes arbitrary social norms on living individuals as a result of a normative intention and a normalizing decision.[18] Here the meaning of "norm" is the same as the Latin *norma*: a straight angle that allows one to "straighten" something. It is this sense of social normativity that lies at the basis of Foucault's famous studies on disciplinary power and its normalizing effects.

Canguilhem's theory of normative order takes as its starting point the radical difference between biological and sociological normativity. For Canguilhem, a living individual is normal, but never normalized. At the same time, Canguilhem is interested in a feature of sociological normativity that makes society be more than a machine. According to his famous formula, "a society is both machine and organism."[19] What this means is that when a society tries to organize itself, to plan its operations, it is at one and the same time becoming more machinelike and is transcending its machinic existence. Its technological self-organization is nothing short of the attempt to regulate itself in order to satisfy its own needs in a way that is analogous to a living being:

> We must see above all in planning endeavors the attempts to constitute organs through which a society could estimate, foresee and assume its needs instead of being reduced to recording and stating them in terms of accounts and balance sheets. So that what is denounced, under the name of rationalization—the bogey complacently waved by the champions of liberalism, the economic variety of the cult of nature—as a mechanization of social life perhaps expresses, on the contrary, the need, obscurely felt by society, to become the organic subject of needs recognized as such.[20]

Foucault's theory of biopower—as opposed to his theory of disciplinary power—is based on Canguilhem's discovery of society's attempts to mimic the biological normativity of the individuals that compose it: "social regulation tends toward organic regulation and mimics it without ceasing for all that to be composed mechanically."[21] Just like Canguilhem argues that the living individual will always "enliven" social norms by appropriating them creatively,[22] so Foucault will argue that biopower manifests itself in the form of subjectivity of the entrepreneur, who is always "innovating" and taking risks on the basis of the stability of expectations guaranteed by social normalization.

Having said this, I do not mean to belittle the fact that Canguilhem's thesis on social normativity also contains an affirmative biopolitical meaning, which he explicitly and rightly contrasts with the (neo)liberal attack on state regulatory activity. Canguilhem suggests that the attempt to plan economic production, far from being a rigid, machinelike barrier to entrepreneurial, creative activity, as neoliberals maintain, in reality indicates the attempt of the state to overcome itself as a machine in order to become a political "body" that is more "living," that is characterized by what I call a "surplus" of life. Such a political body would be one in which norms cease to function like disciplinary controls in order to become what Agamben calls "form-of-life," a coincidence of individual *bios* with social *zoe*. This suggestion of a deeper and more fundamental coincidence between planning and (surplus) life, opens the possibility of an affirmative, post-Marxist conception of biopolitics that is opposed to the neoliberal appropriation of biological normativity which resolutely tends toward decreasing the capacity of political (state) planning of the economy. I shall argue below that Foucault adopts not only the negative conception of biopower to understand neoliberal governmentality, but also this affirmative, non-liberal biopolitics.

For now I merely wish to indicate how close Canguilhem's reflections are in relation to Hayek's conception of spontaneous social orders—despite Canguilhem's belief that his notion of social normativity was not compatible with liberalism's critique of social planning (which may be partly due to a confusion with regard to how one understands the terms "organization" and "planning" in the traditions within which Canguilhem and Hayek were both working). As I shall discuss in the next section in more detail, Hayek polemicizes against the "planning" of society because this renders all social order a matter of "organization," and thus reduces individuals to being "cogs in the wheel" of the great machine of society. For Hayek, social organization does not take into account the creative potential of all individuals and fails to see that the best way to coordinate this creativity is by empowering it through spontaneous orders of exchange or commerce, which he calls *catallaxy*, exemplified by the free market. Only the latter orders make society more like a "living" thing, what Hayek calls a "Great Society."[23]

Foucault takes up these intuitions of Canguilhem and defines a norm as that kind of regulation of society which moves it from its state of being a machine to its state of being a (quasi-)living organism: the norm is a regulation which seeks "an ordered maximization of collective and individual forces" (*WK*, 24). Norms, the regulation of governmentality, thus correspond to the biologization of law; to a modeling of law onto the internal normativity of life, with the result that "civil society" appears as "self-regulated." More specifically, whereas a law forbids certain *acts*, but leaves untouched their subject, the norm instead *generates an individuality*. Foucault gives the example of the regulations of modern sexuality which transform someone who commits an act of sodomy into "a personage . . . a type of life, a life form, and a morphology, with an indiscreet anatomy and possibly a mysterious physiology . . . the homosexual was now a species" (*WK*, 43). In other words, normalizing technologies of biopower are productive of subjectivities understood as a "mode of specification of individuals." Norms transform every individual into a specimen, and conversely groups of human beings become subspecies in and through this individualization.[24] This is the key to the way in which biopower resolves the task of coordinating the individual and the community by governing the "conduct" of "populations."

Modern political rationality is a question of normalization, and normalization means the generation and government of "conducts" of populations (or subspecies) which, at one and the same time, maximize individual forces and collective forces, and integrate the individual into the life of the collective. Biopower is therefore the set of norms that establish the "conduct of conducts" (*DE*, 237). One can understand this famous formula for governmentality as a logical extension of Max Weber's intuition that rationalization consists in an "autonomous" *Lebensführung* (conduct of life), following the secularization of the idea of vocation. Foucault is here offering biopower as an explanation for how individual actions can be coordinated into a social order allowing for stable expectations and intentions. Now, according to Hayek coordination is the central problem of economics. For both Foucault and Hayek, then, the most rational social order is achievable only on condition that individual behavior is conducted as close as possible to the self-regulation according to which life is lived: in a play on words, the shift from Weber to Foucault and Hayek is a shift from a "Lebens-*führung*" (understood as the conduct qua "ethic" of an individual life, a *bios*) to a "*Lebens*-führung" (understood as the conduct qua "government" of a species life, a population endowed with *zoe*). Whereas in Weber, the "spirit of capitalism" depends on a "Protestant ethic" that charges the individual with giving a vocation to its life (*bios*), in Foucault and Hayek it is life itself (*zoe*) that provides the norms that constitute the individuality or subjectivity required by the capitalist economy. The difference is that Hayek embraces this rationalization, while Foucault criticizes it. In other words, Foucault's theory of biopower offers a new basis for the critique of political economy, and it is the only one—as I show below—which situates itself at the level of the ontology of the economic because it treats the fundamental economic "problem" of the coordination of expectations and its "solution" provided by the free or competitive market.

In the genealogy of governmentality which Foucault develops after the first volume of the *History of Sexuality*, he traces back the opposition between law and order to a much earlier stage than the rise of sovereign power and of a "juridical monarchy." The form of biopower which establishes "conducts" for individuals such that they can "naturally" coordinate themselves and so achieve a stable social order, or a true "civil society," has its origin in what Foucault calls the ideal of pastoral power, a technology of power and of norms he associates with the Jewish and Christian traditions of theocracy and divine providence where God is to men like a shepherd is to his flock. Against this pastoral power, Foucault opposes what he calls "political power." This is not a "sovereign" power, but, to the contrary, the power that makes law into the sole legitimate basis for the constitution of social order. Undoubtedly, such a "political" conception of power originates with the republican and democratic traditions of Greece and Rome, and is recovered in the West thanks to thinkers like Marsilius of Padua, Machiavelli, Spinoza, and Harrington.

Whereas pastoral power "governs men," according to Foucault political power is not at all about governing men, rather it is fundamentally about making law (or giving oneself a constitution) so that no man will be ruled (*STP*, 115–21). Without citing him, Foucault is alluding to Cicero's famous saying that one subjects oneself to the law so as not to have to obey another person, that is, so as not to have masters (and in that way confirm one's natural status as *sui iuris*). By way of contrast, the pastoral "idea of governing people is certainly not a Greek idea, and nor do I think it is a Roman idea" (*STP*, 122). Foucault draws a clear opposition between political and pastoral power: "the pastor is not fundamentally a man of the law. . . . The Greek citizen . . . is only prepared to be directed by two things: by the law and by persuasion . . . the general category of obedience does not exist in the Greeks" (*STP*, 173). Conversely, pastoral power is essentially the establishing of a relation of "complete subordination" between two persons (*STP*, 175). Complete subordination or dependence is antithetical to the law because it means establishing a "relationship of submission of one individual to another individual": "Christian obedience is not obedience to a law . . . but subordination to someone because he is someone" (*STP*, 175). Christian pastoral power appears to be the exact opposite of the republican principle that (constitutional) laws make for freedom. Laws and opinions (persuasion) are the basis of political power, whereas the government of conducts is the basis of pastoral power.

The law, in the Greco-Roman tradition, has an internal reference to the value of independence, or what Foucault calls "mastery of self [*maitrise de soi sur soi*]" (*STP*, 184); whereas the order that is generated by norms has an internal reference to the value of dependence. Self-mastery, in turn, has an internal relation to the freedom to form an opinion about public or political matters. Foucault's last Courses were dedicated to the task of explaining what kind of alternative "technology of self" or ethos is required in order to exercise this freedom of opinion (or *parrhesia*) and achieve this mastery of self, which is in turn the sole condition for being ruled by laws and not by men, that is, the sole condition of what we call the republican ideal of political freedom. He sought his answers in the parrhesiastic practices of Greek democracy and Socratic philosophy, because "when one submits oneself to a philosophy professor, in Greece, it is in order to succeed in becoming master of oneself at a certain moment, that is to say to reverse this relationship of obedience and to become one's own master" (*STP*, 177): "The Socratic injunction 'take care of yourself' [means] 'make freedom your foundation through the mastery of yourself' " (ECS, 301). Thus the fundamental opposition in Foucault's late thought is that between a politico-philosophical "care of self" versus an ideal of divine providence or government, where one "lets" one's needs be "taken care of" by a normative order that transcends the individual and on which the individual must depend. The key task thus becomes that of tracing these two forms of "care of self" in the republican and liberal conceptions of the rule of law, respectively. When Foucault speaks of "becoming one's own master" he is clearly referring to the Roman republican tradition where the expression meant becoming *sui iuris*, or capable of living under laws because one has the power to give laws, that is, having the power of a citizen. Foucault's critique of governmentality is oriented by a republican, not by a liberal, political ideal.

The Problem of Coordination and Hayek's Reconciliation of Law and Order

Understood from within the above horizon of an opposition between Greco-Roman political power and Christian pastoral power, the reconciliation between law and order that defines neoliberal governmentality according to Foucault is nothing short of an attempt to develop a concept of law which appropriates the republican status of being *sui iuris* and places it at the service of the capitalist political economy. The juridification of politics in neoliberalism is intended to legally regulate (i.e., to conduct) the behavior of every individual into a new situation of dependence and insecurity with respect to a spontaneous social order that no individual can master or even comprehend, and that provides for the needs of individuals only insofar as it remains uncontrolled by and incalculable to every individual. This conception of a spontaneous order that grows behind the backs of the self-interested pursuits of individuals, an order which cannot be mastered and on which everyone is absolutely dependent, is called by Hayek *catallaxy* or "free market."

Is this conception of the free market a secularized version of divine providence, as Agamben has recently noted?[25] Is political economy the last refuge of divine government and pastoral power, or is it rather the definitive proof that "God is dead"? The fate of the idea of divine providence in modernity opens up an enormously complex problem in the history of ideas which remains far from being resolved. But in my opinion, Hayek's neoliberal discourse depends far more on a rhetorical feat consisting in presenting its secularized pastoral ideal of a normative order through the republican vocabulary of law (*nomos*) found in the Greek and Roman traditions than through the adoption of Christian ideas on providence. It is indicative that neoliberalism owes its origin to the polemics of the Austrian School of economics against the defenders of planned economies starting in the early 1930s and lasting through the 1950s. Von Mises and Hayek compared the ideal of a planned economy to wanting to organize and plan society on the basis of what one mind knows about all other minds rather than on the basis of the knowledge that is spread throughout society and its individual members. Such a planned economy would require belief in the existence of a divine mind that foresees all accidents and variations and can plan accordingly; it also requires belief in a group of human philosophers who have foresight into the divine mind and can impute true "class consciousness" on the rest of the ordinary mortals. Thus, during those years, Hayek mixed the critique of providentialism and anti-Platonism with a critique of Marx's historical materialism. Rhetorically, neoliberal thinkers opposed such (supposed) Platonic–Marxist reliance on (secularized versions of) divine providence with the evolutionary cunning of a spontaneous order based on the unconscious interaction between many minds, and the selection of the best ideas through the mechanism of competition.[26]

One of the clearest examples of this attempt at hijacking the republican tradition is found in Hayek's use of *nomos* in his last main work, *Law, Legislation and Liberty*, written during the 1970s. Hayek argues that the Greek word *nomos* should not be translated as *lex* (this is how Cicero translated it), but as *ius* (the equivalent of *Recht* in the sense of a "normative order" as I have explained it above). In this way, the ancient ideal of the "rule of law" (*nomos basileus*) is linked with what Hayek calls "judge-made law" and is explicitly opposed to legislation made through political procedures, such as parliamentary legislation, which in turn is based on a conception of separation of powers, and ultimately on constitutionalism.[27] Neoliberalism is that discourse of governmentality which places political power, that is, the power to make law, at the mercy of "political economy." The meaning of "political" in "political economy" is very precise: it refers to this rhetorical transformation of republican laws into liberal norms, and the consequent rise of *judge-made laws* over *citizen-made laws* as basis of the constitution of a social order.

It is striking to see the degree to which Hayek's thought conforms to Foucault's distinction between law and order. Hayek's innovation consists in distinguishing between two fundamental ways of understanding the regularity of expectations and intentions that characterizes any normative social order: on one side, there is *nomocratic* regularity, which is achieved by the deliberate creation of laws; on the other side, there is *spontaneous* order, which no one creates by design and which lacks all external purpose.[28] The term *catallaxy* is drawn from the Greek verb *katallattein* which means a peaceful way of "connecting" people and making possible "exchanges" between them. The order of free markets, but also the order of the World Wide Web, are examples of *catallaxy*.

Since his early work in economics, Hayek believed that the central problem of economics consists in explaining the coordination between rational actors, each having the capacity to make their own plans of action in order to maximize gains and minimize losses. While still engaged in economics, during the 1920s and early 1930s Hayek had seen that the classical theory of market equilibrium between sellers and buyers rested on the assumption that all actors shared the same knowledge of the objective situation. According to his biographer Bruce Caldwell, it was in the early 1930s that Hayek came to question this assumption, once he became convinced that the knowledge of any given actor always remained subjective or perspectival, and thus variable and error-prone. The fallibility of the knowledge of economic actors forces Hayek to abandon the search for purely economic explanations to the condition of market equilibrium and instead shift his attention to the legal–political causes of equilibrium.[29] It is at this stage in his development that Hayek discovers the *nomos* as an essential moment of free-market economics. Basically, Hayek transforms economics into the study of normative or nomothetic orders: "The central concept of liberalism is that under the enforcement of universal rules of just conduct, protecting a recognizable private domain of individuals, a spontaneous order of human activities of much greater complexity will form itself than could ever be produced by deliberate arrangement."[30] Neoliberalism is impossible without this creative reappropriation of the idea of *nomos* or substantive "normative order" first introduced into the vocabulary of twentieth-century jurisprudence by Schmitt.

In Hayek's mature account, the contradictory opposite of a spontaneous social order, represented by the free market, is not the juridical law or *nomos* but the idea of a political "organization," that is, the idea of manmade laws designed to bring individuals together by giving them a common purpose. Hayek's central premise is that the spontaneous order of the market is *only* compatible with a restricted conception of the juridical law understood as *nomocratic*, and which is opposed to a *telocratic* conception of the law as an organization or constitution of a community. Nomocratic rules are what

Hayek calls judge-made law and which he opposes to "legislation" or sovereign- and parliament-made laws. While the former are rules of individual conduct which indicate what ought not to be done, the latter are rules of organization that say positively what must be done, that is, they prescribe a form of life in common.[31] In Hayek's rhetoric, judge-made laws never command anyone to do anything, they merely demarcate areas of noninterference: they establish what belongs to each, they do not state what everyone has in common. For Hayek, only the action of an individual can be just or unjust, depending on whether the act is in accordance with the judge-made law. But since the way in which a free market distributes goods obeys no one's intention, there is no sense in saying that the market is either just or unjust. The preoccupation with distributive justice, and thus the desire to interfere politically in the workings of the market, is for Hayek exclusively to be placed on the shoulders of a telocratic conception of the law as organization of the state, that is, on the public law understood as a political constitution:

> a progressive permeation of private law by public law in the course of the last eighty or hundred years, which means a progressive replacement of rules of conduct by rules of organization, is one of the main ways in which the destruction of the liberal order has been effected. ... This tendency has been most explicitly seen and supported by Adolf Hitler's "crown jurist" Carl Schmitt who consistently advocated the replacement of the 'normative' thinking of liberal law by a conception of law which regards as its purpose the "concrete order formation" [konkretes Ordnungsdenken].[32]

Hayek blames those rules that organize citizens into a state, what the republican tradition has called the idea of a political constitution, for what he takes to be the irrational demand that the outcomes of the market be judged according to the principles of distributive justice. To add insult to injury, Hayek attempts to smear this republican, constitutional understanding of law by identifying it with Schmitt's understanding of *nomos*, thus in one swift move erasing the debt his own neoliberal idea of *nomos* owes to Schmitt and placing it on the shoulders of republicanism.

If this interpretation is correct, then the reconciliation of law and the spontaneous order of the market is only achievable because Hayek offers a truncated conception of law, which denies any constitutional, that is, political implications to the system of law, and makes public right subservient to private law. In a sense Hayek reverses the Kantian order between "conclusive right" and "provisional right": for Kant, all private right was merely provisional until public right was based on a true republican constitution, on the basis of which what was provisionally distributed in the form of private property to natural individuals prior to the state could be conclusively redistributed to citizens in a republic and in a federal organization of republics. For Hayek, instead, all "conclusive right" or constitutional law is but a means to establishing private property as a "provisional" right of consumers and entrepreneurs. The juridical framework of neoliberalism requires that law be understood explicitly in antirepublican terms (all the time picking up the rhetoric of republicanism): in neoliberalism, the law is no longer intended to organize citizens as law-giving subjects into a free people (*civitas*). Instead, the law favors negative liberty ("free choice" and the "pursuit" of self-interest) which, in turn, compels subjects to conduct themselves with respect to each other by following those legal norms that structure the spontaneous order of the free market (*societas*). This neoliberal conception of law refuses to see citizens as equal members of a people, in accordance with a constitution. Instead, it sees them as nothing more than specimens of a population who are subject to a normative order: a normative order on which they become entirely dependent (*alieni iuris*).

Policing the Economy: The Meaning of Nomos in Neoliberalism

Foucault asserts that in neoliberal governmentality "the law operates more and more as a norm, and that the juridical institution is increasingly incorporated into a continuum of apparatuses whose functions are for the most part regulatory" (*WK*, 144). By losing its political or constitutional significance, the "judge-made law" of neoliberalism becomes part of national and transnational *administrative* orders: the law falls under the norms of what Foucault calls, after von Justi, *Polizeiwissenschaft* (the science of public policy). There is an internal relation between judge-made law and policing activity. What Foucault shows is that the private space liberal and neoliberal systems of law defend from state or political intervention is not a normative vacuum, but rather becomes the space for "security" provided by the normalizing activity of the police.[33] By police Foucault means all *dispositifs* or arrangements that provide "security" for the free circulation of things, persons, and information essential to the existence of a *catallaxy* or free market, and providing "insurance" for the unpredictable outcomes of the transactions on the free market.[34] Neoliberal government, which has as its fundamental goal the assuring of competitive and transparent free-market mechanisms in society that use legal norms to regulate the conduct of individuals, exercises biopower by "insuring the lives" of individuals through a series of controls that operate on (civil) society and assign the task to each individual to produce a "surplus" of biological life.[35] Citing Foucault:

> The aim of the police is the permanently increasing production of something new, which is supposed to augment the citizens' life and the state's strength. The police govern not by the law, but by a specific, a permanent and a positive intervention in the behaviour of individuals.[36]

In this sense, it is not an exaggeration to conceive of the police, in neoliberalism, as a name for all *dispositifs* that provide for "life insurance," in the widest sense of the term.

Insurance is needed because the liberal or negative liberties which are the outcome of the limits imposed by the system of law and by the system of political economy on the sovereignty of the state, do not, as such, turn the private space into a space of security. The laws of the state are, of course, intended to prevent individuals from "harming" one another, but for liberalism it is illegitimate to legislate in order to "secure" the lives or the happiness of individuals. This is evident in Mill, whose "harm principle," which is the sole criterion of state law-making, should precisely not exclude all kinds of experimentations, and therefore all kinds of insecurity, with regard to one's form of life, irrespective of whether the results turn out to be harmful or beneficial for the individual herself. As Hayek puts the point:

> Not all expectations can be protected by general rules, but even that the chance of as many expectations as possible being fulfilled will be most enhanced if some expectations are systematically disappointed. This means also that it is not possible or desirable to prevent all actions which will harm others but only certain kinds of actions.[37]

In civil society, it is the biological life of the individual which is exposed to a new field of "insecurity" generated by the very unpredictability and spontaneity which characterizes spontaneous orders.[38] It is not only a matter of the obvious insecurity into which workers are cast,[39] but also, on the side of the owners of the means of production, the hegemony of financial capital and the so-called democratization of credit has led to the use of financial instruments, such as derivatives, that are intended to generalize the risk of an investment as a form of "insuring" a return, not to speak of theories, such as those of Hyman Minsky, that postulate financial instability as a prerequisite of investment strategies. In general, the radical lack of assurance that investments will turn a profit is demanded by the neoliberal idea of "competition" which is said to characterize the form or *eidos* of a free-market economy.[40] It is precisely because the rules of just conduct protect the individual only to the extent that they expose her to further harm that insurance or the underwriting of risk becomes fundamental to neoliberal normativity. In the absence of social justice, neoliberalism provides models that seek to approximate insurance coverage for all which reflects the universal exposure to catastrophic risk.

On my reading, neoliberalism for Foucault names a kind of discourse which attempts to insure the biological or species life of the individual against the "risks" to which it has been exposed in civil society, that is, amid a society that no longer needs to fear the sovereign power of the state. The norms of police power or biopower produce this "insuring" of the biological life of each individual against the risks congenital with civil society. The police generates a "surplus value," not of capital but of biological life itself. As Foucault says, the interventions of the police are intended to "supply [men] with *a little extra life*—and by so doing supply the state with a *little extra strength*. This is done by controlling communication, that is, the common activities of individuals (work, production, exchange, accommodation)" (OES, 319). On this hypothesis, only when the biological life of the individual is placed under total observation and control (in my terms: is "insured") does the negative liberty which the self-limitation of sovereignty grants its subjects no longer become a source of insecurity, which is activity-inhibiting, but rather invites the individual to become enterprising, to live in a "free and responsible" way that unleashes what political economists call the "competition" that lies at the heart of all production of surplus value in late capitalism. That is also why Foucault can say that the Panopticon is not only the model of disciplinary power, but also remains "the general political formula" of liberal biopolitics (*BB*, 67). Thus, if the legal intervention into political economy discussed above accounts for the "juridification" of the neoliberal normative order, then the generation of security and "life insurance" accounts for the "biologization" of the neoliberal normative order. Both together make possible the "spontaneous" coordination of conducts characteristic of political economy.

Law as Resistance: People versus Population in Foucault

The idea of "surplus life" allows me to make my way to a tentative conclusion by returning to the problem of the biological model of normative order in Canguilhem with which I began this chapter. Implicit in Canguilhem's suggestion that the planning of political economy could be understood as the attempt by the state to make itself less like a machine and more like a living organism, is the idea that surplus life need not be only the result of the deregulation of the economy and increased policing of society, as advocated by neoliberalism, but can also be attained by an increase in the political capacity for self-organization (or political constitution) of a people and a citizenry. After all, it is a leitmotif of republican thought that a political constitution endows the political body with an organization that permits every part of the people to engage in a permanent rebirth of itself in and through its political action, and this permanent rebirth of itself is the content of its political "life." Something of this intuition is also found in Foucault's attempt to open up the possibility of an affirmative biopolitics which takes advantage of the normativity of living beings in order to resist social normalization and reach a more creative relation to norms, a normative creativity that is at the antipodes of the normativity of the entrepreneur. On this hypothesis, political resistance would take the form of a communal reappropiation of what I have been calling "surplus life," which is expropriated from the political and economical life of the people by the neoliberal *nomos* and partitioned off into the various policed subpopulations. Generally speaking, this is the opening that was taken up by the thinkers associated with the Italian reception of Foucault, mainly Giorgio Agamben,

Antonio Negri, and Roberto Esposito. In what follows, I merely indicate why Foucault's opening for the possibility of an affirmative biopolitics is inscribed within a revolutionary tradition of republican thought.

The illusory reconciliation of law and order in the neoliberal normative order is possible because the law is cut off from its roots in a conception of the political self-organization of a people (i.e., the republican idea of constitutionalism), and turned into "judge-made law." Simultaneously, the neoliberal *nomos* makes legislation into a function of the policing of conducts and the generation of security in the forms of assurance and insurance of biological life. The explosion of legislative activity and constitution making in neoliberal regimes is due to the fact that only the law makes "acceptable" the "essentially normalizing power" of the police.[41] But if power-as-law remains the standard for the legitimacy or rational acceptability of power also in neoliberalism, then the neoliberal reconciliation of the antinomy between law and order inevitably generates an antinomy of its own: the more the law is employed in its policing function, the less it will be able to be employed in its political function, that is, as a means of (self-)organizing a free people. In this way, every surplus of security is necessarily accompanied by a deficit of political legitimacy.

The surplus of life on which the entrepreneurial conduct relies is paid at the price of a widening deficit of legitimacy for the legal system and for the legislative powers of the state. Recently, neoliberalism has attempted to pacify this contradiction by projecting the conduct of the entrepreneur outside the sphere of civil society and into the public sphere of the state: hence successful entrepreneurs become prime ministers or presidents, promising to run the country as they ran their companies. But this attempt will also backfire: for turning the entrepreneur into a model for the lawmaker can only accelerate the process of turning the state into a private company with disastrous consequences for its capacity to generate the very acceptability needed by those normalizing police practices. The current lack of "representativeness" on the part of legislators is merely a symptom of the fact that the "laws" they claim to make have long ceased being laws in the republican sense of the term. Thus their demand that a people should grant them its support can only be met with attempts on the part of the people to take back their legislative power and become, in a direct manner, what republicanism always said they were, namely, the constituent power of society. The rising popularity of "direct democracy" initiatives in civil society is a symptomatic response to the antinomy generated by neoliberal jurisprudence.

It is this sort of antinomies that led Foucault in the last years of his life to return to a republican logic of political rationality according to which the sovereignty of the state is set limits by a system of law which gives expression to the existence of an "innate right" to have civil and political rights. In the republican understanding of natural right, the innate right to have rights is a right to belong as a member of a constituent people that gives itself law. The "innate right" to be a member of a people is *the only right that cannot be adjudicated by a judge-made law.* That is why Foucault insists on maintaining the "old" category of a people: "the people are generally speaking those who resist the regulation of the population, who try to elude the apparatus by which the population exists, is preserved, subsists, and subsists at an optimal level. This people/population opposition is very important" (*STP*, 44). Foucault calls this republican understanding of rights "revolutionary" and opposes it to the liberal understanding of rights. On the republican model of rights, the legitimacy of the state is a consequence of the self-limitation of the art of government before a new "field" of freedoms (rights), whose "nature" the state does not command. The question becomes: to what understanding of living nature does this "innate" right to rights correspond? At the end of the first volume of *The History of Sexuality* Foucault says that when biological life becomes the issue of politics, as it does in liberal governmentality, then political struggles and resistances to normalizing power take the form of a struggle for a whole series of new rights, such as "the right to life, to one's body, to health, to happiness, to the satisfaction of needs . . . the right to rediscover what one is and all that one can be" (*WK*, 145). I do not think that Foucault thereby meant to reject these struggles for new rights: they are the "political response" to the return of pastoral power in neoliberalism.[42] What Foucault attempts to provide in his last years is an account of the new subjectivity that can bear these new biopolitical rights. This search leads him from the Kantian question of critique, which for him is the question of "how to be governed less," back to the Greek and Roman understanding of mastery of self as a technique and work that one performs on oneself in order to put the surplus of life to another, more social and creative use. But this also entails rooting the "innate" right to have all of these new civil rights on the features of biological life that are shared by human beings, as a living species, with other living species, and that exploit the powers of biological life to resist the normalization imposed by social norms. The "innate" right to be part of a "people" cannot rely on the prior construction of a public space of mutual recognition structured by civil and political rights, for a people precedes such a space. It has become necessary to think the biopolitical roots of the innate right to have rights, the right to form a people, which of necessity—since it is shared by the entire human species—will no longer be a territorial conception of a people. The task of reconstructing a cosmo-political republicanism which is adequate to the age of biopower after Foucault remains unfinished.

PART FOUR

Philosophy as Ethics and Embodiment

TEN

Parrhesia between East and West: Foucault and Dissidence

Simona Forti

In the lecture dedicated to the Socratic concept of *parrhesia*, given on February 22, 1984, in the Course titled *The Courage of Truth*, Michel Foucault warmly recommended Jan Patočka's book *Plato and Europe*: "Of all modern books on the history of philosophy—he states—this is the only one that confers a crucial role to *epimeleia heauton*" (*CT*, 127). In fact, Patočka discerned in the idea of "care of the self" as "care of the soul," the root of European rationalism. Of course, Foucault states, Patočka's book was fundamental, but it nevertheless adhered to a notion of the soul still tied to a dualistic conception of the human from which one should want to take leave.

What I will attempt to argue in this essay is that Foucault's comment was in a way doubly misleading: first of all, because Patočka's notion of the soul does not at all repeat a metaphysical dualism, but, mainly and more interestingly for us, because it tended to suppress the profound affinity between Patočka's concept of dissidence and Foucault's concept of "counter-conduct." My point is that the idea of the "care of the soul," as intended by

Patočka, and the idea of "life-within-the-truth"—as intended by other dissident Patočkian thinkers, such as Václav Havel—played a role in shaping Foucault's later ideas, centered on the notions of "care of the self" and of *parrhesia* (fearless speech; to speak frankly, to tell the truth in the face of power). I have absolutely no intention of reconstructing Patočka's and Foucault's philosophical development, but, rather, I want to emphasize a theoretically virtuous circularity between philosophical practice as dissidence, in Patočka's sense, and the rethinking of the relationship between subjectivity, power, and truth put forward by Foucault. Looking at Foucault's late Courses through Patočka's idea of dissent, on the one side, and looking at Patočka's idea of philosophical dissidence through Foucault's notion of *parrhesia*, on the other side, sheds new light on each of them. Patočka no longer appears as the thinker of a new Platonic–Christian humanism and Foucault no longer appears the bearer of a nihilistic relativistic aestheticism of life.

Not many interpreters have reflected on the crucial nature of this exchange and the potential that it opens up for a sui generis exploration of the pathologies of power and, especially, of the role that subjectivity plays in sustaining or rejecting them. Certainly, looking back today at the philosophical and political ideas of the "dissidents" is in some ways easier than in the past as the climate during the Cold War led to a polarization that made the judgment of positions that were not unilaterally on one side or the other more difficult. Often labeled as liberal and anticommunist, and often identified with a humanistic and existential Christianity, the thought of Eastern European intellectuals, in its critical importance, has been enormously neglected. It was not simple for Western intellectuals—above all the French, who at that time were working to deconstruct humanistic rationalism and the morality connected to it—to understand and welcome the sometimes naive use that the Eastern European philosophers often proposed of Husserlian phenomenology and of the notion of the "life-world."

As the text of the Collège de France's Courses testify, Foucault paid increasing attention to what was happening in the countries of East-Central Europe, particularly Poland and Czechoslovakia. We also know that his works were smuggled into Prague and distributed among intellectual circles, especially those engaged in the *Charta 77* experience.[1] Many *samizdat*, even those of quite diverse ideological and theoretical roots, were directly inspired by Foucault's works. Having learned of the strong resonance of his texts within the seminars and the *samizdats*, Foucault expressed his wish to participate. After several failed attempts, his journey to Prague was eventually organized: he was expected there in the spring of 1984, but by then was extremely ill and was unable to make the journey. It was without a doubt a political interest that inspired Foucault: the intellectual activity of Czechoslovakia was a "disorganized" and "scattered" open challenge to the regime which could not fail to interest him. Nevertheless, there was also a more profound theoretical element which he had in common with the dissenters: a political critique formulated in philosophical terms which called into question both the dichotomous and demonic view of power and the myth of passive and innocent obedience. In short, in the circularity taking place between that historical experience, *ethos of truth*, and philosophy, Foucault had the possibility of observing how a subject can constitute itself as a force field of ethical and political resistance and as a locus of retrospective action against the pressures of a system of domination.

"To be pregnant," Patočka said at the end of the 1960s, "a philosophical thought, whatever it may be, should take a position on the front line."[2] Patočka's life, of course, might be taken as an example of *parrhesia*. Arrested by the political police, Patočka was struck down by a brain hemorrhage following a series of grueling interrogations, the last of which, on Sunday, March 13, 1977, lasted more than ten hours. While there can be no doubt about the political significance of his death, there nevertheless remains an unsolved question: what philosophical meaning can be attributed to it? Was it, perhaps, a sacrifice made in the name of the good which, according to many interpreters, defines the Christian horizon of the Prague thinker?

Patočka's language sometimes deceives, so much so that many have numbered the philosopher among the supporters of a renewed Christianized Platonism, in which the notion of "soul" would be the main indicator. However, I am convinced that Patočka's "a-subjective phenomenology," as he defines his own philosophy, which sees existence as "movement," does not imply a religious presupposition, but a radical theory of the *polemos* (conflict) whose meaning has an ethical and political value.[3]

In the 1973 book *Plato and Europe*, the text cited by Foucault, Patočka diagnosed the crisis of European culture as obliviousness to the notion of soul.[4] An invention of the Greek philosophers, whether regarded as mortal or as immortal, the soul was still something which one "had to take care of." This was in fact the only way in which mortals could become immortals. Immortality was not the essence of the soul. It was an *energy*, an *activity*, a *movement* triggered by a specific way of being and perceiving by the *psyche*. In this sense, for Patočka the soul is that which enables one to overcome the simple dualism of the mythical world, the dualism between the everyday and the divine.

Here, then, even in the text on Plato, the distinction emerges which recurs in all of his works: the difference between the "forces of the day" and the "forces of the night." The *conflict* between these forces—which constantly recurs in different forms in every human life—*is the movement of existence*:[5] a disturbance which shakes us from the guarantees of the forces of the day and exposes us to the truth that reveals the precariousness of our life. Philosophy and thinking, then, mean "caring for the soul"; and "the care of the soul" is nothing but the possibility that opens the way, for humans, to go beyond their natural horror toward death; beyond the natural fear which mythology talks about. Pre-Socratic philosophy—chiefly Heraclitus's *logos*—thus discovered the "care of the soul" to be that opportunity given to man alone to question himself and reality. The Platonic doctrine brought this exercise to the pinnacle of its expressive potential.

To be sure, Patočka's language, still so heavily marked by classical metaphysical terms, disguises, especially in *Plato and Europe*, his philosophically heretical intent. In other words, his intention to revive the notion of a soul was a guard against relativism, but also as a barrier to any substantialization of thought, either Christian or rationalistic. In the *Heretical Essays*, published in 1975, the awareness of duality and *polemos* acquires all the weight of ethical and political demands. In this work, the crisis of European rationalism fully shows itself in the figure of the wars of the twentieth century.[6] In reality, Patočka states, we are not simply facing the advent of the "kingdom of the night." The wars for the domination and partitioning of Europe were aimed at making the continent a giant complex of energy at the service of the "kingdom of the day." It was therefore "the forces of the day," those forces that claim to work for progress and to seek peace, "which for four years sent millions of humans into hellfire."[7] What have the bloody wars of the twentieth century and the ideologies that inspired them taught us? What "secret'" of the time is Patočka revealing to us? It is this: that a distorted rapport between life and death reached the apex of perversion in the twentieth century. For the individual, "the forces of the day," life, is everything. It is the absolute value. But, from the standpoint of the "forces of the day," for that power and strength that accumulate life and energy, the life of the individual does not exist.[8] Indeed, both of them act as if death did not exist.

So Patočka's ultimate message is unequivocal: life, not death, was the century's great undisputed "grande dame," the life that monopolizes and captures both individuals and communities. The "powers of the day" thereby lose their pristine innocence, and become the carriers of a power which moves downward toward a final event of death. Not unlike Foucault, who interrogated biopolitics, a politics which brought about death in the name of life, Patočka accused the absolutism and maximization of life for being a powerful instrument of death. If looked at from an ontological perspective, Patočka appears to conclude, such forces have not only haunted the twentieth century, but it was only in the twentieth century that they managed to bring about the complete separation between death and life, in such a way as to make life into the complete opposite of death. In the pages of the *Heretical Essays*, the reciprocal otherness of life and death is one of the most powerful questions. So, just for having denied its nocturnal face, its inextricable link with death, life is submerged by violence and death. Denied, death returns, but in the guise of devastation. By closing one's eyes to death, by never ending with the "preparations for life," as Musil says, death takes possession of life.

An appeal to offer our civilization a faint possibility of change, of leaving behind the hegemony of force, comes to light in all the *Heretical Essays*. The call to return to a different relationship between life and death is mediated today, in contrast to ancient philosophy, by the words of those who, shaken by the experience of war, have been able to grasp its deeper meaning.

So, then, what is Patočka telling us? That there are two ways in which one can relate life and death, ways which are radically incompatible. The first is that assumed by all the wars of the twentieth century and which continues to act not only in post-totalitarian regimes, but also under the surface of Western liberal democracies. To this way of thinking, death, the dead, are no more than the necessary tribute paid for the affirmation of life, the price paid for the stabilization of life. It is the cost demanded by the forces of the day to which in reality we all feel bound. Such forces are in the final analysis constituted and empowered by our ties, our needs, by everything that roots life together in a system of safeguards and protections. The government of the forces of the day objectivizes our lives by promising to satisfy daily needs: in a word, by promising a way of life without any threat.

To the eyes of those who have been at the front, however, the truth of a different relationship between life and death has been glimpsed. Only in this sense can one say that the sacrifice of the victims had a value: it has served to liberate us from the objectifying power of the forces of the day. Granting an "absolute meaning" to the power of those who have died does not mean either sanctifying their "sacrifice" or believing that it is the ultimate ethical conduct. Rather, it means recognizing that those deaths cannot and should not be justified in the name of anything else. "Dying for" socialism and communism, "dying for" a race or for democracy, are only masks exploited by life to increase its power. Now, if death is instead accepted as constitutive of our individual lives, even the "sense of life" can be rethought.

Closer to Heraclitus than to Plato or Christianity, Patočka says that, just like for those who experienced combat in war, there is another way of linking life and death together. First of all, those people know that death is not the nothingness that the forces of death claim it to be, the nothingness that they constantly use to enslave us while at the same time denying its relevance. Only by recognizing the inevitability of the night can we overthrow, or at least distance ourselves, from the absolutist sense of the day conferred by the logic of power; only in this way do we manage to deconstruct all the stories and calculations that maximize life. This is an experience that can be had only individually, but makes no sense if it cannot be shared and communicated. On it rests the "solidarity of the shaken."[9] It is the solidarity among those who, having had all their assumptions shaken, can no longer view them as obvious. It is a solidarity that transcends all forms of belonging, a solidarity which cannot be identified with any "class," profession, nationality, or culture. It is the community of those who have been able to understand what is at stake in life and death and therefore in history, and are able to understand that history *is* this conflict between *naked life*, shackled by fear, and "life at the peak," which sees clearly that life and peace have an end. Only the individual capable of understanding this and capable of change, by a sort of *metanoia* (conversion), is a "spiritual man."

I do not believe that Derrida, in *The Gift of Death*,[10] is right: in Patočka, self-sacrifice does not have only a religious meaning. When Patočka speaks of a place and a time for change, when he speaks of the subject of responsibility, he does not speak of a sense of an otherworldly salvation, of an eschatological finale. At stake, indeed, is a *metanoia*, but an unusual one which has no other place and time than those of the attitude of the self to itself. This is a person who "lives in truth" for the simple reason that he knows that the *care of death* cannot be disassociated form the care of life. And if a way out of the collapse of European history can be conceived by recalling the past, it is not a religious past, but rather the philosophical past: in particular, to that "care of the soul" (*epimeleia*) which from the beginning characterized Patočka's ideas as a *negative Platonism*.

The theme of the *epimeleia* in fact stems from a series of writings from the mid-1950s posthumously published in a text titled "Negative Platonism."[11] These essays contain incontestable evidence of Patočka's attempts to distance himself, from the beginning, from every attempt to create an integral humanism as a possible escape from nihilism. More clearly than in the book devoted to *Plato and Europe*, and in a less dramatic way than in the *Heretical Essays*, in these pages it is already beyond doubt that the soul should not be understood in a metaphysical sense. "Care of the soul" refers to the "movement of distancing ourselves from what we are immersed in." The soul is the place of "philosophizing," if by philosophy we mean the action of a life which leaves itself and returns to itself. From Socrates, philosophy was therefore not seen as a guide for a soul journeying toward the eternal truth. Rather it is the *praxis* of interrogation which triggers the process of thought. Such a perspective has no other objective than to avoid the identification of life with one of the simple opinions provided by its context. Patočka's Socrates is therefore the heretic who shakes the foundations of Greek society; he is the merciless critic of all those who believe they have the truth and of those who presume to be able to deduce absolute rules from the *doxa*.

In other words, "negative Platonism" is something completely different from the metaphysical Platonism on which Western philosophy has built its structure. Patočka's approach certainly owes a debt to Nietzsche and Heidegger, but while they rejected the Platonic works in toto, Patočka instead—not unlike Arendt and Foucault—saves and enhances the dialogues from which it is possible to extract an autonomous "Socratic moment." The Heideggerian "step back from metaphysics" cannot, according to Patočka, get over Socrates.

Socratic philosophy is a "negative philosophy" not only because it refuses to assume any positive content of truth, but also because it appropriates negativity as a condition of being able to be free. Socratic freedom, according to Patočka, entails being capable of a distance, of a shift, of overcoming all types of objectivization. The greatness of Socrates, in short, was his ability to maintain the transcendence of the given reality without ever reaching a point that would put an end to actual transcending. In contrast to positive Platonism, which believes in the possibility of a path of elevation up to the idea, negative Platonism never claims to go beyond concrete, historical experience. It simply retains its awareness of its transience. Patočka compares Socratic freedom to the notion of *chorismos* (separation), used earlier by Heidegger in his *Introduction to Metaphysics* to try to explain the separation between idea and reality. Now, Patočka's *chorismos* does refer to a separation, but not of two realms coordinated or bound by a third that comes to embrace them. *Chorismos* is the separation itself or, better, it denotes the very movement of separation.[12]

We find the same idea of transcendence and movement at the center of the *Heretical Essays in the Philosophy of History*. There is nevertheless an undeniable continuity between these early writings on Socrates and the essays of the mid-1970s, in which the figure of the dissenting intellectual takes form. "The spiritual man," he wrote in those years, "is a man who exposes himself to the negative."[13] It is he who lives without roots. It is he who has the sense of wholeness, a totality that is not anything objective, but the device of "a dis-objectivizing power." For this reason it cannot be translated into a doctrine of truth nor into a doctrine of good. But not for this is it arbitrary. Our capacity for truth depends on our ability to distance ourselves, to free ourselves from the clutches of objects. The call to truth is the call to freedom.[14]

Patočka's Socrates, viewed through the lens of Heidegger, intertwines freedom and truth. Truth means, as with Heidegger, "leaving things be" but also (and principally) indicates a movement of life that is constituted as an *ethos*. Truth here is the ethical freedom that in the first instance allows us to challenge the given norm and to distance ourselves from the naivety of passed-on convictions. The soul—we may say using other terms—is a process of subjectivation, not too far from the care of the self as *parrhesia* in Foucault's later works. It is a practice of continuous questioning by the subject of himself/herself and his/her conditions, of his/her having become what he/she is and of why reality is configured in its present form. While Patočka did not abandon the term "soul," a heavily connoted term, he used it mainly in the Greek sense of a specific skill or ability. This is, in other words, the sign that stands for the action of transcendence,[15] in the sense of being continuous differing. Becoming ethical subjects means to succeed in perceiving a difference, the difference between life as it is presented to us and life in its commonality with death, and being able to make this tension into the "non-ecstatic" and "non-orgiastic" antidote to the power of the everyday.

The significance of the words which have been used by metaphysics receive a radical deconstruction in Patočka's work. The soul—at least as I see it—is not a substance separate from the body, neither is it something that survives the body and that can aspire to eternal life. *It is that which in the subject constantly offers resistance.* It is the movement which distances itself from the power of things, from the authority of politics, from the blackmail of violence, from the pressure of the desire of life. In a word, it is the power to resist another power.

There is no space in this context to follow the traces of Patočka's appeals to the "spiritual man," to "philosophy" as "care of the soul," and to the "community of the shaken" into the political works written by many of the intellectuals who gravitated around *Charta 77*. Think, for example, of the best account of daily life at the time of real socialism[16] given in *The Power of the Powerless*, the little masterpiece by Vàclav Havel—perhaps the most direct heir of Patočka's philosophy.[17] The essay is not simply a manifesto calling for action, but is intended to show how a network of relationships is made denser, starting from *below*, by compromise on top of compromise, until eventually it confirms and strengthens the system of domination.[18]

Every person, individually, by accepting the rules of the game—as done by the greengrocer who exhibits, without any political faith, a sign saying "Workers of the world unite" in his window, next to the onions—allows that system to continue.[19] Without the obedience of the greengrocer, the obedience of the office worker would be called into doubt; without the conformity of the office worker, that of the teacher would be at risk; and so on, in an endless feedback loop. Each proposes something for the next to repeat because everyone believes the other has the same expectation. In this way, through seemingly innocent gestures, each contributes to the construction of the bleak landscape of everyday life. And the easy absolution that everyone accords himself is, according to Havel, a deception, because each by his conformity compels the other to accept power. Certainly, all are obedient victims of the system, but by acting in this way they are also guilty parties. When a person adapts to the circumstances, he collaborates to the perpetuation of the same. "They do what is done, what is appropriate to do, but in that way they confirm that it is all appropriate and should be done." Thus in essence, "everyone helps everyone else to remain obedient."[20] Havel never tired of repeating that the "life-within-the-lie" cannot be reduced to a domination that the few impose on the many, but is something that harnesses everyone and which everyone helps to create. In other words, there is in each of us a part that agrees with, in fact, desires such a system: that part which blocks the free and risky gesture of the self—the action of what Havel defines the "better me"—in favor of an objectivizing compliance.[21]

As in the case of Patočka, Havel's language could undoubtedly give the impression that his text was a dialectic between the authentic and inauthentic, all the more so when he used a phrase so provocative and seemingly naive as that of "living-within-the-truth." Milan Kundera, who argued against Havel from the time of the Prague Spring, did not hesitate to make him the target of fierce criticism. His major work, *The Unbearable Lightness of Being*, could be read as a long polemic against Havel, which complicates the ethical position of dissent. Kundera asks: When is it possible to distinguish, especially at the level of everyday life, between a "life-within-the-lie" and a "life-within-the-truth"? The circularity between truth, freedom and dissent, in short, is a much more thin line. The entanglement of life and power is close to the point of being intractable.

Much more than for Havel, for Kundera, as for Foucault, power relations are, before any other determination, relationships between bodies, and are therefore inevitable. They illuminate the psychological dynamics which, once triggered, remain for the most part constant, and govern as much private situations as they do political events. Many of Kundera's characters experience, as Lacan might have suggested, relations of power as if they continued the encirclement of the individual by the mother, as if they were prolonging that first and fundamental balance of power. Obedience to power is of course transmitted by means of coercion and fear, but also by a subordination that is, so to speak, spontaneous, driven by an ambivalent and vertiginous power, almost as if it were "an irresistible desire to fall." This is what can push us toward the magic circle and its attractive force. It can count on a subject with a troubled identity that, riven with conflicting forces which he does not want to recognize, is often the obstacle to its own release. Many of Kundera's characters thus remain stuck in relationships that produce negativity and suffering.

Kundera's microphysics, so to speak, produces the polemic against Havel, and his supposed belief in authenticity, well beyond the parameter of political relationships, to envelop, as we have said, personal relationships and, what's more, of a certain kind of "impolitical" critique of communism. The critique made by Kundera is in reality a more profound and radical challenge. It relates not only to communism, but concerns all the "European, religious, and political faiths," all the visions that begin from the assumption that the world is just and being is good. Kitsch, ultimately, is no more than "this categorical agreement with being." From this perspective, he criticizes the "position" of the dissident as a bearer of authenticity, even though he himself does not hesitate to put forward a scathing critique of his times, and of the political regime under which he has lived. He laments the disappearance of the tragic. This is the sense of his indictment of kitsch that we find in the memorable pages of *The Unbearable Lightness of Being*, pages which became, against the intention of their author, emblematic of the dissident philosophy.

In its original ontological meaning, kitsch consists in the action that eliminates from the visible sphere everything that in human existence may appear essentially intolerable. It is the "empire of the positive." As a categorical agreement with being, the kitsch, for Kundera, has as many names as the answers which claim to resolve the question of being. It can be Catholic, Protestant, or Jewish; fascist, communist, or democratic; national or international; feminist or male chauvinist. But is Kundera's condemnation of kitsch really so far from the "life-within-the-truth" thematized by Havel in the footsteps of Patočka? Is it not also the contraposition between tragic and kitsch a way of speaking about that way of life which tries to disturb the unquestioned rule of life? We might also try to think of it as an "aesthetic of existence," in Foucault's sense; that is, as the choice of an *ethos* shaking up the "categorical agreement with being." It is in fact the movement of subtraction and disidentification from the rule of a hegemonic life, a free gesture—as he confirms—that alone may be able to break the vicious circle of the objective guilt.

For those who have read Michel Foucault's later Courses the parallels are obvious: the experience of dissent and its philosophical thematization are not without consequences for the way in which Foucault rethought the relationship between subjects and power, beginning in the second half of the 1970s. There are many traces of this theoretical relationship.

In the lectures at the Collège de France in 1977–78, *Security, Territory, Population*, Foucault spoke of different forms of revolts, insubordinations, and disobedience, preferring the term "counter-conduct" to the term "dissent." In that context, he made clear reference to the historical experience of Eastern Europeans.[22] Foucault explicitly defined the countries of Eastern Europe and the Soviet Union as "systems of generalized obedience" which he explained in terms of their being among the contemporary examples of pastoral power.[23] This reference to dissidence, or whatever Foucault wanted to call it, therefore provides a special conceptual lens through which to observe what is happening and which forces move between subjects when they enter into a relation of power. Subjects and power give birth to a network of relations within which there flows an energy which continuously redesigns established configurations. But the reference to the possibility of "counter-conducts" as forms of dissidence seems now to confute one of the most recurring criticisms directed at the French philosopher, namely, that of not leaving any space for resistance and freedom, within the diffusion of the relationships between power, truth, and subject. The subject, according to Foucault's critics, thus would have no possibility of critique since the criterion of truth was taken from him or her: every truth, in fact, is the result of a configuration of the knowledge–power relation.

Of course, for Foucault there is no society without power relations, that is, without strategies through which men seek to determine the conduct of others. However, he gradually articulated a clear analytical distinction between "strategic games between liberties," "technologies of government," and "states of domination."[24] The criteria for evaluating a system of power, that is, for deciding whether to accept it or reject it, lies in the distance that separates it from a "state of domination": the highest point of subjective dependence. Relations of power, in fact, exist only insofar as subjects are free, in other words, when they can change the situation. And it was in the name of this freedom that Foucault, in his last lectures, opened a passage toward the possibility of a different relationship between subjects and power.

Before drawing conclusions, let us pause for a moment to reflect on the 1978 Course, *Security, Territory, Population* which places us before a crucial junction. In the opening lectures, Foucault presented a historical research on the "art of governing," an art that flourished from the beginning of the sixteenth century. But his "survey" ended by posing a question concerning pastoral power that was more philosophical than historical. The thesis is as strong as it is historically questionable: between "the government of souls," or the "economy of souls," of early Christianity, and the "government of men," which marks the boundary in which Western politics operates, there is a deep connection that must be interrogated. The Christian pastorate, in contrast to the Jewish pastorate and that of the pre-Christian East from which it drew inspiration, marks a decisive break with the classical Greek universe. The Christian shepherd is a guide, who does not however aspire to gain power over a political community: he cares only for the safety of his sheep, each and every one of them. He affirms their salvation primarily by giving them nourishment, driving the flock toward better pastures and making sure that all the animals eat properly. So we are therefore faced with a power that seeks the good. No longer, however, the good of the city in its primarily political meaning as in Greece, but the good understood as the well-being of those who wish to be led and therefore accept subordination. In short, pastoral power is one that takes care of people, that helps, that is concerned, that seeks to prevent pain, that goes after lost sheep and cares for those which are injured and suffering (*STP*, 120). The shepherd is not in himself the supreme power, but rather is the intermediary between the flock and salvation and, as such, does not act for his own glory or for wealth, but toils selflessly for others, even to the point of sacrifice. Thanks to the mediation of Christianity, particularly after it was institutionalized as the state religion, the structural establishment of pastoral power which was so foreign to Greco-Roman thought spreads throughout the Western world. What appears to have been passed over in modern politics, and marks a permanent feature of our political universe, is the structure of a relationship based on the dependence–salvation exchange, and it is not important whether salvation should be interpreted as immortality of the soul or as the material well-being of the people (*STP*, 130).

But how did this particular configuration enter history? What are the cogs which, fitting perfectly into one another, have made the relationship of care and protection not only the political relation par excellence, but also the standard of all right conduct? "The Christian pastorate," Foucault said in his lecture on February 22, "has organized something completely different that seems to me to be foreign to Greek practice, and this is what we could call an instance of 'pure obedience': obedience as a unitary highly valued type of conduct in which the essence of its *raison d'être* is in itself. What I mean is this . . . that Christianity is not a religion of the law; it's a religion of God's will, a religion of what God wills for each in particular" (*STP*, 174). How then does this obedience put down roots in the heart of the subject to become his permanent state and ultimate goal?

In the 1978 lectures the term *apatheia* acted as a marker of this transition between the two ways, the ancient and the Christian, of perceiving the relationship of subordination.[25] *Apatheia*, as it was transmitted from the Greeks and Romans to the Christian Fathers, would come to acquire through the latter a meaning quite different from the original. Instead of control, exercised over the passions by reason, for ancient Christianity, absence of passions, *apatheia*, meant renouncing one's own judgment and will. There is no doubt that for Foucault this was a crucial shift: Christian *apatheia* as an abstention from the persistent practice of self-judgment and self-will, as something handed over to the protection of a pastoral guide, really seemed to be the engagement point of the elevation of a condition of "integral dependence" to a virtue that would be transmitted over the centuries. This virtue is not an obedience to the law of the city or of reason, but it is the obedience of someone to the one who guides him. This relation of dependence succeeded in establishing itself, first, in the institutional structure of the Church, and then asserted itself *as a structural model, as the standard for establishing and organizing relationships of power between men*. If it has proved itself so pervasive and persistent it is because it was an extremely powerful tool of subjective individualization: a subjectivation built on the model of submission.

The government of men is thus ready to become the network of continual deference to the responsibility of others: in the power game of sheep and shepherds nobody acts according to his own will or judgment. The pastor, in fact, does not guide the "sheep" for the pleasure he derives from leading, he does not command for the sake of making decisions and overcoming resistance. No, the pastor is the servant and minister of the truth and salvation of others, being willing in turn to obey, to receive his salvation and his truth from someone else. In the network of reciprocal cross-exchange between acts of obedience, in that "field of generalized obedience," as Foucault called it, commanding or ruling is nothing more than a way of fulfilling the duty of obedience. In the final analysis, therefore, there is no place where the responsibility and final decision regarding the control of conduct or the guidance of conscience resides, but only an infinite plot of dependency.

After focusing on the problem of the "government of men," it was as if Foucault became convinced of the necessity of writing a new *Genealogy of Morals*. We can say that with the 1978 Course Foucault undertook a journey that, in the footsteps of Nietzsche and thanks to the stimulus of the philosophy of dissent, led him to analyze the game of power *in* the subject, with the aim of probing from within the origins of that "scandalous" virtue of obedience and of conformist conduct, which is the strongest adhesive with which to cement relationships of power into relationships of domination. As he reminds us in *The Hermeneutics of the Subject*, the birth of conscience is a complex process in which the "obligation to tell the truth about oneself," which is identified with the necessary condition for salvation, plays a crucial role. In the Courses given in the early 1980s,[26] and also in various conferences of the same period,[27] Foucault's interest moved from the general structure of pastoral power to that of its system—inherited from

Greco-Roman antiquity—which brings the subject to produce "acts of reflective truth" with a view to salvation. According to early Christian texts, we cannot be the judges of ourselves. Self-examination is subordinated to the continuous calling into question of one's own thoughts and the absolute obedience to authority.

In short, these lessons provide one of the most sophisticated philosophical approaches for that "normativity of non-judgment" which is the pivot around which the possible alternative genealogy of the link between the subject of *parrhesia* and power revolves. In a very similar way to Nietzsche, Foucault also thought that obedience, meekness, and conformity emerge whenever the human being is unable to bear the weight of his internal conflict, and he expunges it by creating a dualistic regime. Hence the need of the self to view salvation as a return to the one, to the one of the self or the one with God, guaranteed by the mediation of pastoral authority. The human being is therefore engaged in a relentless struggle against himself to achieve his salvation, which can be reached by fully submitting to the power of divinity, and the power of its ministers. It is quite clear that Foucault is not talking simply of a form of subjectivation limited to the early Christian world, but of a disposition that, although secularized and freeing itself from theology, will endure through the ages. Here, then, is how the interplay between the subject and power is structured in the West. Power, in order to determine the conduct of others, requires submission and obedience; submission and obedience, in turn, answer the need of the individual who, in order to find salvation from death, requires something external to him, whether it be God or a norm. At this point, in bringing to light the structure of the obedient subject, so to speak, the physiognomy of another possibility of subjectivation cannot fail to shine through. This is what Foucault will attempt in his Courses devoted to *The Care of the Self* and to *parrhesia*.

In short, it is as if Foucault was looking within the folds of ancient ethics for a way according to which the relationship between subject, truth, and salvation can form a different constellation, different from that which structures the geometry of the obedient subject, of the subject that supports and feeds a power liable to turn into a state of domination. For this Foucault must search for indications of an extremely fragile balance: a way to allow different forces to live together within the subject, while avoiding the possibility that an external saving power would bring them back to unity. This is the ethic of Foucault's self: an ethic that seeks possible points of subtraction and disidentification from the normativity of power. The challenge is therefore to understand in what way the subject organizes herself internally as a holder of contrasting strengths and in what way she can ensure, as far as she can, autonomy and independence.[28] In other words, the question is in what way can a place of dissidence be found?

In *The Hermeneutics of the Subject*, we can follow two leads: the subject's relationship with salvation and his/her relationship with death.[29] These are the themes that return strongly in the Courses on *parrhesia*. Now, what does "saving oneself" mean in the ethical texts of the Hellenistic philosophies of the first and second centuries? It means, first of all, equipping oneself to become a safe place. Foucault pointed out that salvation never referred to the drama of an event that makes a leap from the negative to the positive (*HS*, 160): "This means that the term salvation does not refer to anything that is not life itself" (*HS*, 162). Salvation seen as the overcoming of death, of the pursuit of eternity, of another world, is never what is at stake. When the subject finds in the domain of self the certainty that nothing can disturb it, when it has fortified itself to the point of self-sufficiency—this is how Foucault read the ideals of ataraxy and autarchy—it has reached its salvation: "One saves oneself for oneself, one saves oneself in virtue of oneself, one saves oneself to not arrive at nothing if not at oneself" (*HS*, 163). If the type of salvation to which Hellenistic and Roman thought strived for was far from that represented by the city in classical philosophy, it was nevertheless distant from all religious aims that, being inseparable from a dualist conception of existence, had to hypothesize a dramatic transition from the false to the true, from nothing to being.

The Hellenistic salvation is a resistance tempered and forged in an ongoing deconstruction of what one identifies with. What emerges from the texts of Epictetus, Seneca, and Marcus Aurelius is the importance of different strategies which have similar results: to dissect contingent identities to perceive one's unique position within the world. Even for this one needs philosophical *askesis*. Principally, this requires the *meditatio malorum* that can be learned by putting oneself under the guidance of a teacher. Meditating on death is, in such a culture, a very powerful dislocation of identity. The thought of death shakes the subject, makes him restless, throws him into disarray but at the same time prepares and fortifies him.[30] Far from being an escape or an excuse to give up critical thinking, the thought of death, unlike in Christianity, enhances both judgment of the present and the ability to review the past. It is, in other words, a fragment—that of Hellenistic and Roman ethics—which Foucault draws out of history as an example of how a *bios* manages to become an *ethos* and how an *ethos* can become *praxis*. For Foucault, the ethics of late antiquity are therefore an example of "virtualization" of subjective identity, that allow us the opportunity to see that there is not only one way to become a subject. If one is not born a subject, but becomes one, then the constitutive practices of the self are not only those which in the history of the "rational animal" have proved successful.

Foucault's call to "se déprendre de soi-meme" in *The Use of Pleasure* is a call to break away from those parts of the self, from those ways of being and acting that keep us tied to powers which seem intolerable, or which we simply no longer recognize. Herein lies the need to choose an *ethos* and give oneself a form, a *bios*. This is not an aesthetic choice, in the sense of "making a work of art out of your life," but instead is a recognition of oneself as a space in which one *can* accept or resist the pressures of domination. In the difficult task of giving shape to one's life, of giving an *ethos* to our *bios* outside of universal norms, *parrhesia* is an expression of the self that gains increasing importance in Foucault. In *The Hermeneutics of the Subject* the ethic of *parrhesia* had already made its appearance as a political practice that opposes adulation of the powerful. In this context, the effect of the truth activated by the speaker is primarily ethical. The *parrhesia* starts from below and rises to strike those at the top. It is not important that the content of the utterance corresponds to the truth, so long as the parrhesiast gains legitimacy on ethical grounds. The parrhesiast states a truth in the form of a personal opinion, showing himself to be a witness. Confidence in the veracity of his words derives from the fact that he confirms through his actions his belief in the truth of what he says. He tells the truth, showing that agreement between the facts and words is a perfect unity of *logos* and *bios*.

With the Course begun in 1983 and published as *The Government of Self and Others*, but mainly in his last lectures before his death, recently published under the title *The Courage of the Truth*, Foucault shifted his gaze to an *immediate* relationship between life and truth, even more radical than that proposed by Stoic ethics. From the *parrhesia* of Creusa in

Euripides, up to that of the Cynics, passing by Socrates's *parrhesia* as philosophy, the criterion for establishing the truth of a parrhesian argument was the close correlation between *logoi* and *erga*. The ethical characteristics which denote the authentic *parrhesia* nevertheless remain constant: courage, risk (to the point of endangering one's life), and outspokenness distinguish the parrhesiast from other residents of the city. If in the lectures of 1982 a division was established between "knowledge of the self" and "care of the self," now, in 1984, the "care of the self" is strongly connected to the *parrhesia*. This is a crucial point in Foucault since, in my opinion, Socrates spells out very clearly the two antagonistic ways of becoming a subject. The first path, marked by Pythagorism, outlines the requisite path from impurity to purity, from contingency to eternity.[31] The subject can constitute itself as the subject of truth only if it becomes the vessel of a revealed truth. The second path is instead connected to *parrhesia*, which identifies truth-telling as a practice that is free and sustained solely by the courage of saying what one believes to be true: a courage that requires a constant monitoring of one's own judgment.

Plato's dialogue *Laches* offers a different view from that of the *First Alcibiades*: in *Laches* the care of the soul opens a perspective which gives rise to the "aesthetic of existence" as a capacity to confront political power through the medium of *parrhesia*. Here courage plays a central role. It has to do in fact with fighting fear, in the sense of controlling fear by the simple exercise of virtue. Several hallmarks of the parrhesian life come together in the figure of Socrates presented in this dialogue: the courage to stand alone against power, the risky exposure of citizens to the Assembly, the care of the self that becomes a call for others to speak the truth freely. Socrates is all of these things together. In contrast to the *First Alcibiades* and the *Apology*, in the *Laches* Socrates is a parrhesiast not only because of what he says, but also for the way of life he pursues. Here is the Socratic "aesthetic of existence": the attempt to transform one's life into a place where the truth can be seen through gestures, actions, and choices. He incessantly interrogates himself even on pain of death. This is an exercise in the art of distinction. Socrates in the *Laches* becomes the master of *parrhesia* not so much because he is wise but because there is no contradiction between his speech and his *bios*. "Care of the self," *parrhesia*, the ability to distinguish between good and evil as well as courage are all intimately connected. Foucault found these elements on the horizontal plane of a *praxis* that besides being ethical could simultaneously become political.

Foucault never tired of returning to the alternatives represented by the *First Alcibiades*, on the one hand, and the *Laches* on the other. The *Alcibiades* establishes power in the *psyche* as an ontological reality separate from the body, which corresponds to a mode of self-knowledge as contemplation of a reality that points beyond the senses. Living in the truth, for this view, means to lead the soul to its own way of being: that of participating in the divine. In other words, this option is that of metaphysical subjectivity, of that discourse which reveals man's essence and what he must do to comply with it. Ethics, in this perspective, dictates the rules of conduct to which the human being must adhere in order to join the matching ontological foundation. However, it is possible—and this is in fact the path of the *Laches*—to find another interpretation of the *didonai logon*, of giving an account of oneself. This is the way of the aesthetic of existence, in the sense of a way of life chosen as the exemplary life, the only possible way to immortalize oneself. In other words, one becomes a subject, one subjectivizes oneself, directly and exclusively through the actions one performs and the words one utters. From the perspective of the *Laches*, living in the truth signifies assuming the risk of telling people that they need courage to acquire a certain form of life.

Despite how much Foucault drags us into a conflict that at times can seem forced, the message he sends is clear. One does not become a subject only as a passive recipient of an external truth. There is no subjectivization in merely subjecting oneself to a power that "saves" by eradicating negative aspects of the self once and for all. But one can become and remain a subject also through an uninterrupted effort of ethical judgment. Foucault is telling us that with Socrates Western culture has offered us two possibilities: one which draws truth from the ethics of the other life and one which is built around the possibility for a life to be otherwise. This, then, is what is at stake in Foucault's research between the folds of tradition: finding a way to achieve a possible interruption of those devices that through power establish a vicious circle of domination. Foucault's aspiration is not to construct a collective subject that will restore the political good in history, nor a negative utopia or an "inoperative community" (Agamben). His is not a search for a multiple and endlessly nomadic identity (Negri). Foucault rather seeks the path toward a possible "ethical revolution": the unique revolution of a *bios* that manages to become an *ethos*, and of an *ethos* that can become *praxis*, the practice of a continuous exercise of freedom.

Removing oneself from the rules of the game, interrupting the *inertia* of the everyday, detaching oneself from one's identifications with powers, all these are practices that can in some contexts be extremely dangerous. The "life-within-the-truth," far from being a purely mental activity, is an "athleticism of judgment"—to put it in Foucault's words; it is the assumption of that *ethos* which refuses to consent to the "categorical agreement with being" by expunging "the negative"; an *ethos* which remains faithful to its own internal *polemos*. Patočka would say that *ethos* which doesn't deny the "forces of the night." Because salvation—salvation from our negativity—comes not from history nor from the system that feeds our life. Salvation from power, a power that becomes domination, can only emerge from ethics, from the choice of an *ethos* as a way of life and a way of thinking.

In many respects, then, the pages of Foucault's final Courses lead us to an ethical subject, to a kind of "anarchical constitution" of the self, in the literal sense of the term: a self which, while constantly attempting to distance itself from external authorities, while resisting the desires of internal unification and pacification, still relates to itself and to others and takes full responsibility for the present in which it lives. Because being a subject not only means shielding oneself from the pressures and orders that come from the outside; it also means knowing how to bring and maintain conflict and division within oneself, within the self. It is in this sense that we must understand Foucault's often repeated claim that the revolution will either be ethical or it will never be.

ELEVEN

The Embodiment of Truth and the Politics of Community: Foucault and the Cynics

Vanessa Lemm

This chapter investigates Foucault's analysis of the philosophical life of the Cynics in *The Courage of Truth* from the perspective of the Nietzschean question: how can truth be incorporated or embodied (*einverleibt*)? In order to consider philosophy as a form of life (*bios theoretikos*) and not merely as a doctrine or a science, the question of how truth can be lived or materialized in the physical body is obviously crucial. As a form of the true life (*la vraie vie*), philosophy competes with political life (*bios politikos*), which is based on opinion. The competition or *agon* between the philosophical life and the political life provides the background for Foucault's analysis of *parresia*, that is, frank speech or truth-telling, in his last two volumes of Courses, *The Government of Self and Others* and *The Courage of Truth*. Whereas both Foucault and Arendt can be read as defenders of the philosophical life because of its ethical–political effects, Arendt argues that the Socratic philosophical life is a life that allows a distance to the body, and in so doing poses a resistance to what Esposito calls the closure of the political body on itself, which is characteristic of "totalitarian" politics.[1] By way of contrast, in Foucault's analysis of the Cynics we find an idea of the philosophical life in which truth is revealed or manifest in the material body of life (*CT*, 172). Moreover, Foucault sets up the idea of the philosophical life as the true life in the Cynics against the Platonic–Socratic ideal of the philosophical life. This chapter takes up Esposito's immunitary logic of biopolitics in order to argue that whereas the Platonic–Socratic philosophical life exemplifies an ascetic ideal that reflects an inherently immunitarian idea of politics, the philosophical life of the Cynics uses the communitary resources of embodiment so as to unite life (*zoe*) and philosophy in a cosmopolitical form of life (*bios*). Foucault saw in this ideal of a philosophical life the resources to resist the modern liberal government of life by opening up the horizon of a new politics of community.

The Embodiment of Truth

In Nietzsche, the question of truth is inseparable from the question of life, and, indeed, the value of truth itself can only be determined against the standard of biological life. Nietzsche reverses the traditional understanding of philosophy by putting forth the claim that truth does not have a value in itself but, rather, its value depends on whether it enhances or diminishes the power of life. This claim has important implications for Nietzsche's understanding of philosophy and of the figure of the philosopher. The philosopher's life (*bios*) and his or her discourse on truth are no longer understood as separate things: truth is no longer the object of a doctrine or a science, but of a form of life in which thought and life (*zoe*) must be considered in their unity.[2] In his description of the general characteristics of the Cynics, Foucault makes a similar point by underlining that the Cynics were the first to pose the problem of the naturality or vitality of the philosophical life (*CT*, 168). In the Cynics, the practice of philosophy comes hand in hand with the task of manifesting truth in and through one's body, in and through the visibility of material existence (*CT*, 172). Here the challenge of the philosophical life is to bring back culture to nature, leading back (*re-ducere*) *bios* to *zoe*, and it is this truth of *zoe* which is reflected in the philosophical way of life embodied by the Cynics.

For the Cynics, the "reduction" of *bios* to *zoe* is an essential part of their understanding of truth-telling (*CT*, 171).³ However, this reduction should not be understood simply as a return to nature, rather it is a return that reveals *zoe* as *bios*, where *zoe* is understood to be that force which gives style and form to life (*CT*, 172). Moreover, this form of life (this *bios* of *zoe*) reflects the way in which truth is visible in the gestures and body of the Cynics. The Cynics turn life into the vehicle of truth and truth into the vehicle of life, bringing forth a perfect communion between life and truth, such that the body gives form to truth and truth gives form to the body. Foucault refers to this relation between life, truth, and the body as a manifestation of truth by the body, an alethurgy of truth (*aléthurgie*) (*CT*, 172).⁴

Nietzsche thematizes the reduction of *bios* to *zoe* under the *topos* of *homo natura*: the retranslation of the human being to nature found in Aphorism 230 of *Beyond Good and Evil*.⁵ According to Nietzsche, humans cannot bear the idea that their so-called cultural achievements are not products of human civilization, that is, the result of an emancipation from nature, but instead are artifacts of nature reflecting life's needs and necessities. For humans the idea of being subject to the necessities of life undermines their sense of freedom and their need to dominate and rule over nature. Hence, they desire to be misled and to mislead themselves about the "frightening basic text of *homo natura* [*schreckliche Grundtext homo natura*]" (*BGE*, 230). Nietzsche envisages the philosopher of the free spirit as someone whose passion for truth and knowledge seeks to "translate the human being back into nature" (*BGE*, 230). What characterizes these free spirits is an "excessive honesty [*ausschweifende Redlichkeit*]" that reminds us of Foucault's Cynics and their striving toward a continuity of community between nature (life) and truth. For both Foucault's Cynics and Nietzsche's free spirits, the affirmation of the necessities of life is a vehicle of liberation and cultivation that overcomes the human being's need for freedom as domination. Just as with the Cynics, Nietzsche claims that this new truth about *homo natura* will affect a "transformation [*Umwandlung*] of the human being" (*KSA*, 9:11 [141]), for it reveals that affirming the necessities of life liberates the human being to continuously create and re-create its own conditions of existence beyond the struggle of self-preservation (for domination) toward a just and common life.

The embodiment of truth in the Cynics provokes a reversal of traditional understandings of the philosophical life as a true life. This reversal is also thematized by Nietzsche in Aphorism 11 of *The Gay Science*, where he gives a first formulation of the question of how truth can be embodied.[6] In this aphorism, Nietzsche puts forth the claim that "the task of *embodying knowledge* and making it instinctive is still quite new" and that this task is "seen only by those who have understood that so far we have incorporated only our *errors* and that all of our consciousness refers to errors!" (*GS*, 11). The philosopher in Nietzsche has to reverse the current, conventional understandings of truth by showing that all we have so far called truth are nothing but errors and illusions. Thus, for both the Cynics and Nietzsche, the philosopher is the subject and object of a radical critique of civilization showing that its entire canon of values whether moral or epistemological are based on false assumptions. If life so far has been made possible by embodying errors, then the challenge of the Cynic philosopher is to show that life can be enhanced also by literally embodying knowledge or truth. Only when truth can be lived and be manifested physically in and through one's body does it constitute true knowledge rather than mere illusion. Here we find Foucault's image of the cynic as a figure of enlightenment: the philosophical life of the Cynics and their truth is situated ahead and beyond humanity, leading it toward its enlightenment (*CT*, 172).

According to Foucault, the philosopher's task of reversing all values is a political task. Foucault underlines that the Cynics need to be understood within the more general context of a critique of political *parrhesia*, which is found not only in the Cynics but also in Plato. Whereas political *parrhesia*, exemplified by the democratic man, reflects nothing but errors and shared opinions, philosophical life needs to prove itself as the only true life, the only form of life that has access to truth. With the Cynics, this political challenge is complicated by the claim that political *parrhesia* can only be truly overcome by a philosophical life that embodies truth, rather than by a philosophical life where truth and body are separate and exclude each other, as in the Platonic–Socratic ideal of the philosophical life (*CT*, 159). In my view, what both political *parrhesia* and Platonic–Socratic *parrhesia* have in common is that in their political constructions, truth figures as an immunitary device.[7] Platonic–Socratic *parrhesia* is a means that separates life and truth, nature and culture, animal and human. Democratic *parrhesia* functions in a similar way by separating difference and equality, individuality and unity, otherness and identity, *polis* and "barbarians." Instead, I argue that truth-telling in the Cynics (and in Nietzsche) is a function of community where life and truth, difference and equality, otherness and identity are understood as part of a shared continuity of life, as elements of a politics of community.[8]

In Nietzsche, the task of embodying truth is further complicated by the insight into the fact that errors (*Irrthümer*) are advantageous and species-preserving (*arterhaltend*): "It seems that one was unable to live with it; that our organism was geared for its opposite: all its higher functions, the perception of sense and generally every kind of sensation, worked with those basic errors that had been incorporated since time immemorial" (*GS*, 110). On this account, the power of knowledge is not determined according to the degree of truth it reflects but, rather, according to its age, its degree of incorporation (*Einverleibtheit*), and its character as a condition of life (*Lebensbedingung*) (*GS*, 110; see in comparison *KSA*, 11:34 [247]). Similar to Foucault's analysis of the Cynics, the philosopher in Nietzsche is confronted with an impossible task: he or she seeks to embody truth such that truth becomes manifest in the body of life, but it turns out that the very body of life is not capable of such an embodiment, of living with truth. Life needs errors and illusions rather than truth to the extent that truth destroys life. Or, in the words of Nietzsche, the philosopher's "new insights [*neue Erkenntnis*]" are dangerous and "damaging [*schädigend*]" for life (*KSA*, 9:11 [320]). This is why taking on the task of embodying knowledge requires before all courage: the courage to expose one's life to the danger of truth, even if this means risking one's life, the death of life. This challenge, no doubt, reminds us of the philosophical heroism emphasized by Foucault in his general characterization of the Cynics (*CT*, 197–211).

From this Nietzschean perspective, political life already deeply incorporates life-preserving errors in the form of its ruling opinions or principles of legitimacy. In the contest against the political life, the philosophical life faces the dilemma of having to prove the impossible, namely, it needs to show that the embodiment of truth is more life-enhancing than political life and its deeply incorporated life-preserving errors. The philosopher succeeds in this struggle against the political life and its incorporated errors if he or she can demonstrate that the need for "error" can be overcome. Overcoming here literally means to overcome a form of political life and to bring forth a new, altered form of political life. Whereas the former is closed and immunitary to nature and nonhuman life, the latter is a political life open to the variety of the cosmos. The Cynic philosopher holds up a cosmopolitical vision of human life against the identity politics of the *polis*.[9] In the words of Foucault, the philosopher succeeds when he or she can show that the true life is an altered and altering life: "Will not the true life be a radically and paradoxically other life [*la vrai vie ne va-t-elle pas etre une vie radicalemente et paradoxalement autre*]" (*CT*, 245). Beyond the critique of civilization, the literal creation of an other, altered life constitutes the affirmative aspect of the philosophical life as a truly embodied life. Foucault grasps the political dimension of this other life by the formula "an *other* life for an *other* world [*une vie autre pour un monde autre*]" (*CT*, 287). However, neither for the Cynics nor for Nietzsche can there be a final solution to the paradoxical dilemma of embodying truth. Both understand the task of manifesting truth in and through one's physical existence as an ongoing self-experiment, an open-ended challenge requiring the self to continuously alter itself and others such that this world becomes an altered world.

Embodiment, Immunity, and Community

The affinity that Foucault sees between his attempt to turn the philosophical life toward alterity and the Cynics' attempt to return to *zoe* is best understood from within the context of a Nietzschean conception of life as will to power. In his recent reading of will to power, Esposito claims that for Nietzsche life is an irresistible drive to become more, to overcome and reach beyond itself. Life is will to power because it incessantly strives toward the outside of life which continuously alters and exceeds the limits of its own being. Therefore, life is never identical with itself for it continuously negates and destroys itself in its striving for self-alteration: "before being in itself, the body is always against, even with respect to itself."[10] For Esposito, this impulse of life (*zoe*) to transcend itself toward the creation of a form of life (*bios*) is also a striving toward a common life, or what he refers to as *communitas*.[11] However, given the self-destructive potential inherent in life's striving toward justice and community, life needs a strategy for self-preservation which essentially protects it against its becoming other, against its alteration. This strategy of self-preservation is the strategy of immunization, or what Esposito also refers to as *immunitas*. One of the most prominent examples of the strategy of immunization referred to by Esposito is Nietzsche's conception of the ascetic ideal which simultaneously negates and preserves life (*GM*). According to Nietzsche, the ascetic ideal reflects an embodiment of truth which successfully manages to preserve life through the negation, suppression, and subjection of the impulses of life. As such the ascetic ideal weakens or makes life as will to power sick, thereby turning its embodied truth into a vehicle of health for the self-preservation for the weak. Nietzsche confirms that the ascetic ideal has successfully turned the negation (sickness) of life into an affirmation of life by making the negative productive. But he also warns against the paradoxical and self-contradictory nature of immunity. In the end, the embodiment of truth in the example of the ascetic ideal shows that the attempt to protect life through negation fails: instead of preserving life through sickness, it makes life sicker, ultimately destroying the life it sets out to protect (*GM*, 3:13). Hence Esposito raises the question of whether it is possible to preserve life other than by way of immunization.

In my view, Nietzsche directly addresses this question raised by Esposito in his immunitary and communitary conceptions of embodiment. As I argue elsewhere, Nietzsche distinguishes between two different conceptions of embodiment which are diametrically opposed to each other: on the one hand, we have embodiment as a strategy of immunity; on the other, embodiment as a strategy of community.[12] When Nietzsche describes processes of embodiment that play an immunitary function, he recurs to a semantics of appropriation (*Aneignung*) (*AOM*, 317),[13] as for example in *BGE*, 259. Instead, when he speaks of embodiment as a strategy of community, then he refers to processes of creative transformation (*HL*, 1; *KSA*, 8:11 [182]).[14] Whereas the former is associated with the exploitation (*Ausbeutung*), subjugation (*Unterdrückung*), and domination (*Herrschaft*) of the other, the latter is associated with the ennobling inoculation (*HH*, 224), differentiation, and pluralization of life stemming from the encounter with the other as precisely that force which cannot be incorporated, that which resists an annihilating incorporation (*Einverleibung*) (*KSA*, 11:36 [22]). Furthermore, whereas in the first case the process of *Einverleibung* is understood as a process of life through which ever more powerful wholes (*Ganzheiten*) are constituted and preserved by the annihilating and excluding incorporation of the other; in the second case, *Einverleibung* is depicted as driven by a receiving and hospitable force, an openness to the other which furthers the pluralization and diversification of life.

Nietzsche's description of the philosophers of the Stoa beautifully captures the idea of embodiment as an annihilating inclusion of the other. The Stoics represent an idea of philosophy as the tyrannical drive to recreate the world according to its own image. Here, philosophy is an expression of the will to power as a drive toward the creation of the world, exemplified by the philosophers of the Stoa who want to incorporate (*einverleiben*) and prescribe (*vorschreiben*) into nature their own ideals and morality (*BGE*, 9). This tyrannical drive of philosophy is nothing but a reflection of the drive of life, of "all that which is alive," namely, to grow and to become more (*BGE*, 230). Nietzsche identifies the "basic will of the spirit [*Grundwillen des Geistes*]" as the power "to appropriate the foreign" (*BGE*, 230). In this movement of appropriating the exterior world (*Aussenwelt*), what stands in the foreground is the equalizing power of incorporation. In this spiritual constitution of the world, one recognizes a strong inclination "to assimilate the new to the old, to simplify the manifold, and to overlook or repulse whatever is totally contradictory" (*BGE*, 230). The objective of the spirit is to incorporate new "experiences," "to file new things in old files" (*BGE*, 230). In other words, it aims for growth and the feeling of greater, increasing power (*Gefühl der vermehrten Kraft*). Here, incorporation designates a means of domination through which a given form of life extends its power over the other, incorporating the foreign, new, and different into an already existing whole, thereby reducing it to an instance of the known, old, equal, and identical. My claim here is that the interaction or contest (*agon*) that Cynics stage against both political life and Platonic philosophical life (ascetic ideal) is an illustration of Nietzsche's "ennobling inoculation" or embodiment as a strategy of community.

Nietzsche maps these two diametrically opposed forms of embodiment onto a distinction between two types of philosophers and philosophies: a philosophy that needs truth as a soothing medicine to cure sickness and a philosophy in which truth figures as a sign of health. In the first case, those who practice philosophy out of a state of sickness need their truth as a soothing medicine. In the second case, those who practice philosophy out of a state of health understand their truth as an expression of an abundance of life forces. While in the former truth is a means of self-preservation protecting the philosopher against the contingencies of life, in the latter, the contingencies of life are embraced and affirmed as instances of truth themselves providing an occasion for the growth and alternating expansion of life.

This distinction in Nietzsche has a strong affinity with Foucault's distinction between the Platonic–Socratic tradition and the Cynic tradition (*CT*, 125–27). According to Foucault, the Platonic–Socratic tradition is characterized by the idea of the philosopher as someone who conducts or leads the human beings toward the truth of their souls understood as a metaphysical entity one discovers in the practice of care of self. In the second, we have the idea of philosophy as a challenge of life, where one continuously has to prove one's truth by giving one's life a certain style or modality. In the former tradition, philosophy places itself under the paradigm of knowledge of the soul where this knowledge becomes an ontology of the self. In the latter, philosophy is a challenge, an experiment or test of life (*bios*), where life is the matter and object of an art of the self or an aesthetics of existence. Foucault claims that the Cynics were the first ones who took seriously the problem of life as an object of the care of self and hence are the starting point of this different praxis of philosophical activity (*CT*, 125–27).

Under the Platonic–Socratic model of a philosophical life, the objective of the care of the self aims at a separation of the soul from the body where the soul is understood as an ontological entity distinct from the body. In other words, the Socratic idea of the philosophical life is an idea of truth, where the embodiment of truth has an immunitary function, separating truth and life, soul and body, aspiring toward the purity of the soul, protecting it from the deviating influence of the instincts and passions of the body on the individual's capacity of truth-telling. Truth-telling here becomes a metaphysical discourse on the nature or essence of the human being, laying the foundation for an ontological understanding of the human being from which an ethics or rules of conduct can be deduced (*CT*, 159–61). The metaphysical character of truth in the Platonic–Socratic idea of the philosophical life carries its contest (*agon*) against political life inwardly, as a retreat into the private sphere (the citadel), be it that of the individual soul or that of a particular prince, where the role of the philosopher is to lead or care for the prince. In contrast to the Platonic–Socratic tradition, truth-telling with the Cynics does not link up with a metaphysical discourse but rather with the necessity to give life a visible, public, or common form. Here truth-telling has to define the visible form a human being gives to his or her life. It requires the "courage of truth" to expose one's physical existence to the challenge of giving it a form or a style.

Foucault and the Politics of Community in the Cynics

Foucault distinguishes four criteria of the true life found in classical Greek thought (*CT*, 218–19). First, there is the idea of the true as the non-hidden, the non-dissimulated, in other words, the completely visible. Second, there is the idea of the true as that which does not receive any addition or supplement. The true is pure and without any mix-up. Third, the true is what is right, correct (*droit*), as in straight and opposed to detours. Truth as rectitude, but also as what is in accordance to the law (*nomos*). Finally, the true is what exists and endures without change or alteration. Truth is incorruptible and always identical to itself. In Plato, these four criteria are reflected in his ideal of life without mix-up between good and bad, pleasure and suffering, vice and virtue. In opposition to the life of the democratic man, the philosophical life is a life of purity, unity in conformity with principles and laws of nature. The true life is a sovereign life subject to perfect mastery of the passions of the body, a life of complete happiness and satisfaction. According to Foucault, the Cynics subject this Platonic ideal of the philosophical life as happiness and blessing to a radical critique questioning the very value of Platonic life which is reflected in the Cynics' principle of "alter the value of the currency" (*CT*, 227). For Foucault the philosophy of the Cynics is a philosophy of rupture, interruption, and transvaluation.

In my view, this transvaluation of values and exteriorization of philosophy can also be understood as an attempt to turn philosophy as an immunitary device into the vehicle of community. The Cynics enact what I call the strategy of community. Community here refers to the process whereby a defense is erected against an excess of immunity, thus leading to an auto-immunitarian release of the *munus* or common. This auto-immunitary strategy describes quite well the Cynics' mode of proceeding: first, they adopt an immunitary principle (for example, the four characteristics of the true philosophical life), then they embody this principle as a form of life in which the practice of care of the self and truth-telling turns the self toward the other (*munus*), instead of separating it from the body and the body of the others. This auto-immunitary embodiment is like a defense against the above immunitary principle. This is the paradox of the "scandal" of cynical truth: it leads to their violent and radical exclusion on the part of instituted, official philosophy, but, at the same time, this immunitary exclusion of the Cynics on the part of the *polis* paradoxically leads to the exclusion of the principles of truth that they embodied and were otherwise accepted as doctrine. By excluding the Cynic embodiment, the *polis* opens up the horizon for a transformation of values, the alteration of the self and of the *polis* itself. The result is the "scandal" that arises once the Cynic embodiment breaks up the immunities of the *polis* and of the Platonic philosophical life, and opens up the horizon of an altered true life, the true life of community.

The Cynics take up the theme of the true life as the non-dissimulated life by altering and transvaluing this idea through what Foucault refers to as the "scandal" of truth (*CT*, 253). The rule of non-dissimulation is not anymore the application of an ideal principle of conduct, but, on the contrary, becomes the manifestation, the "mise-en-scène" of everyday life's materiality by leading a life that is radically public, exposed and visible to all at all times. The Cynics prove through their way of life that life belongs to no one and everyone at the same time. Life is *munus*, radically common. At the same time, the radical application of the principle of non-dissimulation brings about a reversal of the very same principle demonstrating that the life of the Cynics, a life that is truly faithful to the idea of truth as non-dissimulation, is a life that is always in the process of becoming other, different, strange, and in this sense is always changing identity and cannot remain self-same.

According to the Cynics, life reflects and is all that nature has given to life, and hence what nature has given to the human being cannot be something bad or something to be rejected, excluded, and eliminated from the public life of the *polis*. This attitude is in stark contrast to the Platonic–Socratic and Stoic traditions, where everything related to nature, the body, passions, desires, life are excluded from the public life of the *polis* and pushed back into the private sphere. The Cynics affirm nature, life, and its gifts as irreducibly other, and it is this otherness which manifests itself in the true life of the Cynics. After all, the Cynics teach that one is born a Cynic and cannot become one through education and culture: this is both a literal embodiment of the Socratic–Platonic idea of living in accordance to natural right or natural law, and yet it is also a reversal of the Platonic claim that one becomes a philosopher only through an arduous process of education (which is in turn different from the education that the city provides its citizens through tragic poetry). The Cynics abolish the public/private division by dissolving the immunitary barriers of civilization, thus opening up the possibility for a public life that is truly communal. From the perspective of the Cynics, nature is not the problem, but the immunitary devices of civilization such as human habits, conventions, and opinions which first debase life and nature, in order to then exclude and expulse them from the *polis*. When the principle of truth as non-dissimulation is embodied by *zoe*, it turns out that leading a true life requires rejecting all the habitual limits and traditional barriers of shame.[15] For what the human being has received from nature needs to be transvalued rather than being excluded; it needs to be affirmed as a good instead of being excluded as an evil. The Cynics show in their way of life that nature is nothing to be ashamed of, but on the contrary a gift that needs to be appreciated and affirmed (*CT*, 254). The life of the Cynics reflects a revaluation of *zoe* which liberates the principle of non-dissimulation from all the conventional ideas of shame.

With respect to the idea of truth as independence without mix-up reflected in an independent life that does not contain any addition that is unaltered and perfectly identical to itself, the Cynics operate a similar reversal by embodying the very same principle. In Plato this idea is known as a life of purity, beauty, and perfection of the soul, a soul that has been completely separated from material life and the body. In the Stoics and Epicureans it becomes the life of independence, self-sufficiency, and self-rule. In the Cynics, on the contrary, the life of independence takes the form of the indifferent life reflected in the figure of radical poverty, a poverty that is, according to Foucault, real, active, and infinite (*CT*, 257). It is real insofar as it does not simply content itself with the idea of independence understood as an indifference toward what might or might not occur, to the realm of contingency. On the contrary, poverty is a continuous challenge that requires endurance and courage to live according to the principle of independence. It is in this sense that poverty is infinite or indefinite: the Cynics are continuously striving toward a reduction of supplements and needs, until they reach or find what is truly indispensable for life. Poverty as such requires a process of continuous self-experimentation and work on the self.

Again, the outcomes of this embodiment of the idea of truth as independence are radical and paradoxical insofar as the latter, rather than producing a harmonious life of beauty and peace, produces a life characterized by its ugliness and humiliating dependence. The Cynics revalorize the most basic necessities of life, exposing themselves, making themselves completely dependent while paradoxically leading a life of independence; a dirty, ugly life, defined by misery and humiliation (*CT*, 259). From here comes the famous comparison of the life of the Cynics with the life of dogs. Again, we can see the idea of *munus* active in the life of the Cynics, the Cynics are entirely exposed and dependent on the gifts of the other to the point that they cannot preserve themselves anymore, they have destroyed and overcome all immunitary devices of self-preservation and are entirely subject to the goodwill of the other (who give them food, for example).

The materiality and fragility of life, exposed in the way of life of the Cynics, is reaffirmed by them also under the idea of slavery. While slavery is rejected by the *polis* as the most base, unfree, and inhuman form of life, with the Cynics slavery is affirmed and appreciated. It reflects their belief that life, all life, can never be fully self-sufficient and self-ruled. True independence rests on the gift of another, on the communal relation between humans and nature where what is given falls outside of a logic of profit and calculation. Here, life is maintained in community with the other rather than through separating devices of immunization.

Finally, by embodying the principle of independence through the form of poverty, the Cynics become subjects of a bad reputation. For the Cynics the systematic practice of humiliation, insults, and dishonor is reversed into a positive conduct that has meaning and value. The more one can stand the humiliation through the other, the greater becomes the pride of the Cynics, for the Cynic proves through his example of life that he is truly sovereign and master of himself, having even resisted and overcome the worst, namely, being excluded from the public life of the *polis*. He has shown that the greater community of cosmic life is what preserves his life and not the *polis* (*CT*, 262).

The third idea of truth as the life of rectitude, a life in conformity with *logos* and *nomos*, becomes in the Cynics a life in conformity with the law of nature. Nature as opposed to conventions is the only acceptable standard against which to measure a true life (*CT*, 263). Here, the standard of nature is the human being's animality. Whereas traditionally the animality of the human being had been excluded, the Cynics raise it to the highest measure of human achievement. Animality becomes a model of life and individual conduct based on the idea that what the animals do not need, the human animal should not need either. Whereas previously the needs and necessities of life were considered to be a sign of weakness that subject the human being to slavery now, by applying the standard of animality, this idea is reversed and liberated. Now the human being is liberated from needs, since all needs of nature can also be satisfied by nature and since the human being does not need anything else above and beyond. Living according to the standard of animality is liberating (*CT*, 265). According to Foucault, animality in the Cynics is a reductive form of life but also prescriptive. Animality is not understood as a simple given, but as a task, an ethical challenge to live according to the needs of one's own animality. Animality becomes the moral as well as the material model of existence. Animality as a task or challenge becomes a principle of culture. The life of *zoe*, that is, the *bios* of *zoe*, is a life where *bios* is not imposed on animal life (*zoe*) like a second nature but where *zoe* brings forth out of its own resources a *bios*.

Finally, we have the idea of the true life as a sovereign life. In the Socratic ideal, the sovereign life is a life in complete possession of itself, where no fragment or element of the self escapes the mastery and control of the self. The sovereign life is a life of pleasure, a self-fulfilled life. At the same time, this life is beneficial to others and comes along with an obligation typically represented either in the relationship between the master and pupil or in the image of the hero or genius of culture, a benefactor of all humanity. In this context, we find Foucault's theme of the Cynic as an anti-monarch, an anti-king who receives his kingdom not through external circumstances as in the case of Alexander the Great, but through the will of the gods. The Cynic does not become king by way of education and cultivation but is born a king by way of simply being human. In the Cynics' understanding of sovereignty, being selected by a god comes with an obligation, a mission, namely, to take care of the others. Taking care of others does not simply mean to lead the other through discourses or by offering an example of life, but to truly take care of them, even if this means sacrificing one's own life. It is a hard and difficult mission that requires giving up oneself, renouncing oneself. Interestingly, Foucault points out that the most frequent model of intervention of the Cynics is the medical one as opposed to the legal one. The Cynics heal the other such that they can become truly happy and healthy. This intervention is difficult and requires the aggressiveness and willingness to fight and combat. The Cynic does not do good to the other through leading an exemplary life, but because he fights for the other; he is useful because he bites and attacks. The Cynic fights for humanity as a whole, with the objective of changing the world with respect to its moral attitudes and values, but, at the same time, changing the habits, conventions, and forms of life (*CT*, 280). The ultimate task of the Cynic consists in addressing the whole of humanity by fighting with, for and at times against it in view of revolutionizing the world (*CT*, 294). Such a task can only be appointed by a god, and living up to it means facing the four challenges of the true life as the Cynics understand it. Thus the Cynics become the universal missionaries of humanity that watch out and over it. They carry forth the responsibility for humanity as a whole, for the whole of humankind (*CT*, 301). Foucault insists that with the Cynics, the care of the self as well as the conduct of oneself is inseparable from the care and conduct of others, such that changing the world for the Cynics means changing how humans conduct themselves in the world (*CT*, 313).

Following these four principles or characteristics of the true life and their reversal by the embodiment of those characteristics in the Cynics, Foucault asks whether the Cynics have not successfully demonstrated that the true philosophical life is another life than that lead by the majority of men in the *polis* and by the philosopher in particular. The true life is paradoxically and radically other than all traditionally accepted forms of existence (*CT*, 245). My hypothesis, on the other hand, is that the otherness of the Cynics is nothing but the common shared by the political life and the Socratic philosophical life but not recognized by either one. The political life immunizes *doxa* by protecting opinion against truth; the Socratic philosophical life immunizes truth by protecting it against opinion. The Cynic form of life overcomes this division between political life and philosophical life by showing the commonality between both forms of life, thus undoing their mutual immunization. Thus, the Cynic contestation of Platonic–Socratic philosophical life appears as an attempt to popularize philosophy because it breaks down the immunity of truth. Conversely, the Cynic contestation of political life appears as an attempt to establish cosmopolitanism because it breaks down the immunitary defenses of the *polis* against foreigners.

Perhaps it is in these two features, the making popular of the philosophical life and the making cosmopolitan of the political life, that lies the key to the famous encounter between Alexander the Great, who was a student of Aristotle, and Diogenes the Cynic. After all, Alexander the Great brought an end to the hegemony of the Greek *polis* in establishing his Hellenistic, cosmopolitan empire, and this may explain his attraction to Diogenes's attack on the immunity of the *polis* in the name of a new world politics or cosmopolitanism. On the other hand, when Alexander the Great comes to see Diogenes to offer him whatever he wants, and the Cynic answers that he merely wishes Alexander to stop casting a shadow on him and move out of the sun's way, the message is also clear: the sun here represents the divine; the rays of the sun are the election by god of its true representative on earth, and these rays are for Diogenes, not Alexander. Political sovereigns are merely the passing clouds that interfere with the true enlightenment of the Cynic form of life.

NOTES

INTRODUCTION
VANESSA LEMM AND MIGUEL VATTER

1. We refer to the following Courses: *Lecons sur la volonté de savoir* [1970–71] (French ed. 2011, English trans. 2013), *La société punitive* [1972–73] (French ed. 2013), *Les Anormaux* [1974–75] (French ed. 1999, English trans. 2004), *Il faut défendre la société* [1976] (French ed., 1997, English trans. 2003), *Sécurité, territoire, population* [1977–78] (French ed. 2004, English trans. 2007), *Naissance de la biopolitique* [1978–79] (French ed. 2004, English trans. 2008), *Du gouvernement des vivants* [1979–80] (French ed. 2012), *L'Herméneutique du sujet* [1981–82] (French ed. 2001, English trans. 2005), *Le gouvernement de soi et des autres* [1982–83] (French ed. 2008, English trans. 2011), *Le gouvernement de soi et des autres, Tome 2: Le courage de la verité* [1983–84] (French ed. 2009, English trans. 2011).
2. For a recent account of the shortcomings of this interpretation, see Nealon, *Foucault beyond Foucault*.
3. An exception to this general statement is the early thematization of governmentality prior to the publication of the Courses by scholars who attended in person Foucault's lectures, for instance, Burchell, Gordon, and Miller, *Foucault Effect*. This first reception of the idea of governmentality is later systematized in works such as Dean, *Governmentality*. In this first reception, the connection with biopolitics either is absent or not made a central element in the interpretation of governmentality. Another systematic analysis of Foucault's turn to the problem of governmentality is found in Lemke, *Eine Kritik der politischen Vernunft*; and expanded in Bröckling, Krassmann, and Lemke, *Gouvernamentalität der Gegenwart*. As the subtitle of this last work (*Studien zur Ökonomisierung des Sozialen*) indicates, at this point in time the German reception of the late Foucault was oriented toward the "economization" of Foucault's conception of power and its linkage to post-Marxist thought. Biopolitics was not mentioned, and there was no problematization of the discourse of law and

rights, as in the Anglo-American reception of late Foucault. With respect to biopolitics, this changed in Lemke, *Gouvernamentalität und Biopolitik*; and Lemke, *Biopolitics*.

4. This is also the approach preferred by Davidson, *Emergence of Sexuality*; in the same Canguilhemian vein, see Rheinberger, *Epistemology of the Concrete*.

5. Neither Downing, *Cambridge Introduction to Michel Foucault*; nor Gutting, *Cambridge Companion to Foucault*, discusses Foucault's last production; governmentality and biopolitics do not feature at all. Fitzpatrick and Golder, *Foucault's Law*, is a significant contribution to the study of Foucault's conception of law, but its approach does not center on the problem of government. Other recent attempts to take stock of Foucault's turn to governmentality are Krasmann and Volkmer, *Michel Foucaults "Geschichte der Gouvernementalität" in den Sozialwissenschaften*; Purtschert, Meyer, and Winter, *Gouvernementalität und Sicherheit*; and Galzigna, *Foucault oggi*. But these collections do not focus on the relation between neoliberalism and biopolitics as fundamental, and do not center their treatment of Foucault's thought on his later Courses. O'Leary and Falzon, *Foucault and Philosophy*, discusses Foucault's relation to various key philosophical thinkers but unrelated to the problem of government; the collection also does not address the role of Greek philosophy in the late Courses.

6. For a good description of this problem of internal coherence of Foucault's discourse, see Esposito, *Bios*.

7. For "theologically" informed interpretations of Foucault, see Carrette, *Foucault and Religion*; and Carrette and Bernauer, *Michel Foucault and Theology*. For a recent attempt at bringing together Foucaultian and Weberian analyses of governmentality in relation to Calvinism and early modern state-building, see Gorski, *Disciplinary Revolution*. See also Steiner, "Foucault, Weber, and the History of the Economic Subject." The problem of government is central in Marzocca, *Perché il Governo*, although the Weberian connection to religion is downplayed.

8. See, for instance, Lazzarato, *Lavoro immateriale*; Bazzicalupo, *Il governo delle vite*; and Cooper, *Life as Surplus*.

9. On this point, see the useful collection of essays in Dillon and Neal, *Foucault on Politics, Security, and War*.

10. Schmitt, *Nomos of the Earth in the International Law of Jus Publicum Europaeum*, 68.

11. For an interpretation of the *katechon* in a biopolitical sense, see Esposito, *Immunitas*, 52–79.

12. A different application of Foucault's attention to the connection between biopolitics and neoliberalism is now given by those who understand biopolitics or a "politics of life" in terms of "biological citizenship," as in

Rose, *Politics of Life Itself*; and Fassin, "Another Politics of Life Is Possible." These analyses of the relation between biotechnology and neoliberal policy are conducted without reference to the problem of normative order (or *nomos*).

13. See Barry, Osborne, and Rose, *Foucault and Political Reason*; Moss, *Later Foucault*. Several essays in the latter volume address directly the relation of Foucault to liberal rule of law, but do not do so from the perspective of the problem of government, which only makes fleeting appearances in the book. The former volume is not exactly about Foucault's work on governmentality but freely draws from what was then known about the Courses in order to offer an "analytics of liberal political reason" (*Foucault and Political Reason*, 7). These authors draw on another connection between Foucault and Weber in order to understand governmentality, namely, the Weberian analysis of the relation between politics and "systems of expertise," especially social-scientific expertise (*Foucault and Political Reason*, 12). The result is that their idea of "governmentality" is still very much tied to the state as a consumer of public policies; there is no conception of liberalism as a normative network of extra-, supra-, and infra-legal regulations of life.

14. On philosophy as a form of life, Foucault was influenced by Hadot, *Philosophy as a Way of Life*. But Hadot does not understand the relation between normativity and philosophical life from the context of the problem of government.

15. On the new approach to Foucault and the question of liberal rights, see Golder, "Foucault and the Unfinished Human of Rights."

1. THE FOURTH AGE OF SECURITY
FRÉDÉRIC GROS

1. See Wittgenstein, *Lectures and Conversations on Aesthetics, Psychology, and Religious Belief*.
2. See Foucault, *STP*, 285–310; *The Government of Self and Others*, 1–24; *CT*.
3. For treatments of medieval millenarianism and the problematic of Empire, see Carozzi and Taviani-Carozzi, *La fin des temps*; Cohn, *The Pursuit of the Millennium*; Delumeau, *Une histoire du paradis*.
4. Spinoza, *Political Treatise*, 290.
5. Locke, *Second Treatise of Government*, 111.
6. Hobbes, *Leviathan*, 129.
7. See Aron, *Peace and War*.
8. On this new idea of security, see Kaldor, *Human Security*. I refer to my discussion of this theme in Gros, "Nouvelles menaces, nouvelles sécurités"; and Gros, "Désastre humanitaire et sécurité humaine."

2. THE LAW OF THE HOUSEHOLD: FOUCAULT, NEOLIBERALISM, AND THE IRANIAN REVOLUTION
MELINDA COOPER

1. This is not to deny the decisive role played by the United States in creating the Afghan mujahideen during the Cold War, nor to underplay the ongoing collusion of the United States in sustaining sectarian divisions among Shi'ite and Sunni forces in occupied Iraq. Least of all should it obscure the ongoing U.S. relationship with Saudi Arabia—the principal financier of Wahhabi and Salafi ultraconservatism throughout the Middle East, South Asia, and North Africa. See Ahmad, "Islam, Islamisms, and the West."

2. Foucault, "A Powder Keg Called Islam," 241.

3. Prasad, "Why Is France so French?"; Behrent, "Liberalism without Humanism."

4. Afary and Anderson, *Foucault and the Iranian Revolution*.

5. Minoo Moallem has written an illuminating study of this symbolic division of labor (male asceticism and female piousness) in revolutionary and postrevolutionary Iran. See *Between Warrior Brother and Veiled Sister*.

6. Mitropoulos, "Oikopolitics, and Storms," 72.

7. Foucault, "Dialogue between Michel Foucault and Baqir Parham," 186.

8. Ibid., 185.

9. Foucault, "What Are the Iranians Dreaming About?" 205.

10. Foucault, "A Revolt with Bare Hands," 211.

11. Ibid., 211.

12. Foucault, "What Are the Iranians Dreaming About?" 207.

13. Ibid., 205.

14. Foucault, "Tehran: Faith against the Shah," 203.

15. Afary, *Sexual Politics in Modern Iran*, 239.

16. Ibid., 234–49; Shahidian, *Women in Iran*, 53–58.

17. See on this point, Olivier Roy, who notes that "unlike the Sunnis, the Shiites have an institution that can determine who is the most learned, the best Muslim, the guide. Since there is a supreme religious authority in Shi'ism, this authority should hold supreme state power. Thus the exercise of power should fall to the supreme clerical authority. This does not mean that the clergy governs directly as a body: although the guide is a cleric, he does not represent the clergy, he is above all institutions, for he is nothing less than the representative of the hidden twelfth imam" (*Failure of Political Islam*, 173). Roy describes the Islamic Republic of Iran as a "constitutionalist theocracy" (177). Riesebrodt offers a slightly different interpretation: "One cannot speak here ... as one can in relation to Protestant fundamentalism, of a tension between republicanism and democracy but only of a hierocratically controlled republicanism with elements of rule by plebiscite" (*Pious Passion*, 142).

18. Khomeini, *Sayings of the Ayatollah Khomeini*. Cited by Dabashi, *Theology of Discontent*, 476.

19. Foucault, "Foucault's response to Atoussa H.," 210. For a full account of this exchange, see Afary and Anderson, *Foucault and the Iranian Revolution*, 91–94.

20. Ibid., 143.

21. See Behrent, "Liberalism without Humanism," for a detailed discussion of the context in which Foucault delivered these lectures. Behrent explains that there already existed a considerable degree of receptiveness to the new neoliberal doctrine among political elites in France. In his lectures at the Collège de France, Foucault drew much of his source material from the work of one of France's most prolific champions of the new economic liberalism, Henri Lepage, who in 1978 had published *Demain le capitalisme*, a four-hundred-page primer on the major currents within neoliberalism. I should note here that I disagree with Behrent's thesis that Foucault's later work was receptive to the precepts of neoliberalism. My argument is rather that Foucault fashioned an ethical response to neoliberalism via his work on the Iranian Revolution and the care of the self.

22. Becker's early attempts to rethink the economics of crime, racial discrimination, education, and sex can be found in "Crime and Punishment"; *Economics of Discrimination*; *Human Capital*; and *Treatise on the Family*. See also "An Interview with Gary Becker."

23. Becker, *Treatise on the Family*, 1.

24. Foucault is here citing Lepage, *Demain le capitalisme*, 346, who is in turn citing Migué.

25. In this respect, he is no doubt guilty of the orientalist conceit which consists of reading the contemporary politics of the Middle East through the lens of premodern Europe and classical Greece. Foucault's projection of the classical *oikos* onto modern-day Iran was not without foundation, however, in the actual positions taken by the Islamist faction in Iran, which was itself deeply committed to restoring a nostalgic politics of the proper household, through the reimposition of divine law in everyday life.

26. Becker, *Treatise on the Family*, 242.

27. For details on this process, see Sedghi, *Women and Politics in Iran*, 102–20. Sedghi notes that in "the early phases of Western industrialization, women participated primarily in industry, due to higher levels of investment and capital accumulation in this sector. It was during the later periods that women became predominant in the service sector. In the developing world, women's absorption in the service sector can be explained in terms of its relatively greater expansion or insufficient demand for women's labor in industries. The growth of the services and the availability of new jobs pushed more Iranian women to join the service sector" (120).

28. There is not sufficient space here to explore the "logic" or rather conditions sustaining this slippage of terms. It is a slippage, however, that can also be found in the early Marx, who in the *Manuscripts of 1844* compares the alienation of labor in general to a form of prostitution. The possibility of this slippage is inscribed in the very terms in which labor is defined in the first place—the notion of alienable property in the body is borrowed from Hegel's dialectic of subject and object which is in turn indebted to a *Philosophy of Nature* that configures sexual difference as an alienation of the male body from itself. See Marx, *Economic and Philosophic Manuscripts of 1844*; Hegel, *Philosophy of Nature*.

29. On the convergence between Marxist and Islamist discourses on this point in particular, see Shahidian, *Women in Iran*. Shahidian quotes the following telling statement from the Minority Faction of the leftist Fedayeen, that is, the faction that did not collaborate with the Islamist regime: "The toiling women of our homeland are well aware that the liberation promised by . . . supporters of the bourgeoisie, these lackeys of imperialism and the anti-people regime of the Shah, is nothing but the freedom to exploit more, and the liberty to sell the luxury imperialist goods at the expense of plundering the toilers; it is nothing but spreading the penetration of degenerate imperialist culture. Their defense of women's liberation means defending prostitution, drug addiction, setting up houses of lust and a thousand other manifestations of capitalist culture" (230).

30. Azari, "Sexuality and Women's Oppression in Iran."
31. Translation modified.
32. Pomeroy, "Introduction," 41.
33. Aristotle, *Politics*, 14 [I.9 1257b 40–1258a 10].
34. Translation modified.
35. It is important to stress that Foucault uses the expression "sovereignty" of the self (*souveraineté sur soi*) in the French edition of the *Use of Pleasure*. See Foucault, *Histoire de la sexualité*, 2, 107, 109. Given Foucault's prior engagement with the political concept of sovereignty and given the resonance of the term in twentieth-century political theory, this choice cannot have been accidental. The term is lost in the English translation.
36. Detel, *Foucault and Classical Antiquity*, 142.
37. See Detel's comments on the punishment of adultery (ibid., 142, 147).
38. Pecora, *Households of the Soul*, 175.
39. On Foucault's encounter with Bani-Sadr, see Afary and Anderson, *Foucault and the Iranian Revolution*, 70. For close readings of the "monotheistic economics" of Bani-Sadr, see Dabashi, *Theology of Discontent*, 367–408; Katouzian, "Shi'ism and Islamic Economics"; Katouzian, "Review"; and Behdad, "Disputed Utopia." For general discussions of twentieth-century Islamic economics, see Tripp, *Islam and the Moral Economy*; and Kuran, *Islam and Mammon*.

40. Bani-Sadr, *Eqtesad-e Tawhidi*, 392. Cited by Roy, *Failure of Political Islam*, 137.

41. Bani-Sadr, *Fundamental Principles and Precepts of Islamic Government*, 30.

42. For an illuminating discussion of the notion of *tadbir al-manzil* in medieval Islamic philosophy, see Essid, *Critique of the Origins of Islamic Economic Thought*, 81, 179–82.

43. Baeck, "Economic Thought of Classical Islam," 111.

44. Baeck, "Aristotle as Mediterranean Economist," 100–102.

45. Valibeigi, "Banking and Credit Rationing under the Islamic Republic of Iran"; Behdad, "Post-revolutionary Economic Crisis," 101.

46. Afary, *Sexual Politics in Modern Iran*, 277–84.

47. Azari, "Sexuality and Women's Oppression in Iran," 135–36; Riesebrodt, *Pious Passion*, 128.

48. Agamben, *Il regno e la Gloria*.

49. Schmitt, *Nomos of the Earth in the International Law of the Jus Publicum Europaeum*, 345.

3. THE RISKS OF SECURITY: LIBERALISM, BIOPOLITICS, AND FEAR
THOMAS LEMKE

1. The background of the interview and Foucault's wider interest in the structure of the social security system is analyzed in Lebaron, "De la critique de l'économie á l'action syndicale."

2. See *SMD* and *WK*. The notion of biopolitics appeared for the first time in Foucault's work in a lecture he gave in 1974 (Foucault, "Birth of Social Medicine," 137).

3. Disciplinary technology and security technology differ not only in their objectives and instruments and in the date of their historical appearance, but also in their institutional localization. The disciplines developed inside individual institutions like the army, prisons, schools, and hospitals, while the state organized and centralized the regulation of the population from the eighteenth century on. In this context, demographic data were collected on the population and the tabulation of wealth, and statistical investigations of average life expectancy and rates of disease and death were carried out. Thus it is possible to distinguish "two series: the body–organism–discipline–institutions series, and the population–biological processes–regulatory mechanisms–State" (*SMD*, 250).

4. Foucault, "About the Beginning of the Hermeneutics of the Self," 204.

5. See *BB*, 317. This theoretical displacement goes along with a shifting changing account of liberalism during the same period. Michel Senellart shows that in a text he wrote in 1977, Foucault still conceived of liberalism quite traditionally as "the model of liberalism–legalism: freedom–law" (Foucault

quoted by Senellart, "La question du libéralisme," 55). In the lectures on liberal governmentality only two years later he no longer analyzes liberalism along juridical terms but rather takes political economy as the guiding principle (ibid.).

6. Lemke, "Freiheit ist die Garantie der Freiheit."
7. Bonnafous-Boucher, *Un libéralisme sans liberté*.
8. See Opitz, "Zwischen Sicherheitsdispositiven und Securitization."
9. See Ewald, *Histoire de l'État providence*, 51–57.
10. In an interview in 1978 that was published under the title "The Crisis of Disciplinary Society" Foucault explained that it seems to be "obvious that we have to say good-bye to the disciplinary society such as it exists today" (Foucault, "La société disciplinaire en crise," 533).
11. Foucault, "Désormais, la sécurité est au-dessus des lois," 367.
12. Foucault, "Lettre à quelque leaders de la gauche," 390.
13. Cited by Macey, *Lives of Michel Foucault*, 396.
14. Foucault, "Préface in Mireille Debard et Jean-Luc Henning, *Les juges kaki*," 139.
15. See Lemke, Krasmann, and Bröckling, "Gouvernementalität, Neoliberalismus und Selbsttechnologien."
16. Demirović, "Liberale Freiheit und das Sicherheitsdispositiv."
17. Bröckling, *Das unternehmerische Selbst*.
18. Hardt and Negri, *Empire*, 323, 339.
19. Have, "Geneticization"; Conrad, *Medicalization of Society*.
20. Petersen and Wilkinson, *Health, Risk, and Vulnerability*.
21. Legnaro, "Aus der Neuen Welt."
22. Massumi, "Everywhere You Want to Be: Introduction to Fear."
23. Davis, *Ecology of Fear*; Holert, "Angst essen Seele auf."
24. O'Malley, "Uncertain Subjects," 465.
25. Legnaro, "Aus der Neuen Welt"; Wacquant, "Ordering Insecurity." See also Weldes et al., *Cultures of Insecurity*.
26. Frankenberg, "Nochmals," 61.
27. Nadesan, *Governmentality, Biopower, and Everyday Life*, 202; Chappell, "Rehearsals of the Sovereign."
28. Legnaro, "Konturen der Sicherheitsgesellschaft"; Singer, *Corporate Warriors*; Monahan, *Surveillance in the Time of Insecurity*.
29. Holert, "Sicherheit"; Heinzelmann and Weinhart, *Auf eigene Gefahr*.
30. For a history of the idea of fear in political philosophy and theory see Robin, *Fear*.
31. Cooper, "Pre-empting Emergence"; Dillon, "Governing Terror."
32. Castel, "From Dangerousness to Risk"; Krasmann, *Die Kriminalität der Gesellschaft*.
33. Hochschild, "Bush Hijacks American Fear."

34. For an extended version of my argument see Lemke, "Critique and Experience in Foucault."

35. Foucault points to the motto of Enlightenment according to Kant: *Aude sapere*, which means "dare to know" or "have the courage, the audacity, to know" (see WE, 306). See also Foucault's lectures on "fearless speech" where he insists that the ancient activity of the truth-teller (the parrhesiast) is connected to risk-taking: "Parrhesia, then, is linked to courage in the face of danger: it demands the courage to speak the truth in spite of some danger" (Foucault, *Fearless Speech*, 18). This is—according to Foucault—intimately linked to "the roots of what we could call the 'critical' tradition in the West" (ibid., 170).

36. Foucault, "Polemics, Politics, and Problematizations," 114. Cf. also SP, 332.

37. Butler, "What Is Critique?" See also Saar, *Genealogie als Kritik*.

38. Esposito, *Communitas*.

39. Esposito, *Immunitas*. See also Esposito, *Bios*; Celikates, "Communitas–Immunitas–Bíos."

40. Foucault, "The Moral and Social Experience of the Poles," 465.

41. Castel, "From Dangerousness to Risk," 289.

4. A GENEALOGY OF BIOPOLITICS: THE NOTION OF LIFE IN CANGUILHEM AND FOUCAULT
MARIA MUHLE

1. For this reading of the notion of "biopolitics" see Geyer, *Biopolitik*; for the critique of a liberal eugenics see Habermas, *Die Zukunft der menschlichen Natur*.

2. See Esposito, "Vom Unpolitischen zur Biopolitik."

3. Even though the main topic of the lectures on the abnormal is the functioning of the disciplinary power under its psychiatric institutionalization, the passage from the disciplinary power to biopolitical power is more explicit here then in *Discipline and Punish*. It is thus possible to affirm that the Foucaultian genealogy of biopolitics starts with these lectures.

4. Bichat does not understand life, as in the traditional vitalist definition, as the actualization of a prefigured principle of life, nor, as in the mechanicist model, as a series of actions and reactions subjected to a determined and therefore calculable causality. He writes of the traditional vitalist notion of life in his *Physiological Researches upon Life and Death*: "Most physicians who have written on vital properties, have begun by seeking out their principle. . . . *The soul* of Stahl, the archeus of Vanhelmont, the vital principle of Barthez, and the vital power of some others, etc. by turns considered as the only centre of all the actions which bear the character of vitality, have been alternately the common base on which have rested all physiological explanations. These bases have been successively overturned" (64). Following Foucault, the classical debate

between vitalism and mechanism is only the surface phenomenon of the archeological dislocation constituted by the opposition between the organic and the inorganic.

5. In *On the Normal and the Pathological*, Canguilhem states that "the normal is not a static or peaceful, but a dynamic and polemical concept" (146). Foucault picks up on this formulation in his lectures on the abnormal: "The norm is not simply and not even a principle of intelligibility; it is an element on the basis of which a certain exercise of power is founded and legitimized. Canguilhem calls it a polemical concept. Perhaps we could say it is a political concept" (*Abnormal*, 50).

6. Foucault, *The Order of Things*, 250.
7. Agamben, "Absolute Immanence," 233.
8. Ibid., 220.
9. Ibid., 221.
10. Ibid.
11. Agamben, *Homo Sacer*, 6.
12. Ibid.
13. Agamben, *Remnants of Auschwitz*, 85.
14. Agamben, *Homo Sacer*, 181.
15. For an interpretation of Agamben's theory of the *homo sacer* and the state of exception in terms of latency, see Haverkamp, *Latenzzeit*.
16. Agamben, *Homo Sacer*, 4.
17. Bichat, *Physiological Researches upon Life and Death*, 121.
18. Bichat, *Recherches physiologiques sur la vie et la mort*, 232. Translation mine.
19. Canguilhem, *On the Normal and the Pathological*.
20. Ibid., 71, 70.
21. Foucault has analyzed this inversion of vitalism into a "mortalism" in *The Birth of the Clinic*: "The irreducibility of the living to the mechanical or chemical is secondary only in relation to the fundamental link between life and death. Vitalism appears against the background of this 'mortalism'" (145). His reading of Bichat's *Physiological Researches upon Life and Death* and his affirmation of the permanent presence of death in life led him to the reformulation of the notion of illness by that of "pathological life." In his short text on the notion of life in the thought of Foucault and Deleuze, Agamben refers to this notion of life determined by death (life as a reaction to death) as the "first" understanding of life, that will be replaced in Foucault's reflections by life introduced by Canguilhem as the proper domain of error. Against Agamben, I would like to argue that there is neither a *dislocation in the theory of knowledge* nor a *subjective turn* announced by it. Instead, the fundamental relation between life and death prefigures the fallibility of life that gives way to its twofold dynamics and represents the functional model of the governmental.

22. See Macherey, "Normes vitales et normes sociales dans l'Essai sur quelques problèmes concernant le normal et le pathologique de Georges Canguilhem."

23. See Canguilhem, "Vie," 532.

24. Canguilhem, *On the Normal and the Pathological*, 95.

25. Canguilhem attributes such a "propulsive value" to the physiological constants that allow the living to behave normatively in the exposed meaning and opposes them to the pathological constants: "The pathological state, on the other hand, expresses the reduction of the norms of life tolerated by the living being, the precariousness of the normal established by disease. Pathological constants have a repulsive and strictly conservative value" (ibid., 137).

26. For an extended discussion of this hypothesis see Muhle, *Eine Geneaolgie der Biopolitik*.

27. The absence of repression or negation does not presuppose, as Foucault so clearly points out on different occasions, a "better," "humanist," or libertarian form of power. What changes profoundly is that the power over death (that has never reached a bigger extension than in the twentieth century as Foucault recalls) exists as the complementary element (the "counterpart") to the biopolitical strategies that are not directed to the juridical subject, nor the disciplinary individual, but to the biological population. The modern *thanatopolitics* are executed under biopolitical premises, that is, in order to assure the existence of everybody: "Massacres have become vital" (*WK*, 137). The "war of races" is its paradigmatic example.

28. See Lemke, *Biopolitik*, 67.

29. The short analysis that Foucault presents of human rights, the "'right' to life, to one's body, to health, to happiness, to the satisfaction of needs" (*WK*, 145) as "incomprehensible" for the classical juridical system, is to be understood in a similar way. For an extensive discussion see Raimondi, "Diese andere Sache."

30. The first shift being oriented toward "the advancement of learning," that is, the forms of discursive practices that articulated the human sciences, and the second shift that analyzed what it describes as power: "the manifold relations, the open strategies, and the rational techniques that articulate the exercise of powers" (*UP*, 6).

31. For this discussion see Muhle, *Eine Geneaolgie der Biopolitik*, 276–81; Saar, *Genealogie als Kritik*; and Sarasin, *Foucault zur Einführung*. Saar and Sarasin read Foucault's technologies of the self from different perspectives as the turn to the subject and therefore an "antidote" to power.

32. Deleuze, *Foucault*, 92.

33. For the development of the notion of "immunitarian democracy" see Brossat, *La démocratie immunitaire*.

34. Foucault, "Power and Strategies," 142.

5. POWER OVER LIFE, POLITICS OF DEATH: FORMS OF RESISTANCE TO BIOPOWER IN FOUCAULT
FRANCESCO PAOLO ADORNO

1. I am here referring to Foucault's "La politique de la santé au XVIIIème siècle," "Crise de la médecine ou crise de l'antimédicine," "La naissance de la médicine sociale," and "L'incorporation de l'hôpital dans la technologie moderne."

2. Foucault, "La politique de la santé au XVIIIème siècle," 18.

3. Ibid., 23.

4. Foucault, "Crise de la médecine ou crise de l'antimédicine," 43.

5. See Bacon, "De viis mortis, et de senectute retardanda, atque instaurandis viribus."

6. See Agamben, *Il regno e la Gloria*.

7. See Agamben, "Politicizing Death," in *Homo Sacer*, 160–66; and Esposito, *Bios*, 110–46.

8. Foucault assigns this function to racism in the early twentieth century; see *SMD*, 256–59.

9. Esposito, *Bios*, 121. Esposito here takes up and pursues a line of investigation he began in *Immunitas*.

10. Kerenyi, "Introduction," 34.

11. I prefer to read Agamben's problematic distinction between *zoe* and *bios* (see *Homo Sacer*) in terms of Bichat's distinction between an "organic" life, that for us is a vegetative life, and animal life, that is, the relational life, and adopt the difference that James Rachels proposes between a bio*logical* life and a bio*graphical* life. See Bichat, *Physiological Researches upon Life and Death*; and Rachels, *End of Life*.

12. See also Emile Durkheim's classic 1897 work *Suicide: A Study in Sociology*. In his introduction to the PUF edition, Serge Paugam clearly demonstrates the link between the problematization of suicide and the statistical data that, for the first time, allow Durkheim to write a sociological investigation of suicide.

13. Determining the exact moment of death has become an economic problem: see Ziegler, *Les vivants et la mort*, who cites, among others, the 1968 Report of the Ad Hoc Committee of the Harvard Medical School to examine the definition of brain death.

14. Plato, *Phaedo*, 64.

15. Montaigne, "To Philosophize Is to Learne How to Dye," 80. Montaigne quotes Seneca in this essay. See Hadot, *Exercises spirituels et philosophy antique*. See also Hadot, *What Is Ancient Philosophy?* and *Philosophy as a Way of Life*. On the art of dying in early modernity, see Delumeau, "Les *artes moriendi* de la Renaissance et les 'Pensez-y bien' du XVIIe siècle"; Tenenti, *Il senso della morte*

e l'amore della vita nel Rinascimento; Ariès, *Essai sur la mort en Occident du Moyen Age à nos jours*.

16. See Kojève, *Introduction to the Reading of Hegel*; Heidegger, *Being and Time*.
17. See Illich, *Limits to Medicine*.
18. Heath, *Matters of Life and Death*, 22.
19. On this point see Baud, *L'affaire de la main volée*; and Conseil d'État, *Sciences de la vie*.
20. Guidieri, *Ombre*, 57 (translation mine).
21. Ibid., 46.

6. IDENTITY, NATURE, LIFE: THREE BIOPOLITICAL DECONSTRUCTIONS
JUDITH REVEL

1. On this point, I refer the reader to my work *Le parole e i poteri*; and to a more recent article in French, "La naissance littéraire de la biopolitique."
2. Foucault, "Interview with J. Francois and J. De Wit," 1481.
3. Foucault, "Friendship as a Way of Life," 137.
4. Foucault, "Nietzsche, Genealogy, History," 380.
5. In the 1960s, this anti-naturalism appears sometimes in a literary form within a discourse, which also aims to deconstruct the figure of the classical subject and the privilege of self-identity on the basis of the themes of metamorphosis, transgression, and transmutation. Thus Foucault writes on the subject of the Minotaur, a figure which returns over and over in this period when Foucault speaks about Roussel's writings or the works of Deleuze, that "the space symbolized by the Minotaur is, on the contrary, a space of transmutation.... Its meticulous movement, supported by nature and reason, gives rise to Antiphysis and all the volcanos of madness. It is no longer a matter of the deceptive surfaces of disguise but, rather, of a nature metamorphosed into a depth by the powers of the counternatural" (Foucault, "So Cruel a Knowledge," 66).
6. Foucault, "Human Nature: Justice vs. Power," 29.
7. Foucault, "Foucault: By Maurice Florence," 461.
8. Foucault, "Bio-histoire et bio-politique," 97.
9. Foucault, "Human Nature: Justice vs. Power," 29.
10. On this subject, see Descola's remarkable *Par-delà nature et culture*.
11. Foucault, "La vie des hommes infâmes," 245.
12. Ibid., 248.
13. Foucault, "Sexe, pouvoir, et la politique de l'identité," 1555.
14. Ibid., 1555.
15. Foucault, "Polemics, Politics, and Problematizations," 114.

7. FROM REASON OF STATE TO LIBERALISM: THE COUP D'ÉTAT AS FORM OF GOVERNMENT
ROBERTO NIGRO

1. See Foucault, "On the Genealogy of Ethics."
2. Deleuze, *Foucault*, 94. A few years after Foucault's death, Deleuze tried already to make clear what was at stake in Foucault's last production. By citing some beautiful texts of Foucault, he clarifies the switch from an analytics of power to a topic centered on the question of subjectivation: "The most intense point of lives—Foucault writes—the one where their energy is concentrated, is precisely where they clash with power, struggle with it, endeavor to utilize its forces or to escape its traps" (Foucault, "The Life of Infamous Men," 162, quoted in Deleuze, *Foucault*, 94). Deleuze can tentatively conclude that power does not take life as its objective without revealing or giving rise to a life that resists power. Although somewhat problematic, Deleuze's remark is highly important, since it stresses a crucial passage in Foucault's thought, pertaining to the role the question of subjectivity came to play in his last reflection. Foucault himself has stressed several times the importance of the question of the subject in his work: "I would like to say, first of all, what has been the goal of my work during the last twenty years. It has not been to analyze the phenomena of power, nor to elaborate the foundations of such an analysis. My objective, instead, has been to create a history of the different modes by which, in our culture, human beings are made subjects. . . . Thus it is not power, but the subject, which is the general theme of my research" (SP, 326).
3. Fontana, "Leggere Foucault, oggi."
4. I will limit here my remarks to only a few aspects. See Eribon, *Michel Foucault*, 263–95, for a more detailed account.
5. See Michel Foucault, "The Repressive Hypothesis," in *WK*, 16–49; and *SMD*, Lecture 1 (January 7). On this topic see the interesting remarks by Etienne Balibar, who points out that a true struggle with Marx crosses Foucault's whole work. See Balibar, "Foucault et Marx," 282. See also Lemke, "Marx sans guillemets"; Fontana and Bertani, "Situating the Lectures." I take the liberty here to also refer to my "Foucault, Reader and Critic of Marx"; and "Quelques remarques sur les enjeux d'une confrontation entre Foucault et Marx."
6. Michel Senellart recalls Foucault's personal involvement with the Klaus Croissant affair at the end of 1977. See "Course Context," 372. Among the elements of the historical, political, and intellectual context in which Foucault's lectures are inserted, Senellart also refers to the debates provoked by the defeat of the left in the national elections of March 1978 and to the perspective of the 1981 presidential election. He calls attention to the fact that Foucault's discussion of liberalism and neoliberalism took place within the framework of these debates. Another important phenomenon, the immense effect of which is re-

flected in some passages of Foucault's lectures, is the movement of Soviet dissidence, which then enjoyed increasingly wide support. Last but not least, there were Foucault's reports from Iran for the Italian daily *Corriere della Sera*, where he traveled in the months of September and November 1978 during the Iranian Revolution. He paid attention to the idea of "good government," set out by the ayatollah, and to the dimension of "political spirituality" (ibid., 371–76). These events may have called into question the meaning of revolutionary experience and have contributed to model his discussion of the technologies of the self.

7. See Althusser, "Ideology and Ideological State Apparatuses." If an *Auseinandersetzung* with Marx crosses Foucault's whole work, a productive dialogue with Althusser is at stake as well. One could even argue that Foucault and Althusser engaged in a play of mutual influence throughout their lives. Their theoretical perspectives sometimes overlapped, as with the debate around the human sciences, the philosophical anthropology, and the theoretical anti-humanism in the 1960s. Nonetheless, they also differed at times. See interview with Michel Foucault conducted by Trombadori and "On the Ways of Writing History," where Foucault underlines what distances him from Althusser with regard to his interpretation of the epistemological break and the place of Marx in the history of thought. As for the relationship between Althusser and Foucault with regard to debates on theoretical humanisms in the 1960s, see my afterword to Foucault, *Introduction to Kant's Anthropology*, 127–57; and also my article "La question de l'anthropologie dans l'interprétation althussérienne de Marx." A different perspective on the relationship between Foucault and Marx (also including Deleuze and Althusser) has been recently developed by Isabelle Garo in *Foucault, Deleuze, Althusser, et Marx*. For an in-depth discussion of Althusser's last production, see Vatter, "Machiavelli after Marx." See also Bidet, "Introduction à Idéologie et appareils idéologiques d'État"; Negri, "Pour Althusser." Interesting developments in contemporary thought, based on Althusser's and Foucault's theories in subjection, can be found in Butler, *Psychic Life of Power*, Chapters 3 and 4.

8. See Senellart, "Course Context," 385.

9. In this connection, see Berns, *Gouverner sans gouverner*, for the light his research sheds on contemporary governmental rationality. On his account, neoliberalism develops in a constructivist perspective, for it produces and shapes the reality it tries to govern.

10. This is a very summary overview of the content of the course *Security, Territory, Population*. Foucault also devoted the first three lectures to the study of security apparatuses, involving the space of security, the treatment of the uncertain, and the government of populations. After the detour, mentioned above, he came back to apparatuses of security and liberalism in the very last lecture. Foucault's apparent switch of topics in this course has attracted the attention of many commentators. Mike Gane, for instance, remarks that Foucault "does

not follow his usual methods" in these lectures and "they do not seem to have a convincing overall structure." See "Foucault on Governmentality and Liberalism," 357. A very useful interpretation of these lectures is still the work of Lemke, *Eine Kritik der politischen Vernunft*.

11. In his book *Politiques de Foucault*, Jean Terrel provides an in-depth analysis of all these issues through an examination of the two courses of Foucault. See, in particular, Part 1, Chapter 4: "Le libéralisme en question," 85–149.

12. *STP*, Lecture 9 (March 8). It was also question of Machiavelli in Lecture 4 (February 1), in connection with the discussion of the problem of government in the sixteenth century. Foucault explains that the development of a literature on the arts of government, between the sixteenth and eighteenth century, orbits the rejection of Machiavelli's *The Prince* (*STP*, 127).

13. See *STP*, 316, 337–41.

14. For a detailed discussion of the concept of "prudenza politica" in connection with the debate on reason of state carried out by Italian authors, see Borrelli, *Ragion di Stato e Leviatano*; Borrelli, *Ragion di Stato*; Borrelli, *Non far novità*.

15. At issue here is the relationship between reason of state and forms of disciplinarization. This involves the question about the production of forms of obedience in the subjects and of command over society. Gerhard Östreich in his classical work *Antiker Geist und moderner Staat bei Justus Lipsius (1547–1606): Der Neustoizismus als politische Bewegung* provides an important discussion of these topics, including the question of *Sozialdisziplinierung*. See Östreich, *Neostoicism and the Early Modern State*. Pierangelo Schiera expands on these topics with regard to the question of the *Lebensführung* in Max Weber's work. See Schiera, "La conception Wébérienne de la discipline et le theme de la 'Lebensführung.'"

16. The connection between reason of state and liberalism, with reference to Foucault's analyses, is discussed by Senellart in "Dalla ragion di Stato al liberalismo." In his work, Senellart expands a lot on these topics. He shows that the study of the relationship between mercantilism and political economy paves the way for a different interpretation of reason of state. His interpretation opposes the very influential work by Friedrich Meinecke, *Machiavellism*. Meinecke considered Machiavelli as the inventor of the reason of state (and historicism) and the author who had greatly contributed to the Enlightenment. In Meinecke's eyes, Machiavelli opposed the doctrines of natural law and was allowed to interpret the functioning of power in rational form. Senellart remarks, first, that historicism, which developed in Germany in the nineteenth century, was a reaction against the French Revolution and the theories of natural right which had inspired it; second, he calls into question Meinecke's interpretation since the relationship between reason of state and Machiavellism seems to him more problematic. The reason of state is not, in fact, a concept Machia-

velli developed on his own, but is a notion at work since the twelfth century as *ratio status*. Jurists and theologians in the wake of the Roman public right referred to the *ratio status*. One cannot say that the Middle Ages had ignored it. For the critique of Meinecke, see Senellart, *Machiavellisme et Raison d'État*. Meinecke's work has nowadays undergone several critiques. I mention here only some essential references: Stolleis, "L'idée de la raison d'État de Friedrich Meinecke et la recherche actuelle"; Stolleis, *Staat und Staatsräson in der frühen Neuzeit*; Lefort, *Le travail de l'oeuvre de Machiavel*; Vatter, *Between Form and Event*. On the relationship between medieval thought and the diffusion of reason of state, see Senellart, *Les arts de gouverner*. Senellart outlines the emergence of two pathways, both of them originated in the medieval period through the discussion about the concept of *necessity*. The first one led to the integration of the concept of necessity into a religious–juridical tradition, which gave birth to the Christian reason of state as sketched out by Giovanni Botero. The other pathway enabled the distinction between the concept of *necessitas* and of *ratio status* and led to the work of Machiavelli. For a different perspective about the idea of a substantial continuity between the modern notion of reason of state and that of *ratio status*, see Viroli, "Revolution in the Concept of Politics." The author argues that this kind of continuity is historically incorrect. By also referring to the study of Gaines Post (*Studies in Medieval Legal Thought*, 479), he points out that the medieval reason of state was "right reason" in the sense of "being a reasoning in accordance with the fundamental laws of God and nature." For a more detailed analyses of these issues see also Viroli, *From Politics to Reason of State*. For a different account of these issues see Vatter, "Idea of Public Reason and the Reason of State." The author identifies two different but co-originary senses in the concept of public reason (*ratio publicae utilitatis*): a *reason for the state* and a *reason of the state*. He points out: "On one hand, the concept refers to a reason *for* an estate (*status*) with a superior right or *jus*. . . . On the other, the concept of public reason refers to a reason *of* the estate which is charged with interpreting or deciding, case by case, what the good of the community requires" (246). By also basing his argument on Post's historical reconstruction, Vatter outlines that the *reason of the state* can be identified as a precursor of absolutist *raison d'état*.

17. Naudé, *Considérations politiques sur les coups d'états*. This work was first published in Rome, in 1639, in only twelve exemplars: it is a book on the secrets of State published in secret. See *STP*, 242–55. To reconstruct this debate Foucault mainly exploited the classical work by Etienne Thuau, *Raison d'État et pensée politique à l'époque de Richelieu*.

18. Bartelson, "Making Exceptions."

19. Naudé, *Considérations politiques sur les coups d'états*, 76.

20. Bartelson remarks that it was Locke who paved the way for a modern interpretation of the coup d'état. He made this possible by discussing the concepts

of rebellion and usurpation in his *Second Treatise* (1690). In this way, the modern coup d'état could little by little assume the modern connation of an illegitimate act of usurpation carried out from the outside, never staged from inside the locus of legitimate authority (Bartelson, "Making Exceptions," 324–25).

21. Marin, "Pour une théorie baroque de l'action politique," 10 (translation mine).

22. I leave here aside a number of issues that could be implicated in a discussion about the becoming prince of the multitude, as sketched out by Antonio Negri, and about the tension between the two viewpoints of the people and of the prince, as discussed by Althusser as well. Althusser remarks that "[the Prince] is not himself the people. Equally, the people are not summoned to become the Prince. So there is an irreducible duality between the place of the political *viewpoint* and the *place* of the political force and practice; between the subject of the political viewpoint—the people—and the subject of the political practice: the Prince" (Althusser, *Machiavelli and Us*, 26). See also Negri, *Insurgencies*, 37–97. In the context of our discussion of the coup d'état, these remarks are all the more important since they indicate the possibility to refer to the classical idea of the coup d'état as what still haunts modern times in the form of a revolutionary process. In fact, if the classical coup d'état becomes superfluous with the advent of popular sovereignty (inasmuch as a sovereign people can no longer undertake a coup against itself, logically), there remains nevertheless space for considering it as the internal strength for governmental changes (Bartelson, "Making Exceptions," 338).

23. Schmitt, *Political Theology*, 15. A discussion of the concept of exception, that takes into account the Schmittian background and, by the same token, focuses on reason of state in the sixteenth century (in particular on Naudé's work) is developed by Freund in "La situation exceptionelle comme justification de la raison d'état chez Gabriel Naudé." See also Zarka, "Raison d'État, maximes d'État et coups d'État chez Gabriel Naudé."

24. Schmitt, *Political Theology*, 71. Ottavio Marzocca discusses this aspect of Schmitt's account in the light of Foucault's critique of sovereignty. See *Perché il governo*, 100.

25. See Marin, *Portrait of the King*; Marin, *On Representation*. To some extent, Giorgio Agamben's book *Il regno e la Gloria* can be inserted in the same sequence. Agamben does not mention Marin, but he situates his work in the wake of Foucault's research on the genealogy of governmentality. His focus is on the function of rites, ceremonies, acclamations—in a word, *la Gloria* (glory)—in the exercise of government. If *media* are so important in modern democracies, it is not because they try to control and govern public opinion, but because they administer and dispense glory.

26. See *SMD*, 239–64; and "Right of Death and Power over Life," in *WK*, 134–59. The first references to the notion of biopolitics are to be traced back to

his conferences on medicine delivered in Rio de Janeiro in 1974. See, among them, "The Birth of Social Medicine."

27. Foucault, *Discipline and Punish*, 221.

28. See Foucault, "The Eye of Power," and "About the Concept of 'Dangerous Individual' in Nineteenth-Century Legal Psychiatry." To some extent, Foucault's account of confinement as a police matter, as developed in *History of Madness*, 44–78, may be connected with these analyses. In that context, Foucault clarifies that confinement, as a massive phenomenon, the signs of which are found all across eighteenth-century Europe, was required by something quite different from any concern with curing the sick, namely, by an imperative of labor.

29. An important piece in this genealogy is introduced by the work of Roberto Esposito, *Bios*. By drawing on Foucault's analyses on the biopolitical character of liberalism, Roberto Esposito has shown the intricacy of the relationship between liberalism and Nazism. Biopolitics has often culminated in very deathly results (the event of Nazism is probably the most emblematic one). If Nazism was defeated militarily and politically after the Second World War, so argues Esposito, its defeat was not cultural and linguistic. Nazi politics was centered on political control of *bios*. The human body entered a mechanism of control and appropriation by means of the state politics. Nevertheless, the centrality of *bios* as the object and subject of politics did not disappear after the defeat of the Nazi regime, rather the human body entered a new mechanism of control, characterized by liberal forms of government. Liberalism transferred the property of the human body from the state to the individual. But it still kept on using the same biopolitical vocabulary. So, biopolitics gave birth to two political forms, Nazism and liberalism, state biopolitics and individual biopolitics, whose relationship should be deeply investigated.

30. See Negri and Hardt, *Commonwealth*, 56–63. On these connections, see Lemke, *Gouvernamentalität und Biopolitik*, 77–88. See also Read, "Genealogy of Homo-Economicus."

31. I do not take here into account the semantic shift these notions underwent in the years following 1978. But it would be interesting to remark that while, at the end of the seventies, they were employed in the field of power relations in connection with the problem of the state, at a later time they were referred to power relations in what they imply in terms of conduct of the others and conduct of oneself. See Senellart, "Course Context," 388. See also Gros, "Course Context," 548n30. In the 1980s, Foucault also introduced interesting distinctions between the notions of government, domination, and power as strategic games. This differentiation between three types of power relations is all the more important for it questions a simplistic use of the notion of resistance. As Jean Terrel (*Politiques de Foucault*, 131) points out, if one keeps on using the notion of resistance, one risks coming back to an interpretation of power in

terms of repression. The reactive conception of resistance undermines and masks the productive character of power. See ECS. See also, Lemke, *Gouvernamentalität und Biopolitik*, 47–64. A discussion of the notion of resistance in Foucault's work is found in Dupont, *L'impatience de la liberté*.

32. Foucault, *La société punitive*, 4, 7, 26, 228.
33. Foucault, "La torture, c'est la raison," 390.
34. Foucault, "The Eye of Power," 164.
35. In this connection, see Maurizio Lazzarato's critical remarks on subjectivation and micropolitics in his book *Expérimentations politiques*, 85–143.
36. See Nigro and Raunig, "Molecular Revolution and Event."

8. FOUCAULT AND RAWLS: GOVERNMENT AND PUBLIC REASON
PAUL PATTON

1. Recent histories of this society include Hartwell, *History of the Mont Pelerin Society*; and Mirowski and Plehwe, *Road from Mont Pelerin*. Further references to the institutional and intellectual history of neoliberalism may be found in Jackson, "At the Origins of Neo-liberalism."

2. As he explained in a lecture to the *Société Française de Philosophie* the previous year, the critical attitude that conditioned his "historicophilosophical" analyses of the present did not ask why we are governed at all but how we are governed. The critical question posed was "how not to be governed *like that*, by that, in the name of these principles, in view of such objectives and by means of such methods, not like that, not for that, not by them?" (WC, 44). Behrent argues that the governmentality lectures contributed to the shift in political sensibility that enabled some of those around him, notably François Ewald, to abandon revolutionary politics in favor of direct engagement with the institutions and policies of government ("Accidents Happen").

3. See Behrent, "Liberalism without Humanism," 552–55; Behrent, "A Seventies Thing," 19–20; see also Senellart, "Course Context," 371. Behrent claims that "Foucault's interest in neoliberalism appears to owe much to his attraction to the Second Left" ("Liberalism without Humanism," 553).

4. Behrent, "Liberalism without Humanism," 568; Behrent, "A Seventies Thing," 25.

5. Rawls, *Political Liberalism*, 213.
6. Ibid., xlvii.
7. Ibid., 218.
8. Miguel Vatter traces the origins of the idea of public reason, as this is differently expressed in Rawls and Carl Schmitt, to different components of late medieval concepts of public reason. Although concerned more with the form rather than the content of public reason as Rawls describes it, his argu-

ment is also a powerful case for the importance of a genealogical approach ("Idea of Public Reason and the Reason of State").
9. Rawls, *Political Liberalism*, 137; see also 217, 393.
10. Patton, "Foucault and Normative Political Philosophy," 207.
11. Rawls, *Political Liberalism*, 224; emphasis added.
12. Ibid., 214.
13. Ibid. In "The Idea of Public Reason Revisited" and the introduction to the paperback edition of *Political Liberalism*, he suggests that matters of basic justice would include "questions of basic economic and social justice and other things not covered by the constitution" (Rawls, *Political Liberalism*, xlviiin23; 442n7). In the same text, in the context of discussing the essential features of the public deliberation that characterizes public reason in a liberal democracy, he mentions a range of policy proposals to address "the alleged coming crisis in Social Security": these include such measures as raising taxes, slowing down the growth of benefits levels, raising the retirement age, and imposing limits on "expensive terminal medical care that prolongs life for only a few weeks or days" (ibid., 449).
14. Krouse and McPherson, "Capitalism, 'Property-Owning Democracy,' and the Welfare State," 87.
15. Daniels, "Justice, Health, and Healthcare," 2–3.
16. Ibid., 3.
17. Rawls, *Justice as Fairness*, 139.
18. Jackson, "Revisionism Reconsidered," 418.
19. Meade, *Efficiency, Equality and the Ownership of Property*.
20. Krouse and McPherson, "Capitalism, 'Property-Owning Democracy,' and the Welfare State," 79.
21. Rawls, *Justice as Fairness*, 135–36.
22. Ibid., 138.
23. Ibid., 139.
24. Rawls, *Theory of Justice*, 241.
25. Jackson comments, with reference to Meade, that many of the points made by authors such as Hayek about respecting consumer sovereignty and freedom of occupational choice "found a sympathetic audience at the time among elements of the social democratic left" (Jackson, "At the Origins of Neo-liberalism," 150).
26. DiQuattro, "Rawls versus Hayek," 308.
27. Rawls, *Theory of Justice*, 24213; Rawls, *Justice as Fairness*, 135.
28. Rawls, *Theory of Justice*, 242, 248.
29. Ibid., 243.
30. Rawls summarizes the tasks of government as follows: "I assume that the basic structure is regulated by a just constitution that secures the liberties of equal citizenship (as described in the preceding chapter). Liberty of

conscience and freedom of thought are taken for granted, and the fair value of political liberty is maintained. The political process is conducted, as far as circumstances permit, as a just procedure for choosing between governments and for enacting just legislation. I assume also that there is fair (as opposed to formal) equality of opportunity. This means that in addition to maintaining the usual kinds of social overhead capital, the government tries to ensure equal chances of education and culture for persons similarly endowed and motivated either by subsidizing private schools or by establishing a public school system. It also enforces and underwrites equality of opportunity in economic activities and in the free choice of occupation. This is achieved by policing the conduct of firms and private associations and by preventing the establishment of monopolistic restrictions and barriers to the more desirable positions. Finally, the government guarantees a social minimum either by family allowances and special payments for sickness and employment, or more systematically by such devices as a graded income supplement (a so-called negative income tax)" (ibid., 243).

31. Jackson, "At the Origins of Neo-liberalism," 146.
32. Ibid., 136.
33. Ibid.
34. Ibid., 143.
35. Ibid., 145.
36. See, for example, Roemer, *Future for Socialism*; Ackerman and Alstot, *Stakeholder Society*; Kelly and Lissauer, *Ownership for All*; and O'Neill and Williamson, *Property-Owning Democracy*.
37. Rawls, *Justice as Fairness*, 27.
38. Rawls, *Political Liberalism*, 215.
39. Ibid., 220.
40. This proviso is taken to settle the limits of what he calls the wide view of public political culture as distinct from the background culture of the society in question (Rawls, *Political Liberalism*, 462). So, for example, in "The Idea of Public Reason Revisited" he suggests that anti-slavery campaigners in the US who defended immediate and uncompensated universal emancipation on religious grounds fulfilled the proviso because they were defending basic liberal constitutional values. They could have provided reasons in the terms of a reasonable conception of justice (ibid., 464).
41. This family of reasonable liberal conceptions of justice is characterized by three things: a list of basic rights, liberties, and opportunities, an assignment of priority to these, and a set of measures designed to ensure that all citizens enjoy adequate means to make effective use of their freedoms (Rawls, *Political Liberalism*, 6, 450).
42. Rawls, *Political Liberalism*, 215.
43. Ibid., 13; see also 227.

44. "Views raising new questions related to ethnicity, gender and race are obvious examples, and the political conceptions that result from these views will debate the current conceptions. The content of public reason is not fixed, any more than it is defined by any one reasonable political conception" (ibid., li).

45. Ibid., 452.

46. Ibid., li; emphasis added.

47. Freeman, *Rawls*, 387.

48. Rawls, *Political Liberalism*, 225.

49. Rawls suggests that public reason should not appeal to "elaborate economic theories of general equilibrium, say, if these are in dispute" (ibid., 225).

50. The recognition that settled convictions may change is arguably implicit in Rawls's suggestion that the conception of justice the parties to the original position would adopt "identifies the conception of justice that we regard—here and now—as fair and supported by the best reasons" (ibid., 26). The phrase "here and now" might be taken to indicate that the conceptions of justice that would be adopted by rational and reasonable parties under the restrictions imposed by the veil of ignorance express the considered judgments of a historically specific form of society. As those judgments or convictions change, so too might the details of the conception of justice.

51. Ibid., 226.

52. Ibid., 216.

53. Ibid., 215.

54. Larmore, "Public Reason," 382; Rawls, *Political Liberalism*, 444.

55. Jackson, "Revisionism Reconsidered," 419.

56. Ibid., 421.

57. Ibid., 418.

58. Cited in ibid., 421.

59. Ibid., 422.

60. Rawls, *Political Liberalism*, 382.

9. FOUCAULT AND HAYEK: REPUBLICAN LAW AND LIBERAL CIVIL SOCIETY
MIGUEL VATTER

A longer version of the essay presented here is found in my book *The Republic of the Living: Biopolitics and Civil Society* (New York: Fordham University Press, 2014).

1. For another reading of Hayek through Foucault's categories, see now Spieker, "Defending the Open Society." Spieker concentrates on Hayek's "evolutionary account of order" (311) according to which the free market is the result of a process of "natural selection" between "disciplined" actors and those who are not. But this idea of "discipline" is not connected to Hayek's discourse on law.

Spieker in fact concentrates on Foucault's idea of politics as war in *Society Must Be Defended* rather than in the lectures on governmentality proper. His picture of Hayek is Hobbesian, while mine will turn out to be that of a (modified) Kantian.

2. Foucault's thesis, of course, is that the "free and responsible" subject generated by the order of the market is just a condition for its "normal" functioning (*BB*, 144–50, 172–77). See in general Lemke, *Gouvernamentalität und Biopolitik*, on this kind of normativity in Foucault's conception of biopower.

3. See the discussion of this point in Valverde, "Law versus History."

4. Foucault, "The Political Technology of Individuals," 417.

5. On Foucault's conception of norms, see Legrand, *Les normes chez Foucault*; and Napoli, *Naissance de la police moderne*. Both of these works, though, do not consider the possibility that Foucault recovers a discourse of the law, as opposed to the norm, in an affirmative sense, as I shall argue here.

6. For another argument, with which I find myself in broad agreement, concerning Foucault's alternative and affirmative understanding of law, see Fitzpatrick and Golder, *Foucault's Law*, Chapter 2.

7. Foucault, "The Political Technology of Individuals," 417.

8. Ibid.

9. Not even in such texts where he comes closest to identifying law with ideology, for example in *Discipline and Punish*.

10. Gehring, "Foucaults 'juridischer' Machttyp, die *Geschichte der Gouvernamentalität* und die Frage nach Foucaults Rechtstheorie."

11. Agamben, *Homo Sacer*; Esposito, *Bios*.

12. Patton, "Foucault, Critique, and Rights"; Rose, *Politics of Life Itself*; Fassin, "Another Politics of Life Is Possible."

13. For the early modern republican conception of freedom as *sui iuris* status, see Skinner, *Visions of Politics*, Chapters 11–12; and *Liberty before Liberalism*. For the Kantian conception of *sui iuris*, see Vatter, "The People Shall Be Judge."

14. I do not mean that Foucault is "republican" in the sense in which this term is used, for instance, in contemporary French political discourse, a use which has been recently criticized in Rancière, *Hatred of Democracy*. He is "republican" in a more anarchic sense of the term that has been developed in Rancière, *La Mésentente*, and which I discuss in "Pettit and Modern Republican Political Thought."

15. Canguilhem, *Le normal et le pathologique*; *Études d'histoire et de philosophie des sciences*; and *Vital Rationalist*.

16. Canguilhem, *Vital Rationalist*, 351–84.

17. Le Blanc, *Canguilhem et les normes*, 87.

18. Canguilhem, *Vital Rationalist*, 370; Le Blanc, *Canguilhem et les normes*, 83.

19. Canguilhem, *Vital Rationalist*, 376; Le Blanc, *Canguilhem et les normes*, 87.
20. Canguilhem, *Vital Rationalist*, 374.
21. Ibid., 377. See Muhle, *Eine Genealogie der Biopolitik*, for an excellent reading of Foucault along these lines.
22. Canguilhem, *Vital Rationalist*, 370; Le Blanc, *Canguilhem et les normes*, 91.
23. The current Liberal–Conservative government in power in the United Kingdom is entirely based on turning that country into a "Great Society" in this Hayekian sense. It must be added that Hayek also rejects all organicism—usually opposed to organization—but he does so in ways that do not affect the substantial affinity that his idea of spontaneous order shares with Canguilhem's notion of life's internal normativity.
24. I do not have space here to discuss at greater length how this notion of individualization by way of speciation, and vice versa, depends on the close relation between biopolitical norms and the constitution of a "milieu" or "environment" (*Umgebung/Umwelt*) in which a species can maximize its "standard of life." See the discussion of "milieu" in *STP*.
25. See Agamben, *Il regno e la Gloria*, on divine providence in Scholasticism, where coordination via secondary causes leads to an idea of the "nature of things" which, he argues, is the background for the "naturality" of the economy in eighteenth-century political economy.
26. For examples, see the essays "Two Pages of Fiction" and "The Use of Knowledge in Society" in Nishiyama and Leube, *Essence of Hayek*. On the question of the evolution in Hayek's thought from what Mirowski calls the "abuse of reason" phase to the "evolutionary proto-cyberneticist" phase, see "Naturalizing the Market on the Road to Revisionism." But Mirowski downplays the importance of jurisprudence in Hayek's development and abstracts from biopolitics entirely. He has now reconsidered this last point after reading Foucault's work on governmentality, as evidenced by Mirowski and Plehwe, *Road from Mont Pelerin*.
27. Hayek, "Nomos."
28. Hayek, "Principles of a Liberal Social Order," 366.
29. I here follow Caldwell, "Hayek's Transformation," on the basic thesis on the genesis of Hayek's mature thought.
30. Hayek, "Principles of a Liberal Social Order," 365.
31. Ibid., 372–73.
32. Ibid., "Nomos," 190.
33. It is crucial that Hayek assigns government only one role, namely, the enforcement of norms; thus police action is central for him. All other functions of government, basically providing for needs that individuals or corporations cannot provide for (e.g., public services), are secondary to the state's functions. Both of these functions, when considered together, belong to the meaning of *Polizei* (police) as Foucault understands it.

34. On security and insurance from a biopolitical perspective, see Dillon, "Governing through Contingency"; and Lobo-Guerrero, *Insuring Security*.

35. For this concept, I refer to Vatter, "Biopolitics"; and Cooper, *Life as Surplus*.

36. Foucault, "The Political Technology of Individuals," 415.

37. Hayek, "Nomos," 102.

38. I would place in this context the importance of the interpretation given by Lemke of the relation between Foucault and the project of a critique of political economy. See "Marx sans guillemets"; and *Gouvernamentalität und Biopolitik*.

39. One need only think about how this insecurity of the working classes, their slide into abject poverty and death, is thematized from Malthus and Ricardo to Marx. On the new insecurity of neoliberal capitalism, see Boltanski, and Chiapello, *Le nouvel esprit du capitalisme*.

40. See *BB*, 118–21, on neoliberal regulation of competition. In general, risk and insurance go together—only where there is an assumption of risk does it make sense to take on insurance.

41. Here Foucault's analysis of neoliberalism rejoins Walter Benjamin's critique of *Gewalt* and his unmasking of the police as the "rotten core" of bourgeois systems of law.

42. In this sense, I agree with Patton, "Foucault, Critique, and Rights," 270, that Foucault has a positive discourse with respect to rights, but for me the basis of these new rights is to be understood from the distinction between pastoral and political power, the latter having the ideal of self-mastery (*sui iuris*) at its center.

10. PARRHESIA BETWEEN EAST AND WEST: FOUCAULT AND DISSIDENCE
SIMONA FORTI

1. Michel Foucault never denied his engagement; after 1950 he went to Poland on many occasions. See, for example, the historical reconstruction made by Jeannette Colombel, "Michel Foucault et la dissidence tchécoslovaque"; and Á. Szakolczai, "Foucault passe à l'Est."

2. "Entretien avec Jan Patočka (1967)," 31. Regardless of their different origins—they ranged from rock fans to theologians—all dissidents believed it a duty to oppose the "institutional lie" of the regime and to implement a series of actions and practices that responded to the "life-in-the-truth." In Prague, but also in Brno and Bratislava, everyone knew of the illegal meetings being held. Certain European intellectuals, mostly French—Derrida and Vernant to mention the best known—supported the clandestine groups with funding and "banned" books, but very often also by participating personally in the discussions. It was in this context that the names of authors thought to be "decisive"

for political action emerged. Among them, in fact, most important of all was Michel Foucault.

3. On the notion of "a-subjective phenomenology" see Ricoeur, "Préface aux *Essais hérétiques* (1981)"; Barbaras, *Le mouvement de l'existence*; Barbaras, "Phenomenology and Henology"; Barbaras, *L'ouverture du monde*; Jervolino, "Reading Patočka, in Search for a Philosophy of Translation."

4. On Socrates, see the series of lectures held by Patočka in Prague in 1947, *Socrate*.

5. See Patočka, *Le monde naturel et le mouvement de l'existence humaine*; and *Movement of Human Existence*.

6. Patočka, "Does History Have a Meaning?" 80.

7. Patočka, "Wars of the Twentieth Century and Twentieth Century as War," 119. We also read: "How do the day, life, peace govern all individuals, their bodies and soul? By means of death; by threatening life. From the perspective of the day life is, for all individuals, everything, the highest value that exists for them. For the forces of the day, conversely, death does not exist, they function as if there was no death, or, as noted, they plan death impersonally and statistically, as if it were merely a reassignment of roles. Thus in the will to war, day and life rule with the help of death.... Those who cannot break free of the rule of peace, of the day, of life in a mode that excludes death and closes its eyes before it, can never free themselves of war" (129). On this, see Dodds, *Twentieth Century as War*.

8. Patočka, "Wars of the Twentieth Century and Twentieth Century as War," 125.

9. Ibid., 123.

10. Derrida, *Gift of Death*, in which he considers the Patočka's essay "Is Technological Civilization Decadent, and Why?"

11. On the idea of "negative Platonism," see Evink, "Relevance of Patočka's Negative Platonism"; Ullmann, "Negative Platonism and the Appearance Problem." See also Findlay, *Caring for the Soul in a Postmodern Age*; and Merlier, *Patočka*.

12. Patočka, "Negative Platonism," 193: "*Chorismos* meant originally a separateness without a second object realm. It is a gap that does not separate two realms coordinated or linked by something third that would embrace them both and so would serve as the foundation of both their coordination and their separation. *Chorismos* is a separateness, a distinctness *an sich*."

13. Patočka, "L'homme spirituel et l'intellectuel (1975)," 246 (translation mine).

14. Ibid.

15. On the soul as movement, see Ricoeur, "Préface aux *Essais hérétiques* (1981)."

16. Žižek, *Did Somebody Say Totalitarianism?* 130.

17. On the intellectual biography of Havel, see Keane, *Václav Havel*.

18. Havel was very clear that what could really disrupt the system of oppression was not so much a heroic sacrifice, a grandiose isolated gesture, as an effort made up of small acts which, precisely because they were neither outstanding nor openly political, would be the stumbling block for the regime. This was the regime of the late stages of real socialism, which, as Havel said, no longer worked on the basis of terror, thus making it possible for dissidents to create a small crack in the vicious spiral of fear. First, power now made use of "normal" means directed at establishing implicit and explicit rules, and no longer resorted to a continuous state of emergency. Second, because what was at stake was no longer the conduct dictated by an enthusiastic support of recruits to the ideology truth, but rather the daily survival of the "existential lie": a conduct consisting of a set of external actions, which contributed to the maintenance of the regime no less than to the internalization of the ideological faith and of violent repressive mechanisms.

19. Havel, *Power of the Powerless*, 24.

20. Ibid., 80.

21. Ibid. We also read: "There is in everyone the desire for freedom, for dignity as a transcendence of being, of a free experience of existing, yet at the same time in everyone there is the desire for indistinction, of blending into the crowd" (64).

22. "In fact, maybe the word 'dissidence' is exactly suited for these forms of resistance that concern, set their sights on, and have as their objective and adversary a power that assumes the task of conducting men in their life and daily existence. The word would be justified for two reasons, both of them historical. The first is that in fact the word 'dissidence' has often been employed to designate religious movements of resistance to pastoral organization. Second, its current application could in fact justify its use since, after all, what we [call] 'dissidence' in the East and the Soviet Union, really does designate a complex form of resistance and refusal, which involves a political refusal, of course, but in a society where political authority, that is, the political party, responsible for defining both the country's characteristic form of economy and structures of sovereignty, is at the same time responsible for conducting individuals in their daily life through a game of generalized obedience" (*STP*, 207).

23. "The political struggles that we put together under the name of dissidence, certainly have an essential, fundamental dimension that is refusal of this form of being conducted. . . . The whole pastoral practice of salvation is challenged. . . . We do not want this pastoral system of obedience. We do not want this truth. We do not want to be held in this system of truth. We do not want to be held in this system of observation and endless examination that continually judges us, tells us what we are in the core of ourselves, healthy or sick, mad or not mad, and so on. So we can say [that] this word dissidence really

does cover a struggle against those pastoral effects I talked about last week. And it is precisely because the word dissidence is too localized today in this kind of phenomena that it cannot be used without drawback. . . . I will propose to you is the doubtless badly constructed word 'counter-conduct'—the latter having the sole advantage of allowing reference to the active sense of the word 'conduct.' . . . And then maybe this word 'counter-conduct' enables us to avoid a certain substantification allowed by the word 'dissidence'" (*STP*, 267–68).

24. In one of his most important interviews, given in January 1984, "The Ethics of the Concern for the Self as a Practice of Freedom" Foucault seems to systematize the distinction between power and domination: "The analysis of power relations is an extremely complex area; one sometimes encounters what may be called situations or states of domination in which the power relations, instead of being mobile, allowing the various participants to adopt strategies modifying them, remain blocked, frozen. When an individual or social group succeeds in blocking a field of power relations, immobilizing them and preventing any reversibility of movement by economic, political, or military means, one is faced with what may be called a state of domination. In such a state, it is certain that practices of freedom do not exist or exist only unilaterally. . . . Thus, in order for power relations to come into play, there must be at least a certain degree of freedom on both sides. Even when the power relation is completely out of balance, when it can truly be claimed that one side has 'total power' over the other, a power can be exercised over the other only insofar as the other still has the option of killing himself, of leaping out the window, or of killing the other person" (ECS, 292).

25. On this notion, see also OES.

26. See, for example, the recently published volume of Foucault's 1979–80 Course *Du gouvernement des vivants*. An excellent analysis of the text can be found in Landry, "Confession, Obedience, and Subjectivity."

27. See Foucault, "The Battle for Chastity," and "Technologies of the Self."

28. In *HS*, 140, Foucault argued with the rhetoric of the "return to the self," to the authentic self, observing almost a sort of impossibility of filling such ethical appeals with any content. Nevertheless, he continued, this establishment of just such an ethic is an urgent task, fundamental and politically indispensable, if it is true that, after all, there is no other original or final point of resistance to political power that does not reside in the relation of the self with itself.

29. This does not mean that the Course *The Hermeneutics of the Subject*, held in 1982, inaugurated a self-referential vision of the self. Indeed, the practices and ethical techniques of antiquity—in particular those of the first and second century B.C.E.—demonstrate, to Foucault, that the subject cannot structure itself except with reference to otherness: to the context, to a particular political regime, to the arbiter of conscience, to the teacher, and so on.

30. "The practice, the thought of death is nothing except a means to focus a pitiless look on one's life, thus allowing one to grasp the value of the present, both of implementing the great circle of memory, through which it will be possible to review one's own life and make what it actually is come to light" (*HS*, 163).

31. On this division of ethics see *CT* 55.

11. THE EMBODIMENT OF TRUTH AND THE POLITICS OF COMMUNITY: FOUCAULT AND THE CYNICS

VANESSA LEMM

This essay is based on a paper with the same title given on March 21, 2013, at the University of Western Sydney, Australia. I thank the audience for their questions and comments.

1. See Arendt, *Life of the Mind*; Esposito, *Bios*.

2. This point has been advanced brilliantly by Jacques Derrida in *Éperons*.

3. For Foucault, the reduction of life to itself is one of the main characteristic of the Cynics' way of life. In his interpretation of the Cynics, however, Foucault does not explicitly distinguish between *bios* and *zoe*.

4. For Foucault, the reception of the Cynics during his time for the most part missed the point of Cynic *aléthurgie*. This reception typically represents the philosophy of the Cynics as an example of a radical individualism. In particular, Foucault refers to the works of Heinrich, *Parmenides und Jona*; Tillich, *Courage to Be*; and Gehlen, *Moral und Hypermoral*. For Heinrich, the Cynics embody the "self-determination [*Selbstbehauptung*] of the individual" in its struggle for self-preservation (142); Tillich sees in the Cynics mainly an example of "radical non-conformism" (113); and Gehlen claims that even their cosmopolitanism is nothing but the "other side [*Kehrseite*] of their individualism" (23). According to Foucault, this reception of the Cynics fails to acknowledge what he considers to be their most important contribution to the history of thought, namely, as an example of truth-telling (*parrhesia*), where material life manifests truth, where life is the direct expression of truth (*CT*, 166). It is worth noting that Peter Sloterdijk, whom Foucault mentions but admits not having read at the time of his Course, makes a similar point when he says that "cynicism gives a new twist to the question of how to *say* the truth" (*Critique of Cynical Reason*, 104). And also, "the appearance of Diogenes marks the most dramatic moment in the process of truth of early European philosophy" (102).

5. In what follows, I rely on the following standard abbreviations of Nietzsche's work: *KSA* = *Sämtliche Werke: Kritische Studienausgabe in 15 Bänden* (references provide the volume number followed by the relevant fragment number and any relevant aphorism). All translations of KSA fragments are mine. The following abbreviations are followed by the number of the aphorism: *BGE* =

Beyond Good and Evil; GS = *The Gay Science*; GM = *On the Genealogy of Morals*; AOM = *Assorted Opinions and Maxims*; HL = *The Advantages and Disadvantages of History for Life*; HH = *Human, All Too Human*.

6. For an extended discussion of this question, see Lemm, "Nietzsche, Einverleibung, and the Politics of Immunity."

7. For a different view, see Marzocca, "Philosophical *Parresia* and Transpolitical Freedom." According to Marzocca, Socratic and Cynic *parrhesia* are comparable insofar as they both "remain close to the practice of active citizenship" (135).

8. In my view, the problem with Heinrich's and Gehlen's characterization of the Cynics is that they misinterpret their radicalization of individualism. The philosophy of the Cynics does not reflect an attempt to preserve the individual as Heinrich claims (*Parmenides und Jona*, 142). Instead, it exemplifies the exasperation of the individual as the proprietor of the self in view of restoring a politics of the common. Although André Glucksman does not understand the Cynics in terms of an inversed relation between immunity and community, it is interesting to note that he describes Diogenes as "immune" against the reduction of his philosophical life to some kind of "academic testament": "cynicism is not a form of Diogenism [*le cynisme n'est pas un diogènisme*]. More a way of life than a doctrine, it resists being reduced into dogma, and, should that occur, it immediately generates equivocation [*Plus mode de vie que doctrine, il ne se laisse pas condenser en dogme et quand il s'y prête, il retrouve aussitôt l'équivoque*]" (*Cynisme et passion*, 128).

9. If the cosmopolitanism of the Cynics is nothing but the "other side [*Kehrseite*] of their individualism" as Gehlen claims (*Moral und Hypermoral*, 23), then this is so only because this "individualism" reverses an immunitary idea of the self, which is cut off from the other, into a communitary idea of the self, which is inseparable from and related to the life of the cosmos. On the cosmopolitanism of the Cynics, see also Goulet-Cazé, "Un syllogisme stoïcienne sur la loi dans la doxographie de Diogène le Cynique a propos de Diogène Laërce VI 72," who argues that cosmopolitanism in the Cynics is not a positive call for the realization of a universal human community but an individualist rejection of specific political and social arrangements. Instead, John Moles argues that the cosmopolitanism in the Cynics is a positive idea that not only refers to a special community of peers but indeed to the most universalistic idea of community, which includes also the life of the animals. Moles sees in the Cynic "polity of the cosmos" the "noblest of all the philosophical states [*politeiai*]—indeed, of all the political states—of all antiquity" ("Cynic Cosmopolitanism," 120).

10. Esposito, *Bios*, 84.

11. Esposito, *Communitas*.

12. For an extended discussion of problem of immunity and embodiment in Nietzsche and Esposito, see Lemm, "Nietzsche, Einverleibung, and the Politics of Immunity."

13. Nietzsche, *Human, All Too Human*.
14. Nietzsche, *Untimely Meditations*.
15. On the political implications of the Cynics' overcoming of shame, "the political barb [*Spitze*] of the cynical offensive," see notably Sloterdijk, *Critique of Cynical Reason*, 167.

BIBLIOGRAPHY

Note: For Michel Foucault sources cited parenthetically in the text, see the list of abbreviations in the front matter.

Ackerman, Bruce A., and Anne Alstot. *The Stakeholder Society*. New Haven: Yale University Press, 1999.
Afary, Janet. *Sexual Politics in Modern Iran*. Cambridge: Cambridge University Press, 2009.
Afary, Janet, and Kevin B. Anderson. *Foucault and the Iranian Revolution: Gender and the Seductions of Islamism*. Chicago: University of Chicago Press, 2005.
Agamben, Giorgio. "Absolute Immanence." In *Potentialities: Collected Essays in Philosophy*, 220–39. Stanford: Stanford University Press, 1999.
———. *Homo Sacer: Sovereign Power and Bare Life*. Translated by Daniel Heller-Roazen. Stanford: Stanford University Press, 1998.
———. *Il regno e la Gloria: Per una genealogia teologica dell'economia e del governo*. Torino: Bollati Boringhieri, 2009.
———. *Remnants of Auschwitz: The Witness and the Archive*. Stanford: Stanford University Press, 1999.
Ahmad, Aijaz. "Islam, Islamisms, and the West." In *Global Flashpoints: Reactions to Imperialism and Neoliberalism*, edited by Leo Panitch and Colin Leys, 43–62. New York: Monthly Review Press, 2008.
Althusser, Louis. "Ideology and Ideological State Apparatuses." In *Lenin and Philosophy, and Other Essays*, 127–86. New York: Monthly Review Press, 1971.
———. *Machiavelli and Us*. Edited by François Matheron; translated by Gregory Elliott. New York: Verso, 1999.
Arendt, Hannah. *The Life of the Mind*. New York: Harcourt, Brace, 1978.
Ariès, Philippe. *Essai sur la mort en Occident du Moyen Age à nos jours*. Paris: Seuil, 1975.
Aristotle. *Nicomachean Ethics*. Cambridge: Cambridge University Press, 2000.
———. *Politics: Books 1 and 2*. Oxford: Clarendon, 1995.

Aron, Raymond. *Peace and War: A Theory of International Relations.* New Brunswick, N.J.: Transaction Publishers, 2003.

Azari, Farah. "Sexuality and Women's Oppression in Iran." In *Women of Iran: The Conflict with Fundamentalist Islam,* edited by Farah Azari, 90–156. London: Ithaca Press, 1983.

Bacon, Francis. "De viis mortis, et de senectute retardanda, atque instaurandis viribus." In *Francis Bacon's Natural Philosophy: A New Source,* edited by Graham Rees and Christopher Upton. London: British Society for the History of Science, Monographs, 1984.

Baeck, Louis. "Aristotle as Mediterranean Economist." *Diogenes* 35 (1987): 81–104.

———. "The Economic Thought of Classical Islam." *Diogenes* 39 (1991): 99–114.

Balibar, Etienne. "Foucault et Marx: L'enjeu du nominalisme." In *La Crainte des Masses.* Paris: Galilée, 1997.

Bani-Sadr, Abol Hasan. *Eqtesad-e Tawhidi (Monotheistic Economics).* Place and publisher unknown, 1978.

———. *The Fundamental Principles and Precepts of Islamic Government.* Lexington, Ky.: Mazda Publishers, 1981

Barbaras, Renaud. *Le mouvement de l'existence: Études sur la phénoménologie de Jan Patočka.* Chatou: Éditions de la Transparence, 2007.

———. *L'ouverture du monde: Lecture de Jan Patočka.* Chatou: Éditions de la Transparence, 2011.

———. "Phenomenology and Henology." In *Jan Patočka and the Heritage of Phenomenology: Centenary Papers,* edited by Ivan Chvatìk and Erika Abrams, 99–110. New York: Springer, 2011.

Barry, Andrew, Thomas Osborne, and Nikolas Rose, eds. *Foucault and Political Reason: Liberalism, Neo-liberalism, and Rationalities of Government.* London: UCL Press, 1996.

Bartelson, Jens. "Making Exceptions: Some Remarks on the Concept of Coup d'état and Its History." *Political Theory* 25, no. 3 (1997): 323–46

Baud, Jean-Pierre. *L'affaire de la main volée: Une histoire juridique du corps.* Paris: Seuil, 1993.

Bazzicalupo, Laura. *Il governo delle vite: Biopolitica ed economia.* Bari: Laterza, 2006.

Becker, Gary. "Crime and Punishment: An Economic Approach." *Journal of Political Economy* 76, no. 2 (1968): 169–217.

———. *The Economics of Discrimination.* Chicago: University of Chicago Press, 1971.

———. *Human Capital.* New York: Columbia University Press, 1975.

———. "An Interview with Gary Becker, EconTalk Podcast, July 2006." Library of Economics and Liberty. http://www.econtalk.org/archives/2006/07/an_interview_wi.html (accessed July 30, 2010).

———. *Treatise on the Family*. Chicago: University of Chicago Press, 1981.
Behdad, Sohrab. "A Disputed Utopia: Islamic Economics in Revolutionary Iran." *Comparative Studies in Society and History* 36, no. 4 (1994): 775–813.
———. "The Post-revolutionary Economic Crisis." In *Iran after the Revolution: Crisis of an Islamic State*, edited by Saeed Rahnema and Sohrab Behdad, 97–128. London: Tauris, 1996.
Behrent, Michael C. "Accidents Happen: François Ewald, the 'Antirevolutionary' Foucault, and the Intellectual Politics of the French Welfare State." *Journal of Modern History* 82 (2010): 585–624.
———. "Liberalism without Humanism: Michel Foucault and the Free-Market Creed, 1976–1979." *Modern Intellectual History* 6, no. 3 (2009): 539–68.
———. "A Seventies Thing: On the Limits of Foucault's Neoliberalism Course for Understanding the Present." In *A Foucault for the 21st Century: Governmentality, Biopolitics, and Discipline in the New Millennium*, edited by Sam Binkley and Jorge Capetillo, 16–29. Newcastle upon Tyne: Cambridge Scholars Publishing, 2009.
Berns, Thomas. *Gouverner sans gouverner: Une archeologie politique de la statistique*. Paris: PUF, 2009.
Bichat, Xavier. "Anatomie générale." In *Recherches physiologiques sur la vie et la mort*. Paris: Flammarion, 1994.
———. *Physiological Researches upon Life and Death*. Philadelphia: Smith and Maxwell, 1809.
———. *Recherches physiologiques sur la vie et la mort*. Paris: Flammarion, 1994.
Bidet, Jacques. "Introduction à Idéologie et appareils idéologiques d'État." In *Sur la reproduction*, by Louis Althusser, 5–18. Paris: PUF, 1995.
Boltanski, Luc, and Eve Chiapello. *Le nouvel esprit du capitalisme*. Paris: Gallimard, 1999.
Bonnafous-Boucher, Maria. *Un libéralisme sans liberté: Du terme "libéralisme" dans la pensée de Michel Foucault*. Paris: L'Harmattan, 2001.
Borrelli, Gianfranco. *Non far novità: Alle radici della cultura italiana della conservazione politica*. Napoli: Bibliopolis, 2000.
———, ed. *Ragion di Stato: L'arte italiana della prudenza politica*. Napoli: Istituto italiano per gli studi filosofici; Archivio della ragion di Stato, 1993.
———. *Ragion di Stato e Leviatano*. Bologna: Il Mulino, 1993.
Bröckling, Ulrich. *Das unternehmerische Selbst: Soziologie einer Subjektivierungsform*. Frankfurt am Main: Suhrkamp, 2007.
Bröckling, Ulrich, Susanne Krassmann, and Thomas Lemke. *Gouvernementalität der Gegenwart: Studien zur Oekonmisierung des Sozialen*. Frankfurt: Suhrkamp, 2000.
Brossat, Alain. *La démocratie immunitaire*. Paris: La Dispute, 2003.
Burchell, Graham, Colin Gordon, and Peter Miller, eds. *The Foucault Effect: Studies in Governmentality*. Chicago: University of Chicago Press, 1991.

Butler, Judith. *The Psychic Life of Power.* Stanford: Stanford University Press, 1997.

———. "What Is Critique? An Essay on Foucault's Virtue." In *The Political*, edited David Ingram, 212–28. Oxford: Blackwell, 2002.

Caldwell, Bruce J. "Hayek's Transformation." *Journal of Political Economy* 20, no. 4 (1988): 513–41.

Canguilhem, Georges. *Études d'histoire et de philosophie des sciences.* Paris: Vrin, 1983.

———. *Le normal et le pathologique.* Paris: PUF, 1966.

———. *On the Normal and the Pathological.* Translated by Carolyn Fawcett. Boston: Dordrecht Reidel, 1978.

———. "Vie." In *Encyclopaedia Universalis* 23 (1989): 546–53.

———. *A Vital Rationalist: Selected Writings from Georges Canguilhem.* Edited by François Delaporte. New York: Zone Books, 1994.

Carozzi, Claude, and Huguette Taviani-Carozzi. *La fin des temps.* Paris: Flammarion, 1999.

Carrette, Jeremy. *Foucault and Religion.* London: Routledge, 1999.

Carrette, Jeremy, and James Bernauer, eds. *Michel Foucault and Theology: The Politics of Religious Experience.* London: Ashgate, 2004.

Castel, Robert. "From Dangerousness to Risk." In *The Foucault Effect: Studies in Governmentality*, edited by Graham Burchell, Colin Gordon, and Peter Miller, 281–98. Chicago: University of Chicago Press, 1991.

Celikates, Robin. "Communitas–Immunitas–Bíos: Roberto Espositos Politik der Gemeinschaft." In *Politik der Gemeinschaft: Zur Konstitution des Politischen in der Gegenwart*, edited by Janine Böckelmann and Claas Morgenroth, 49–67. Bielefeld: Transcript Verlag, 2008.

Chappell, Ben. "Rehearsals of the Sovereign: States of Exception and Threat Governmentality." *Cultural Dynamics* 18, no. 3 (2006): 313–34.

Cohn, Norman. *The Pursuit of the Millennium: Revolutionary Millenarians and Mystical Anarchists of the Middle Ages.* Oxford: Oxford University Press, 1970.

Colombel, Jeannette. "Michel Foucault et la dissidence tchécoslovaque." In *Michel Foucault, le jeux de la vérité et du pouvoir: Études transeuropéennes*, edited by Alain Brossat, 163–66. Nancy: PUN, 1994.

Conrad, Peter. *The Medicalization of Society: On the Transformation of Human Conditions into Treatable Disorders.* Baltimore: Johns Hopkins University Press, 2007.

Conseil d'État. *Sciences de la vie: De l'éthique au droit.* Paris: La documentation française, 1988

Cooper, Melinda. *Life as Surplus: Biotechnology and Capitalism in the Neoliberal Era.* Seattle: University of Washington Press, 2008.

———. "Pre-empting Emergence. The Biological Turn in the War on Terror." *Theory, Culture, and Society* 23, no. 4 (2006): 113–35.

Dabashi, Hamid. *Theology of Discontent: The Ideological Foundation of the Islamic Revolution*. New York: New York University Press, 1993.
Daniels, Norman. "Justice, Health, and Healthcare." *American Journal of Bioethics* 1, no. 2 (2001): 2–16.
Davidson, Arnold I. *The Emergence of Sexuality: Historical Epistemology and the Formation of Concepts*. Cambridge: Harvard University Press, 2004.
Davis, Mike. *Ecology of Fear*. New York: Vintage, 1998.
Dean, Mitchell. *Governmentality: Power and Rule in Modern Society*. London: Sage, 1999.
Deleuze, Gilles. *Foucault*. Translated by Sean Hand. Minneapolis: University of Minnesota Press, 1988.
Delumeau, Jean. "Les *artes moriendi* de la Renaissance et les 'Pensez-y bien' du XVIIe siècle." In *La Mort et l'immortalité: Encyclopédie des savoirs et des croyances*, edited by Frédéric Lenoir and Jean-Philippe de Tonnac, 209–24. Paris: Bayard, 2004.
———. *Une histoire du paradis, Tome 2: Mille ans de bonheur*. Paris: Hachette, 2002.
Demirović, Alex. "Liberale Freiheit und das Sicherheitsdispositiv: Der Beitrag von Michel Foucault: Gouvernementalität und Sicherheit." In *Zeitdiagnostische Beiträge im Anschluss an Foucault*, edited by Patricia Purtschert, Katrin Meyer, and Yves Winter, 229–50. Bielefeld: Transcript Verlag, 2008.
Derrida, Jacques. *Éperons: Les styles de Nietzsche*. Paris: Flammarion, 1978.
———. *The Gift of Death*. Chicago: University of Chicago Press, 1995.
Descola, Philippe. *Par-delà nature et culture*. Paris: Gallimard, 2006.
Detel, Wolfgang. *Foucault and Classical Antiquity: Power, Ethics and Knowledge*. Cambridge: Cambridge University Press, 2005.
Dillon, Michael. "Governing Terror: The State of Emergency of Biopolitical Emergence." *International Political Sociology* 1 (2007): 7–28.
———. "Governing through Contingency: The Security of Biopolitical Governance." *Political Geography* 26 (2007): 41–47.
Dillon, Michael, and Andrew Neal, eds. *Foucault on Politics, Security, and War*. London: Palgrave Macmillan, 2011.
DiQuattro, Arthur. "Rawls versus Hayek." *Political Theory* 14, no. 2 (1986): 307–10.
Dodds, James. "The Twentieth Century as War." In *Jan Patočka and the Heritage of Phenomenology: Centenary Papers*, edited by Ivan Chvatìk and Erika Abrams, 203–14. New York: Springer, 2011.
Downing, Lisa, ed. *The Cambridge Introduction to Michel Foucault*. Cambridge: Cambridge University Press, 2008.
Dupont, Nicolas-Alexandre. *L'impatience de la liberté: Éthique et politique chez Michel Foucault*. Paris: Éditions Kimé, 2010.
Durkheim, Emile. *Suicide: A Study in Sociology*. New York: Free Press, 1951.

Eribon, Didier. *Michel Foucault*. Cambridge: Harvard University Press, 1991.
Esposito, Roberto. *Bios: Biopolitics and Philosophy*. Minneapolis: University of Minnesota Press, 2008.
———. *Communitas: The Origin and Destiny of Community*. Translated by Timothy Campbell. Stanford: Stanford University Press, 2010.
———. *Immunitas: Protezione e negazione della vita*. Torino: Einaudi, 2002.
———. "Vom Unpolitischen zur Biopolitik." In *Das Politische und die Politik*, edited by Thomas Bedorf and Kurt Röttgers, 89–104. Frankfurt am Main: Suhrkamp, 2010.
Essid, Yassine. *A Critique of the Origins of Islamic Economic Thought*. Leiden: Brill, 1995.
Evink, Eddo. "The Relevance of Patočka's Negative Platonism." In *Jan Patočka and the Heritage of Phenomenology: Centenary Papers*, edited by Ivan Chvatìk and Erika Abrams, 57–70. New York: Springer, 2011.
Ewald, François. *Histoire de l'État providence*. Paris: Grasset, 1996.
Fassin, Didier. "Another Politics of Life Is Possible." *Theory, Culture, and Society* 26, no. 5 (2009): 44–60.
Feher, Michel. "Self-Appreciation: Or, the Aspirations of Human Capital." *Public Culture* 21, no. 1 (2009): 21–41.
Findlay, Edward F. *Caring for the Soul in a Postmodern Age: Politics and Phenomenology in the Thought of Jan Patočka*. Albany: State University of New York Press, 2002.
Fitzpatrick, Peter, and Ben Golder. *Foucault's Law*. London: Routledge, 2009.
Fontana, Alessandro. "Leggere Foucault, oggi." In *Foucault oggi*, edited by Mario Galzigna, 29–44. Milan: Feltrinelli, 2009.
Fontana, Alessandro, and Mauro Bertani. "Situating the Lectures." In *SMD*, 273–93.
Foucault, Michel. *Abnormal: Lectures at the Collège de France, 1974–1975*. Translated by Graham Burchell. New York: Picador, 2003.
———. "About the Beginning of the Hermeneutics of the Self: Transcription of Two Lectures in Dartmouth on Nov. 17 and 24, 1980." Edited by Mark Blasius. *Political Theory* 21, no. 2 (1993): 198–227.
———. "About the Concept of 'Dangerous Individual' in Nineteenth-Century Legal Psychiatry." In *PEW*, 176–200.
———. "The Battle for Chastity." In *EEW*, 185–98.
———. "Bio-histoire et bio-politique (1976)." In *DE*, 95–97.
———. *The Birth of the Clinic*. Translated by Alan M. Sheridan. New York: Vintage Books.
———. "The Birth of Social Medicine." In *PEW*, 134–56.
———. "Crise de la médecine ou crise de l'antimédecine (1976)." In *DE*, 40–58.
———. "Désormais, la sécurité est au-dessus des lois (1977)." In *DE*, 366–68.

———. "Dialogue between Michel Foucault and Baqir Parham (1979)." In *Foucault and the Iranian Revolution: Gender and the Seductions of Islamism*, edited by Janet Afary and Kevin B. Anderson, 183–89. Chicago: University of Chicago Press, 2005.

———. *Discipline and Punish: The Birth of the Prison*. Translated by Alan M. Sheridan. New York: Pantheon Books, 1977.

———. "The Eye of Power." In *Power/Knowledge: Selected Interviews and Other Writings, 1972–1977*, edited by Colin Gordon, 146–65. New York: Pantheon Books, 1980.

———. *Fearless Speech*. Edited by Joseph Pearson. New York: Semiotext(e), 2001.

———. "Foucault: By Maurice Florence." In *AEW*, 459–63.

———. "Foucault's Response to Atoussa H. (1979)." In *Foucault and the Iranian Revolution: Gender and the Seductions of Islamism*, edited by Janet Afary and Kevin B. Anderson, 210. Chicago: University of Chicago Press, 2005.

———. "Friendship as a Way of Life." In *EEW*, 135–40.

———. *Government of Self and Others: Lectures at the Collège de France, 1982–1983*. Translated by Graham Burchell. New York: Palgrave Macmillan, 2010.

———. *Du gouvernement des vivants: Cours au Collège de France, 1979–1980*. Edited by François Ewald, Michael Senellart, and Alessandro Fontana. Paris: Seuil, 2012.

———. *Histoire de la sexualité, 2: L'usage des plaisirs*. Paris: Gallimard, 1984.

———. *History of Madness*. Translated by Jean Khalfa. New York: Routledge, 2006.

———. "Human Nature: Justice vs. Power (1971): A Debate between Noam Chomsky and Michel Foucault." In *The Chomsky–Foucault Debate: On Human Nature*, 1–67. Edited by John Rajchman. New York: New Press, 2006.

———. "L'incorporation de l'hôpital dans la technologie moderne (1978)." In *DE*, 508–21.

———. "Interview with Michel Foucault: Interview Conducted by D. Trombadori (1978)." In *PEW*, 239–97.

———. "Interview with Michel Foucault: Interview with J. François and J. de Wit (1981)." In *DE*, 1475–86.

———. *Introduction to Kant's Anthropology*. Edited by Roberto Nigro. Los Angeles: Semiotext(e), 2008.

———."Is it Useless to Revolt? (1979)." In *Foucault and the Iranian Revolution: Gender and the Seductions of Islamism*, edited by Janet Afary and Kevin B. Anderson, 263–67. Chicago: University of Chicago Press, 2005.

———."Lettre à quelque leaders de la gauche (1977)." In *DE*, 388–90.

———. "The Life of Infamous Men." In *PEW*, 157–75.

———. "Michel Foucault, une interview: Sexe, pouvoir, et la politique de l'identité: Entretien de M. Foucault avec B. Gallagher et A. Wilson (1982)." In *DE*, 1554–66.

———. "The Moral and Social Experience of the Poles Can No Longer Be Obliterated." In *PEW*, 465–73.

———."La naissance de la médecine sociale (1977)." In *DE*, 207–28.

———. "Nietzsche, Genealogy, History." In *AEW*, 369–91.

———."On the Genealogy of Ethics: An Overview of Work in Progress." In *Michel Foucault: Beyond Structuralism and Hermeneutics*, edited by Hubert L. Dreyfus and Paul Rabinow, 229–52. Chicago: University of Chicago Press, 1983.

———."On the Ways of Writing History." In *AEW*, 279–96.

———. *The Order of Things: An Archeology of the Human Sciences*. New York: Vintage Books, 1994.

———. "The Political Technology of Individuals." In *PEW*, 403–417.

———. "La politique de la santé au XVIIIème siècle (1979)." In *DE*, 13–27.

———."A Powder Keg Called Islam (1979)." In *Foucault and the Iranian Revolution: Gender and the Seductions of Islamism*, edited by Janet Afary and Kevin B. Anderson, 239–41. Chicago: University of Chicago Press, 2005.

———."Polemics, Politics, and Problematizations: An Interview with Michel Foucault." In *EEW*, 111–19.

———."Power and Strategies." In *Power/Knowledge: Selected Interviews and Other Writings, 1972–1977*, edited by Colin Gordon, 134–45. New York: Pantheon Books, 1980.

———." 'Préface': Préface in Mireille Debard et Jean-Luc Henning, *Les juges kaki* (1977)." In *DE*, 138–40.

———. "A Revolt with Bare Hands (1979)." In *Foucault and the Iranian Revolution: Gender and the Seductions of Islamism*, edited by Janet Afary and Kevin B. Anderson, 210–13. Chicago: University of Chicago Press, 2005.

———."So Cruel a Knowledge." In *AEW*, 53–67.

———."La societé disciplinaire en crise (1978)." In *DE*, 532–34.

———. *La société punitive: Cours au Collège de France 1972–73*. Edited by François Ewald, Michael Senellart, and Alessandro Fontana. Paris: Seuil, 2013.

———. "Technologies of the Self." In *EEW*, 223–52.

———. "Tehran: Faith against the Shah (1978)." In *Foucault and the Iranian Revolution: Gender and the Seductions of Islamism*, edited by J. Afary and K. B. Anderson, 198–203. Chicago: University of Chicago Press, 2005.

———."La torture, c'est la raison (1977)." In *DE*, 390–98.

———. "La vie des hommes infâmes (1977)." In *DE*, 237–53.

———."What Are the Iranians Dreaming About? (1979)." In *Foucault and the Iranian Revolution: Gender and the Seductions of Islamism*, edited by Janet Afary and Kevin B. Anderson, 203–10. Chicago: University of Chicago Press, 2005.

Frankenberg, Günter. "Nochmals: Angst im Rechtsstaat." *WestEnd* 3, no. 2 (2006): 55–63.

Freeman, Samuel. *Rawls*. New York: Routledge, 2007.
Freund, Julien. "La situation exceptionelle comme justification de la raison d'état chez Gabriel Naudé." In *Staatsräson: Studien zur Geschichte eines politischen Begriffs*, edited by Roman Schnur, 141–64. Berlin: Dunker und Humblot, 1975.
Friedman, Milton. *Capitalism and Freedom*. Chicago: University of Chicago Press, 1962.
Galzigna, Mario, ed. *Foucault oggi*. Milan: Feltrinelli, 2009.
Gane, Mike. "Foucault on Governmentality and Liberalism." *Theory, Culture, and Society* 25, nos. 7–8 (2008): 353–63.
Garo, Isabelle. *Foucault, Deleuze, Althusser, et Marx: La politique dans la philosophie*. Paris: Éditions Demopolis, 2011.
Gehlen, Arnold. *Moral und Hypermoral: Eine pluralistische Ethik*. Frankfurt: Athenäum Verlag, 1969.
Gehring, Petra. "Foucaults 'juridischer' Machttyp, die *Geschichte der Gouvernamentalität* und die Frage nach Foucaults Rechtstheorie." In *Michel Foucaults "Geschichte der Gouvernementalität" in den Sozialwissenschaften*, edited by Michael Volkmer and Susanne Krasmann, 157–80. Bielefeld: Transcript Verlag, 2007.
Geyer, Christian, ed. *Biopolitik: Die Positionen*. Frankfurt am Main: Suhrkamp, 2001.
Glucksmann, André. *Cynisme et passion*. Paris: Bernard Grasset, 1981.
Golder, Ben. "Foucault and the Unfinished Human of Rights." *Law, Culture, and the Humanities* 6, no. 3 (2010): 354–74.
Gorski, Philip. *The Disciplinary Revolution: Calvinism and the Rise of the State in Modern Europe*. Chicago: University of Chicago Press, 2003.
Goulet-Cazé, Marie-Odile. "Un syllogisme stoïcienne sur la loi dans la doxographie de Diogène le Cynique a propos de Diogène Laërce VI 72." *Rheinisches Museum für Philologie* 115 (1982): 214–40.
Gros, Frédéric. "Course Context." In *HS*, 507–50.
———. "Nouvelles menaces, nouvelles sécurités." *Raisons politiques* 32, no. 4 (2008): 5–7.
———. "Désastre humanitaire et sécurité humaine: Le troisième âge de la sécurité." *Esprit* 3 (2008), dossier "Le temps des catastrophes": 51–67.
Guidieri, Remo. *Ombre*. Milan: Medusa, 2005.
Gutting, Gary, ed. *Cambridge Companion to Foucault*. Cambridge: Cambridge University Press, 1999.
Habermas, Jürgen. *Die Zukunft der menschlichen Natur: Auf dem Weg zu einer liberalen Eugenik?* Frankfurt am Main: Suhrkamp, 2005.
Hadot, Pierre. *Exercises spirituels et philosophy antique*. Paris: Études Augustiniennes, 1987.
———. *Philosophy as a Way of Life: Spiritual Exercises from Socrates to Foucault*. Malden, Mass.: Blackwell, 1995.

———. *What Is Ancient Philosophy?* Cambridge: Harvard University Press, 2002.

Hardt, Michael, and Antonio Negri. *Empire.* Cambridge: Harvard University Press, 2000.

Hartwell, Ronald Max. *A History of the Mont Pelerin Society.* Indianapolis: Liberty Fund, 1995

Have, Henk ten. "Geneticization: The Sociocultural Impact of Gentechnology." In *Genetics and Ethics: An Interdisciplinary Study,* edited by Gerard Magill, 80–100. Saint Louis: Saint Louis University Press, 2004.

Havel, Václav. *The Power of the Powerless: Citizens against the State in Central-Eastern Europe.* Edited by J. Keane. Armonk, N.Y.: M. E. Sharpe, 1985.

Haverkamp, Anselm. *Latenzzeit: Wissen im Nachkrieg.* Berlin: Kadmos, 2004.

Hayek, Friedrich A. "Nomos: The Law of Liberty." In *Law, Legislation and Liberty, Vol. 1: Rules and Orders,* 94–124. London: Routledge, 1973.

———. "The Principles of a Liberal Social Order," "Two Pages of Fiction: The Impossibility of Socialist Calculation," and "The Use of Knowledge in Society." In *The Essence of Hayek,* edited by Chiaki Nishiyama and Kurt Leube. Stanford, Calif.: Hoover Institution Press, 1984.

Heath, Iona. *Matters of Life and Death.* Abingdon: Radcliffe, 2008.

Hegel, Georg Wilhelm Friedrich. *The Philosophy of Nature: Encyclopaedia of the Philosophical Sciences (1830), Part II.* Translated by A. V. Miller. Oxford: Oxford University Press, 2004.

Heidegger, Martin. *Being and Time.* Translated by Joan Stambaugh. Malden, Mass.: Blackwell, 1962.

Heinrich, Klaus. *Parmenides und Jona: Vier Studien über das Verhältnis von Philosophie und Mythologie.* Frankfurt: Surhkamp Verlag, 1966.

Heinzelmann, Markus, and Martina Weinhart, eds. *Auf eigene Gefahr.* Frankfurt am Main: Schirn Kunsthalle, 2003.

Hobbes, Thomas. *Leviathan.* Oxford: Oxford University Press, 1996.

Hochschild, Arlie Russell. "Bush Hijacks American Fear." In *Entstaatlichung und Soziale Sicherheit: Verhandlungen des 31. Kongresses der Deutschen Gesellschaft für Soziologie in Leipzig, 2002, Vol. 1,* edited by Jutta Allmendinger, 110–13. Opladen: Leske + Budrich, 2003.

Holert, Tom. "Angst essen Seele auf." *Jungle World* 45 (October 2001): 24–25.

———. "Sicherheit." In *Glossar der Gegenwart,* edited by Ulrich Bröckling, Susanne Krasmann, and Thomas Lemke, 244–50. Frankfurt am Main: Suhrkamp, 2004.

Iervolino, Domenico. "At the Origins of Neo-liberalism: The Free Economy and the Strong State, 1930–1947." *Historical Journal* 53, no. 1 (2010): 129–51.

———. "Reading Patočka, in Search for a Philosophy of Translation." In *Jan Patočka and the Heritage of Phenomenology,* edited by Ivan Chvatìk and Erika Abrams, 121–34. New York: Springer, 2011

Illich, Ivan. *Limits to Medicine: Medical Nemesis: The Expropriation of Health.* London: Boyars, 1976.

Jackson, Ben. "At the Origins of Neo-liberalism: The Free Economy and the Strong State, 1930–1947." *Historical Journal* 53 no. 1 (2010): 129–51.

———. "Revisionism Reconsidered: 'Property-Owning Democracy' and Egalitarian Strategy in Post-war Britain." *Twentieth Century British History* 16, no. 4 (2005): 416–40.

Kaldor, Mary. *Human Security.* Cambridge: Polity Press, 2007.

Katouzian, Homa. "Review: *The Fundamental Principles and Precepts of Islamic Government* by Abolhassan Banisadr." *Iranian Studies* 16, nos. 1–2 (1983): 81–84.

———. "Shi'ism and Islamic Economics: Sadr and Bani Sadr." In *Religion and Politics in Iran: Shi'ism from Quietism to Revolution,* edited by Nikki R. Keddie, 145–65. New Haven: Yale University Press, 1983.

Keane, John. *Václav Havel: A Political Tragedy in Six Acts.* New York: Basic Books, 1999.

Kelly, Gavin, and Rachel Lissauer. *Ownership for All.* London: Institute for Public Policy Research, 2000.

Kerenyi, Carl. "Introduction." In *Dionysos: Archetypal Image of Indestructible Life,* 1–37. Princeton: Princeton University Press, 1996.

Khomeini, Ruhollah. *Sahifeh-ye Nur.* Vol. 1. Introduction by Sayyid Ali Khamenei. Tehran: Sorush, 1982.

———. *Sayings of the Ayatollah Khomeini: Political, Philosophical, Social, and Religious: Extracts from Three Major Works by the Ayatollah, Valayate-Faghih (The Kingdom of the Learned), Kashfol-asrar (The Key to Mysteries), Towzihol-Masael (The Explanation of Problems).* New York: Bantam, 1980

Kojève, Alexander. *Introduction to the Reading of Hegel.* Ithaca: Cornell University Press, 1980.

Krasmann, Susanne. *Die Kriminalität der Gesellschaft: Zur Gouvernementalität der Gegenwart.* Konstanz: Universitätsverlag Konstanz, 2003.

Krasmann, Susanne, and Michael Volkmer, eds. *Michel Foucaults "Geschichte der Gouvernementalität" in den Sozialwissenschaften.* Bielefeld: Transcript Verlag, 2007.

Krouse, Richard, and Michael McPherson. "Capitalism, 'Property-Owning Democracy,' and the Welfare State." In *Democracy and the Welfare State,* edited by Amy Gutmann, 79–105. Princeton: Princeton University Press, 1988.

Kundera, Milan. *The Unbearable Lightness of Being.* New York: Harper and Row, 1984.

Kuran, Timur. *Islam and Mammon: The Economic Predicaments of Islamism.* Princeton: Princeton University Press, 2004.

Landry, Jean-Michel. "Confession, Obedience, and Subjectivity: Michel Foucault's Unpublished Lectures on the Government of the Living." *Telos* (Spring 2009): 111–23.

Larmore, Charles. "Public Reason." In *The Cambridge Companion to Rawls*, edited by Samuel Freeman, 368–93. Cambridge: Cambridge University Press, 2003.

Lazzarato, Maurizio. *Expérimentations politiques*. Paris: Éditions Amsterdam, 2009.

———. *Lavoro immateriale: Forme di vita e produzione di soggettivita*. Rome: Ombre Corte, 1997.

Lebaron, Frédéric. "De la critique de l'économie á l'action syndicale." In *L'infrequentable Michel Foucault*, edited by Didier Eribon, 157–67. Paris: EPEI, 2001.

Le Blanc, Guillaume. *Canguilhem et les normes*. Paris: PUF, 1998.

Lefort, Claude. *Le travail de l'oeuvre de Machiavel*. Paris: Gallimard, 1972.

Legnaro, Aldo. "Aus der Neuen Welt: Freiheit, Furcht und Strafe als Trias der Regulation." *Leviathan* 28 (2000): 202–20.

———. "Konturen der Sicherheitsgesellschaft: Eine polemisch futurologische Skizze." *Leviathan* 25 (1997): 271–84.

Legrand, Stéphane. *Les normes chez Foucault*. Paris: PUF, 2007.

Lemke, Thomas. *Biopolitics: An Advanced Introduction*. New York: New York University Press, 2011.

———. *Biopolitik zur Einfür*. Hamburg: Junius, 2007.

———. "Critique and Experience in Foucault." *Theory, Culture, and Society* 28, no. 4 (2011): 26–48.

———. *Eine Kritik der politischen Vernunft: Foucaults Analyse der modernen Gouvernamentalität*. Hamburg: Argument, 1997.

———. "Foucault, Governmentality, and Critique." *Rethinking Marxism* 14, no. 3 (2002): 49–64.

———. "'Freiheit ist die Garantie der Freiheit': Michel Foucault und die Menschenrechte." *Vorgänge: Zeitschrift für Bürgerrechte und Gesellschaftspolitik* 40, no. 3 (2001): 270–76.

———. *Gouvernamentalität und Biopolitik*. Wiesbaden: VS Verlag für Sozialwissenschaften, 2008.

———. "'Marx sans guillemets': Foucault, la gouvernementalité et la critique du néoliberalisme." *Actuel Marx* 36, no. 2 (2004): 13–26.

Lemke, Thomas, Susan Krasmann, and Ulrich Bröckling. "Gouvernementalität, Neoliberalismus und Selbsttechnologien: Eine Einleitung." In *Gouvernementalität der Gegenwart: Studien zur Ökonomisierung des Sozialen*, edited by Thomas Lemke, Ulrich Bröckling, and Susanne Krasmann, 7–40. Frankfurt am Main: Suhrkamp, 2000.

Lemm, Vanessa. "Nietzsche, Einverleibung, and the Politics of Immunity." *International Journal of Philosophical Studies* 21, no. 1 (2013): 3–19.

Lepage, Henri. *Demain le capitalisme*. Paris: Librairie Générale Française, 1978.

Lobo-Guerrero, Luis. *Insuring Security: Biopolitics, Security and Risk*. London: Routledge, 2010.
Locke, John. *Second Treatise of Government*. Indianapolis: Hackett, 1980.
Macey, David. *The Lives of Michel Foucault*. London: Hutchinson, 1993.
Macherey, Pierre. "Normes vitales et normes sociales dans l'Essai sur quelques problèmes concernant le normal et le pathologique de Georges Canguilhem." In *Actualité de Georges Canguilhem: Le normal et le pathologique: Actes du Xe colloque international d'histoire de la psychiatrie et de la psychanalyse*, edited by François Bing, Jean-François Braunstein, and Élisabeth Roudinesco, 71–84. Paris: Institut Synthélabo pour le progrès de la connaissance, coll. "Les empêcheurs de penser en rond," 1998.
Marin, Louis. *On Representation*. Stanford: Stanford University Press, 2001.
———. *Portrait of the King*. Minneapolis: University of Minnesota Press, 1988.
———. "Pour une théorie baroque de l'action politique." In *Considérations politiques*, by Gabriel Naudé. Paris: Les éditions de Paris, 1988.
Marx, Karl. *Economic and Philosophic Manuscripts of 1844*. Translated by Martin Milligan. New York: Prometheus Books, 1988.
Marzocca, Ottavio. *Perché il governo: Il laboratorio etico–politico di Foucault*. Rome: Manifestolibri, 2007.
———. "Philosophical *Parresia* and Transpolitical Freedom." *Foucault Studies* 15 (2013): 129–47.
Massumi, Brian. "Everywhere You Want to Be: Introduction to Fear." In *The Politics of Everyday Fear*, edited by Brian Massumi, 3–57. Minneapolis: University of Minnesota Press, 1993.
Meade, James Edward. *Efficiency, Equality and the Ownership of Property*. London: Allen and Unwin, 1964.
Meinecke, Friedrich. *Machiavellism: The Doctrine of Raison d'État and Its Place in Modern History*. New Brunswick, N.J.: Transaction Publishers, 1998
Merlier, P. S. *Patočka: Le soin de l'âme et l'Europe*. Paris: L'Harmattan, 2009.
Mirowski, Philip. "Naturalizing the Market on the Road to Revisionism: Bruce Caldwell's 'Hayek's Challenge' and the Challenge of Hayek Interpretation." *Journal of Institutional Economics* 3, no. 3 (2007): 351–72.
Mirowski, Philip, and Dieter Plehwe, eds. *The Road from Mont Pèlerin: The Making of the Neoliberal Thought Collective*. Cambridge: Harvard University Press, 2009.
Mitropoulos, Angela. "Oikopolitics, and Storms." *The Global South* 3, no. 1 (2009): 66–82.
Moallem, Minoo. *Between Warrior Brother and Veiled Sister: Islamic Fundamentalism and the Politics of Patriarchy in Iran*. Berkeley: University of California Press, 2005.
Moheau, Jean-Baptiste. *Recherches et considérations sur la population de la France*. Paris: PUF, 1994.

Moles, John L. "Cynic Cosmopolitanism." In *The Cynics: The Cynics Movement in Antiquity and Its Legacy*, edited by R. Bracht Branham and Marie-Odile Goulet-Cazé, 105–20. Berkeley: University of California Press, 1996.
Monahan, Torin. *Surveillance in the Time of Insecurity*. New Brunswick: Rutgers University Press, 2010.
Montaigne, Michel de. "To Philosophize Is to Learne How to Dye." In *Montaigne's Essays*, vol. 1, translated by John Florio, 73–92. London: Everyman's Library, 1965.
Moss, Jeremy, ed. *The Later Foucault: Politics and Philosophy*. London: Sage, 1998.
Muhle, Maria. *Eine Genealogie der Biopolitik: Zum Begriff des Lebens bei Foucault und Canguilhem*. Bielefeld: Transcript Verlag, 2008.
———. "Zweierlei Vitalismus." In *Philosophie und Nicht-Philosophie: Gilles Deleuze–Aktuelle Diskussionen*, edited by Friedrich Balke and Marc Rölli. Bielefeld: Transcript Verlag, 2010.
Nadesan, Majia Holmer. *Governmentality, Biopower, and Everyday Life*. New York: Routledge, 2008.
Napoli, Paolo. *Naissance de la police moderne: Pouvoir, normes, société*. Paris: La Découverte, 2003.
Naudé, Gabriel. *Considérations politiques sur les coups d'états*. Paris: Les éditions de Paris, 1988.
Nealon, Jeffrey T. *Foucault beyond Foucault: Power and Its Intensification since 1984*. Stanford: Stanford University Press, 2008.
Negri, Antonio. *Insurgencies: Constituent Power and the Modern State*. Minneapolis: University of Minnesota Press, 1999.
———. "Pour Althusser: Notes sur l'évolution de la pensée du dernier Althusser." In *Futur antérieur, Sur Althusser: Passages*, 73–96. Paris: L'Harmattan, 1993.
Negri, Antonio, and Michael Hardt. *Commonwealth*. Cambridge: Harvard University Press, 2009.
Nietzsche, Friedrich. *Beyond Good and Evil: A Prelude to a Philosophy of the Future*. Translated by William Kaufmann. New York: Vintage Books, 1989.
———. *The Gay Science*. Translated by Josefine Nauckoff. Cambridge: Cambridge University Press, 2001.
———. *Human, All Too Human*. Translated by R. J. Hollingdale. Cambridge: Cambridge University Press, 1986.
———. *On the Genealogy of Morals*. Translated by Carol Diethe. Cambridge: Cambridge University Press, 1994.
———. *Sämtliche Werke: Kritische Studienausgabe in 15 Bänden*. Edited by Giorgio Colli and Mazzino Montinari. Berlin: de Gruyter Verlag, 1988.
———. *Untimely Meditations*. Translated by R. J. Hollingdale. Cambridge: Cambridge University Press, 1997.

Nigro, Roberto. "Foucault, Reader and Critic of Marx." In *Critical Companion to Contemporary Marxism*, edited by Jacques Bidet and Eustache Kouvélakis, 646–62. Boston: Brill Academic Press, 2007.

———. "La question de l'anthropologie dans l'interprétation althussérienne de Marx." In *Althusser: Une lecture de Marx*, edited by Jean-Claude Bourdin, 87–111. Paris: PUF, 2008.

———. "Quelques remarques sur les enjeux d'une confrontation entre Foucault et Marx." In *Cahier de l'Herne: Foucault*, 143–48. Paris: L'Herne, 2011.

Nigro, Roberto, and Gerald Raunig. "Molecular Revolution and Event." *Pages* 8 (May 2011): 115–25.

O'Leary, Timothy, and Christopher Falzon, eds. *Foucault and Philosophy*. London: Wiley-Blackwell, 2010.

O'Malley, Pat. "Uncertain Subjects: Risks, Liberalism, and Contract." *Economy and Society* 29 (2000): 460–84.

O'Neill, Martin, and Thad Williamson, eds. *Property-Owning Democracy: Rawls and Beyond*. Chichester: Wiley-Blackwell, 2012.

Opitz, Sven. "Zwischen Sicherheitsdispositiven und Securitization: Zur Analytik illiberaler Gouvernementalität." In *Gouvernementalität und Sicherheit: Zeitdiagnostische Beiträge im Anschluss an Foucault*, edited by Patricia Purtschert, Katrin Meyer, and Yves Winter, 201–28. Bielefeld: Transcript Verlag, 2008.

Östreich, Gerhard. *Neostoicism and the Early Modern State*. Cambridge: Cambridge University Press, 1982.

Patočka, Jan. "Does History Have a Meaning?" In *Heretical Essays in the Philosophy of History*, edited by James Dodd, 53–78. Chicago: Open Court, 1996.

———. "Entretien avec Jan Patočka (1967)." In *Jan Patočka: Philosophie, phénoménologie, politique*, edited by Etienne Tassin and Marc Richir. Grenoble: Millon, 1992.

———. "L'homme spirituel et l'intellectuel (1975)." In *Liberté et sacrifice: Écrits politiques*, edited by Jan Patočka. Grenoble: Millon, 1990.

———. "Is Technological Civilization Decadent, and Why?" in In *Heretical Essays in the Philosophy of History*, edited by James Dodd, 95–118. Chicago: Open Court, 1996.

———. *Le monde naturel et le mouvement de l'existence humaine*. Dordrecht: Kluwer, 1989.

———. "The Movement of Human Existence (1968)." In *Philosophy and Selected Writings*, edited by Erazim Kohák, 274–84. Chicago: University of Chicago Press, 1989.

———. "Negative Platonism: Reflections Concerning the Rise, the Scope, and the Demise of Metaphysics—and Whether Philosophy Can Survive It." In *Philosophy and Selected Writings*, edited by Erazim Kohák, 175–206. Chicago: University of Chicago Press, 1989.

———. *Plato and Europe*. Stanford: Stanford University Press, 2002.

———. *Socrate: Lezioni di filosofia antica*. Edited by Giuseppe Girgenti. Milan: Rusconi 1999.
———. "Wars of the Twentieth Century and Twentieth Century as War." In *Heretical Essays in the Philosophy of History*, edited by James Dodd, 119–38. Chicago: Open Court, 1996.
Patton, Paul. "Foucault, Critique, and Rights." *Critical Horizons* 6, no. 1 (2005): 267–87.
———. "Foucault and Normative Political Philosophy." In *Foucault and Philosophy*, edited by Timothy O'Leary and Christopher Falzon, 204–21. Chichester: Wiley-Blackwell, 2010.
Pecora, Vincent P. *Households of the Soul*. Baltimore: Johns Hopkins University Press, 1997.
Petersen, Alan, and Ian Wilkinson, eds. *Health, Risk, and Vulnerability*. New York: Routledge, 2008.
Picq, Jean. *Václav Havel: La force des sans-pouvoir*. Paris: Michalon, 2000.
Plato. *Phaedo*. Cambridge: Harvard University Press, 2005.
Pomeroy, Sarah B. "Introduction." In *Oeconomicus: A Social and Historical Commentary*, by Xenophon, 1–101. Oxford: Clarendon Press, 1994.
Post, Gaines. *Studies in Medieval Legal Thought*. Princeton: Princeton University Press, 1964.
Prasad, Monica. "Why Is France So French? Culture, Institutions, and Neoliberalism, 1974–1981." *American Journal of Sociology* 111, no. 2 (2005): 357–407.
Purtschert, Patricia, Katrin Meyer, and Yves Winter, eds. *Gouvernementalität und Sicherheit: Zeitdiagnostische Beitraege in Aschluss an Foucault*. Bielefeld: Transcript Verlag, 2008.
Rachels, James. *The End of Life: Euthanasia and Morality*. Oxford: Oxford University Press, 1987.
Raimondi, Francesca. "'Diese andere Sache': Agamben Foucault und die Politik der Menschenrechte." In *Biopolitische Konstellationen*, edited by Maria Muhle and Kathrin Thiele. Berlin: August Verlag, 2010.
Rancière, Jacques. *Hatred of Democracy*. London: Verso, 2009.
———. *La Mésentente: Politique et Philosophie*. Paris: Galilée, 1995.
———. *The Politics of Aesthetics: The Distribution of the Sensible*. London: Verso, 2004.
Rawls, John. *Justice as Fairness: A Restatement*. Cambridge: Harvard University Press, 2001.
———. *Political Liberalism*. Exp. ed. New York: Columbia University Press, 2005.
———. *A Theory of Justice*. Rev. ed. Cambridge: Harvard University Press, 1999.
Read, Jason. "A Genealogy of Homo-Economicus: Neoliberalism and the Production of Subjectivity." *Foucault Studies* 6 (2009): 25–36.

Revel, Judith. "La naissance littéraire de la biopolitique." In *Michel Foucault, la littérature et les arts: Acts du colloque du Cerisy, juin 2001*, edited by Philippe Artières, 47–70. Paris: Kimé, 2004.

———. *Le parole e i poteri: Dalla trasgressione letteraria alla resistenza politica*. Rome: Manifestolibri, 1996.

Rheinberger, Hans-Joerg. *An Epistemology of the Concrete: Twentieth-Century Histories of Life*. Durham: Duke University Press, 2010.

Ricoeur, Paul "Préface aux *Essais hérétiques* (1981)." In *Lectures 1: Autour du politique*, 74–83. Paris: Seuil, 2001.

Riesebrodt, Martin. *Pious Passion: The Emergence of Modern Fundamentalism in the United States and Iran*. Berkeley: University of California Press, 1993.

Robin, Corey. *Fear: The History of a Political Idea*. Oxford: Oxford University Press, 2004.

Roemer, John E. *A Future for Socialism*. Cambridge: Harvard University Press, 1994.

Rose, Nikolas. *The Politics of Life Itself: Biomedicine, Power, and Subjectivity in the Twenty-First Century*. Princeton: Princeton University Press, 2007.

Roy, Olivier. *The Failure of Political Islam*. Cambridge: Harvard University Press, 2001.

Saar, Martin. *Genealogie als Kritik: Geschichte und Theorie des Subjekts nach Nietzsche und Foucault*. Frankfurt am Main: Campus, 2007.

Sarasin, Philipp. *Foucault zur Einführung*. Hamburg: Junius, 2005.

Schiera, Pierangelo. "La conception Wébérienne de la discipline et le theme de la 'Lebensführung.'" *Scienza e politica: Per una storia delle dottrine* 8 (1993): 73–91.

Schmitt, Carl. *The Nomos of the Earth in the International Law of Jus Publicum Europaeum*. New York: Telos Press, 2003.

———. *Political Theology: Four Chapters on the Concept of Sovereignty*. Boston: MIT Press, 1985.

Sedghi, Hamideh. *Women and Politics in Iran: Veiling, Unveiling, and Reveiling*. Cambridge: Cambridge University Press, 2007.

Senellart, Michel. *Les arts de gouverner: Du regimen médiéval au concept de gouvernement*. Paris: Seuil, 1995.

———. "Course Context." In *STP*, 369–401.

———. "Dalla ragion di Stato al liberalismo: Genesi della 'governamentalità' moderna." In *Foucault oggi*, edited by Mario Galzigna, 190–204. Milan: Feltrinelli, 2009.

———. *Machiavellisme et Raison d'État*. Paris: PUF, 1989.

———. "La question du libéralisme." *Le Magazine Littéraire* 435 (2004): 55–56.

Shahidian, Hammed. *Women in Iran: Gender Politics in the Islamic Republic*. Westport, Conn.: Greenwood Press, 2002.

Singer, Peter W. *Corporate Warriors: The Rise of the Privatized Military Industry*. Ithaca: Cornell University Press, 2007.

Skinner, Quentin. *Liberty before Liberalism*. Cambridge: Cambridge University Press, 1998.

———. *Visions of Politics, Volume II: Renaissance Virtues*. Cambridge: Cambridge University Press, 2002.

Sloterdijk, Peter. *Critique of Cynical Reason*. Minneapolis: University of Minnesota Press, 1987.

Spieker, Jörg. "Defending the Open Society: Foucault, Hayek, and the Problem of Biopolitical Order." *Economy and Society* 42, no. 2 (2013): 304–21.

Spinoza, Benedict de. *Political Treatise*. Translated by Samuel Shirley. Indianapolis: Hackett, 2000.

Steiner, Philippe. "Foucault, Weber, and the History of the Economic Subject." *European Journal of the History of Economic Thought* 15, no. 3 (2008): 503–27.

Stolleis, Michael. "L'idée de la raison d'État de Friedrich Meinecke et la recherche actuelle." In *Raison et déraison d'État*, edited by Yves Zarka, 11–39. Paris: PUF, 1994.

———. *Staat und Staatsräson in der frühen Neuzeit: Studien zur Geschichte der öffentlichen Rechts*. Frankfurt am Main: Suhrkamp, 1990.

Szakolczai, Árpad. "Foucault passe à l'Est: Liens et interactions." In *Michel Foucault, le jeux de la vérité et du pouvoir: Études transeuropéennes*, edited by Alain Brossat, 101–10. Nancy: PUN, 1994.

Tenenti, Alberto. *Il senso della morte e l'amore della vita nel Rinascimento*. Turin: Einaudi, 1997.

Terrel, Jean. *Politiques de Foucault*. Paris: PUF, 2010.

Thuau, Etienne. *Raison d'État et pensée politique à l'époque de Richelieu*. Paris: Albin Michel, 2000.

Tillich, Paul. *The Courage to Be*. New Haven: Yale University Press, 1952.

Tripp, Charles. *Islam and the Moral Economy*. Cambridge: Cambridge University Press, 2006.

Ullmann, Tamás "Negative Platonism and the Appearance Problem." In *Jan Patočka and the Heritage of Phenomenology: Centenary Papers*, edited by Ivan Chvatík and Erika Abrams, 71–86. New York: Springer, 2011.

Valibeigi, Mehrdad. "Banking and Credit Rationing under the Islamic Republic of Iran." *Iranian Studies* 25, nos. 3–4 (1992): 51–65.

Valverde, Mariana. "Law versus History: Foucault's Genealogy of Modern Sovereignty." In *Foucault on Politics, Security, and War*, edited by Michael Dillon and Andrew Neal, 135–50. Hampshire: Palgrave Macmillan, 2011.

Vatter, Miguel. *Between Form and Event: Machiavelli's Theory of Political Freedom*. Boston: Kluwer, 2000.

———. "Biopolitics: From Surplus Value to Surplus Life." *Theory and Event* 12, no. 2 (2009).

———. "The Idea of Public Reason and the Reason of State: Schmitt and Rawls on the Political." *Political Theory* 36, no. 2 (2008): 239–71.

———. "Machiavelli after Marx: The Self-Overcoming of Marxism in the Late Althusser." *Theory and Event* 7, no. 4 (2004): 44 pgs.

———. "The People Shall Be Judge: Reflective Judgment and Constituent Power in Kant's Philosophy of Law." *Political Theory* 39, no. 6 (2011): 749–76.

———. "Pettit and Modern Republican Political Thought." In *Political Exclusion and Domination: NOMOS XLVI*, edited by Melissa Williams and Steven Macedo, 118–63. New York: New York University Press, 2005.

Viroli, Maurizio. *From Politics to Reason of State: The Acquisition and Transformation of Language of Politics, 1250–1600*. Cambridge: Cambridge University Press, 1992.

———. "The Revolution in the Concept of Politics." *Political Theory* 20, no 3 (1992): 473–95.

Wacquant, Loïc. "Ordering Insecurity: Social Polarization and the Punitive Upsurge." *Radical Philosophy Review* 11, no. 1 (2008): 9–27.

Weldes, Jutta, Mark Laffey, Hugh Gusterson, and Raymond Duvall, eds. *Cultures of Insecurity: States, Communities, and the Production of Danger*. Minneapolis: University of Minnesota Press, 1999.

Wittgenstein, Ludwig. *Lectures and Conversations on Aesthetics, Psychology, and Religious Belief.* Edited by Cyril Barrett. Berkeley: University of California Press, 1966.

Zarka, Yves-Charles. "Raison d'État, maximes d'État et coups d'État chez Gabriel Naudé." In *Raison et déraison d'État*, edited by Yves Zarka, 152–69. Paris: PUF, 1994.

Ziegler, Jean. *Les vivants et la mort*. Paris: Seuil, 1975.

Žižek, Slavoj. *Did Somebody Say Totalitarianism? Five Interventions in the (Mis)use of a Notion*. London: Verso, 2001.

CONTRIBUTORS

FRANCESCO PAOLO ADORNO is Professor of Moral Philosophy at the University of Salerno, Italy. He specializes in the thought of Michel Foucault and modern moral and political philosophy. His most recent book is *Le désir d'une vie illimitée: Anthropologie et biopolitique* (Paris, 2011).

MELINDA COOPER is Senior Research Fellow in the Department of Sociology and Social Policy at the University of Sydney, Australia. She is the author of *Life as Surplus: Biotechnology and Capitalism in the Neoliberal Era* (Seattle, 2008); and, with Catherine Waldby, of *Clinical Labor: Tissue Donors and Research Subjects in the Global Bioeconomy* (Durham, 2008). She is currently working on a monograph titled *The Fundamentals of Desire: Post-Fordist Family Values*.

SIMONA FORTI is Professor of Philosophy, University of Eastern Piedmont, Italy. She is the author of books on Hannah Arendt and totalitarianism. Her most recent work is *I nuovi demoni: Ripensare oggi male e potere* (Milan, 2012), with an English translation forthcoming from Stanford University Press.

FRÉDÉRIC GROS is Professor of Philosophy at University of Paris 12, France. He has edited several of Foucault's Courses for Seuil–Gallimard. He is author of several monographs and edited volumes on Foucault. Among his recent works are *States of Violence: An Essay on the End of War* (London, 2010); and *Le principe securité* (Paris, 2012).

THOMAS LEMKE is Professor of Sociology with a Focus on Biotechnologies, Nature, and Society at the Johann Wolfgang Goethe University in Frankfurt,

Germany. His main lines of research are social and political theory, political sociology, biopolitics, and social studies of genetic and reproductive technologies. He is author of several works on biopolitics and Foucault; among his recent works are *Biopolitics: An Advanced Introduction* (New York, 2011); *Foucault, Governmentality, and Critique* (Boulder, 2011); *Perspectives on Genetic Discrimination* (New York, 2013); and *Die Natur in der Soziologie: Gesellschaftliche Voraussetzungen und Folgen biotechnologischen Wissens* (Frankfurt am Main, 2013).

VANESSA LEMM is Professor in Philosophy at the School of Humanities and Languages of the University of New South Wales, Sydney, Australia. She is the author of *Nietzsche's Animal Philosophy: Culture, Politics, and the Animality of the Human Being* (New York, 2009); *Nietzsche y el pensamiento politico contemporáneo* (Santiago, 2013); and several articles on Nietzsche, biopolitics, and contemporary political theory. She has also edited volumes on Hegel and Foucault. She is a founding member of the biopolitics research network BioPolitica.cl.

MARIA MUHLE is Professor of Aesthetic Theory at the Merz Akademie, Stuttgart. She is author of *Eine Genealogie der Biopolitik: Zum Begriff des Lebens bei Foucault and Canguilhem* (Berlin, 2008); and editor of *Biopolitische Konstellationen* (with Kathrin Thiele) (Berlin, 2010).

ROBERTO NIGRO is Program Director at the Collège International de Philosophie in Paris and Senior Lecturer at the Institute for Theory, Zurich University of the Arts (ZHdK), Switzerland. He is editor of Foucault, *Introduction to Kant's Anthropology* (Cambridge, Mass., 2008). A selection of his last publications includes "Pouvoir, violence, représentation," *Rue Descartes* 77, http://www.ruedescartes.org/ (2013); *Ästhetik der Existenz: Lebensformen im Widerstreit* (with Elke Bippus and Jörg Huber) (Zurich, 2013); and *Inventionen, Volumes 1 and 2* (with Isabell Lorey and Gerald Raunig) (Berlin–Zurich, 2011–12).

PAUL PATTON is Scientia Professor in Philosophy at the University of New South Wales, Australia. He has published widely on contemporary French philosophy and Anglo-American political philosophy. He is the author of

Deleuze and the Political (New York, 2000); and *Deleuzian Concepts: Philosophy, Colonization, Politics* (Stanford, 2010). He is editor of *Nietzsche, Feminism, and Political Theory* (New York, 1993), *Deleuze: A Critical Reader* (Oxford, 1996); and coeditor (with Duncan Ivison and Will Sanders) of *Political Theory and the Rights of Indigenous Peoples* (Cambridge, 2000), (with John Protevi), *Between Deleuze and Derrida*, (London, 2003), and (with Simone Bignall) *Deleuze and the Postcolonial* (Edinburgh 2010).

JUDITH REVEL is Professor of Italian and Philosophy at the University of Paris 1 Panthéon-Sorbonne and member of the Laboratoire "Philosophies Contemporaines," she specializes in contemporary French philosophy. Among her recent works are *Michel Foucault: Une pensée du discontinue* (Paris, 2010); (with F. Bruge're, G. le Blanc, M. Gaille, M. Foessel, and P. Zaoui), *Dictionnaire politique a' l'usage des gouvernés* (Paris, 2012); *Un malentendu philosophique: Foucault, Derrida, et "l'affaire Descartes"* (Paris, 2014); and *Foucault avec Merleau-Ponty: Ontologie politique, présentisme et histoire* (Paris, 2014).

MIGUEL VATTER is Professor of Political Science at the University of New South Wales, Australia. He is the editor of *Crediting God: Religion and Sovereignty in the Age of Global Capitalism* (New York, 2010) and author of *The Republic of the Living: Affirmative Biopolitics and Civil Society* (New York, 2014). He is a founding member of the biopolitics research network BioPolitica.cl.

INDEX

affirmative biopolitics, 8–9, 112, 170; republican thought and, 182; subjectivity and, 9
Agamben, Giorgio, 231n48, 234nn7,13–14,16, 236nn6–7, 241n25, 248n11, 249n25; "Absolute Immanence," 81; bare life, 78; form-of-life, 170; *Homo Sacer: Sovereign Power and Bare Life*, 82–83; life definition in Foucault and Deleuze, 81; life, subjectivity and, 81–82; *Remnants of Auschwitz: The Witness and the Archive*, 82–83; state of exception, 10
agon, philosophical life and political life, 208–9
alethurgy of truth, 210
Althusser, Louis, 239n7; state, 129
analytics of power, 129–30
anatomopolitics, biopolitics and, 24–25
Anglo-American reception of Foucault, 2–3
animality, 221
anti-imperialism predictions, 30–31
anti-naturalism of Foucault, 119
antinomy of law and order, 165–74
apatheia, 200–1
archeology of life, 80–82
Arendt, Hannah, 254n1; Socratic philosophical life, 208–9
Aristotle, 230n33; excessive pursuit of pleasure, 48; exchange, 47–48, 54–55; sexual immorality, 48–49

ascetic ideal, 214
Austrian School, 131; neoliberalism and, 174–75

Bacon, Francis, 236n5; medicine and economics, 99; "Of Seditions and Troubles," 101–2; poverty, 102
bare life, sovereignty and, 82–83
Becker, Gary, 32–33, 229nn22–23,26; new household economics, 40–41; social issues, 40–41; *Treatise on the Family*, 44
becoming, subjectivization and, 117–18
Beyond Good and Evil (Nietzsche), 210
Bichat, Xavier, 80, 233n4, 234nn17–18, 236n11; *General Anatomy*, 84; *Physiological Researches upon Life and Death*, 84
bio-ethics, 77–78
biological indifference, 85biological life, 82, 120
biological normativity, 168–69
biologization of law, 171
biologization of life, 121
biology, economics and, 105–6
biopolitical substance of life, 82–83
biopolitical techniques, 79
biopolitics: affirmation of being, 123; anatomopolitics and, 24–25; applications, 113; bio-ethics and, 77–78; biopower and, 2; body as a machine, 78;

281

biopolitics (cont.)
   capitalist production, 5; historicization and, 120; human body and, 78; introduction of, 78–80; liberalism and, 60–63, 131; as life, 86–90; life and, 80–81; life as object, 79; nature in, 118–21; neoliberalism as framework, 163–65; polarity, 77–79; polemical concept, 77–78; of the population, 79; power over life, 122; security and, 23–25, 27–28; sovereign power and, 82–83; species body, 79; state formation, 61; subjectivation, 61. *See also* affirmative biopolitics
biopower, 9, 60; biopolitics and, 2; conduct of conducts and, 171–72; death as resistance, 107–11; *dispositifs* of, 120; legitimacy, 166–67; life and, 106; medicine and economics, 98–101; and mimesis of life, 86–88; resistance, 122–23; technology of security, 60
biopowers, power over life, 122
bios, 107; death and, 108; individual, social *zoe* and, 170; life and philosophy, 13; life as, 9; reduction to *zoe*, 209–10; revolution and, 207
body, as a machine, biopolitics and, 78
Butler, Judith, 72, 233n37, 239n7

Canguilhem, Georges, 234nn5,19, 235nn23,25, 248nn15–16,18, 249nn19–20,22; biological indifference, 85; biological normativity, 8; economic production, 170; *On the Normal and the Pathological*, 81, 84–85; normativity, 8, 95, 168–70; spontaneous social orders and, 170–71; surplus of life, 170
capitalism: biopolitics and, 5; laissez-faire capitalism, 151; welfare-state capitalism, 151
Capitalism and Freedom (Friedman), 153
care of the self/soul, 187–88, 190; *epimeleia*, 193; *Laches* (Plato), 205; *logos* and, 190; *metanoia*, 193

catallaxy, 170; free market, 176
Chicago School neoliberalism, 30, 131, 144; *The Birth of Biopolitics* (Foucault), 31; new household economics, 40–45
Christian millenarianism, 19–20
Christian pastoral power, 173, 199–200
civil society, 5; Foucault's negative view, 166; second nature, 62; security and, 21–22
community, 213–14; Cynics, 217–23; shared obligations and, 73
conduct: counter-conducts/discourses, 94; government and, 142; governmentality and, 7; natural order and, 8; *nomos*, 7–8
conduct of conducts, 3–4; biopower and, 171–72; liberalism, 5; self-conduct, 3
coup d'état, 132–35; transcendent sovereignty, 135
Courses: *Abnormal*, 8, 78; *The Birth of Biopolitics*, 25, 31, 142; *The Birth of Biopolitics* (Foucault), 61; *The Care of the Self*, 202–3; *The Courage of Truth*, 12, 187, 208–9; *The Government of Self and Others*, 11, 167, 204–5; governmentality studies, 2; *The Hermeneutics of the Subject*, 18, 203; *La société punitive*, 139; *versus* other activity, 128; publication, 1; *Security, Territory, Population*, 6, 56, 198–200; *Society Must Be Defended*, 136; *The Use of Pleasure* (Foucault), 204
creativity, life and, 121–24
critique, 72–74; deconstruction and, 113; of identity, Foucault's, 113–18
Cynics, 12–13; animality, 221; community, 217–23; *The Courage of Truth* (Foucault), 208–9; embodiment and community, 215–16; humanity and, 222; humiliation, 220; law of nature, 221; necessities of life, 220; *parrhesia*, 211–12; philosophical life, 209–10; public/private division, 219; security and, 18; slavery, 220; true life, 218–19; truth, 210–11

death: avoidance, 106; *bios* and, 108; denial of, 106, 111; loss of meaning, 106–11; meditations on, 203–4; *melethe thanatou*, 110; modality of dying, power and, 108; politics of, 104–7; relationship with life, 191–93; as resistance to biopower, 107–11; sovereign power and, 104–5; suicide, 108–9; thanatopolitics, 105; *Weltanschauung*, 106
deconstruction: critique and, 113; messianism and, 112; reconstruction and, 123
Deleuze, Gilles, 235n32, 238n2; life, 82; vital force, 94–95
democracy, property-owning, 151–52, 158–59
Derrida, Jacques, 251n10, 254n2; *The Gift of Death*, 193
discipline: governmentality of, 168; power and, 136
Discipline and Punish (Foucault), 3, 78, 115, 137, 142
dispositifs, 4; diplomatic-military, 21; governmental, 92; medicine and, 98–99; security, 23, 27, 83, 90, 93; sexual, 94; way of life and, 117
dissidence, *parrhesia* and, 188–207
divine law, as political ideal, 35–40
Durkheim, Emile, 236n12

Eastern European philosophers, 188–207
economic rule of law, 11, 163–64
economic theology of oikonomia, 56–58
economics: as atheistic discipline, 56; biology and, 105–6; Chicago School, 30; coordination and, 171; Islamic, 52–53; juridification, 164–65; medicine and, 9, 98–101; monetarist counterrevolution, 30; monotheistic in Iranian Revolution, 52–56; new household economics, 32–33; *oikos* and, 46–47; police power and, 101–4; as political discourse, 133; as political rationality, 56, 132, 175

egalitarianism, Rawls, John, 152–54
Einverleibung, 214–15
embodiment of truth: community, 213–17; errors and, 211–13; immunity, 213–17; Platonic–Socratic model, 216–17
Esposito, Roberto, 73, 226nn6,11, 233nn2,38–39, 236n9, 243n29, 248n11, 255nn10–11; *communitas*, 213–14; *immunitas*, 214
Eucken, Walter, 144

Family Protection Law (Iran), 37; commodification of women, 54; revocation, 55
fear: desire and, 68; government of, 66–71; homogeneous groups, 68; pleasure and, 68; security state and, 66; technologies of fear, 68
female pleasure, 50–51
feminization of the welfare state, 58
First Alcibiades (Socrates), 205–6
Fordist/Keynesian household, sexual division of labor, 41–42
Foucault, Michel: Anglo-American reception, 2–3; *The Birth of Biopolitics*, 5, 103–4, 130–31; *The Birth of the Clinic*, 81; *The Care of the Self*, 127; conversion to liberalism, 3; *The Courage of Truth*, 204–5, 208–9; *Discipline and Punish*, 3, 115, 137; focus change, 1–2; *Genealogy of Morals*, 201–2; governmentality, 1–2; Greek philosophy return, 12; *The Hermeneutics of the Subject*, 201–2; *The History of Sexuality*, 3; Italian reception, 2; "Life: Experience and Science," 81; *Madness and Civilization*, 113–14; *The Order of Things*, 80–81, 114; *Parallel Lives*, 122; *parrhesia*, transition to, 11–12; *Security, Territory, Population*, 131, 142; *Society Must Be Defended*, 136; *The Use of Pleasure*, 33, 127; "What Is Critique?", 72; "What Is Enlightenment?", 11; *The Will to Knowledge*, 127. See also Courses

Index

free market: catallaxy, 176; divine providence and, 174; neoliberalism and, 11; Ordoliberalism, 144–45
freedom: liberal government, 143; liberalism and, 64–65, 131–32; regulation, 64–65; security and, 67–68; trade, 64
Freudianism, *The History of Sexuality* (Foucault) and, 129
Freiburg School, 144
Friedman, Milton, 144; *Capitalism and Freedom*, 153

gay rights movement, 115–16; way of life and, 116–17
Gehlen, Arnold, 254n4, 255n9
genealogy of governmentality, 103–4
Genealogy of Morals (Foucault), 201–2
General Anatomy (Bichat), 84
German model, neoliberal governmentality and, 146
global age of security, 26–27
government: common good and, 132; excess, liberalism and, 131–32; of fear, 66–71; formula for, 3; freedom and, 63–64; general context, 61; happiness of individuals and, 103; internal regulation, 62; of the living, 87; of men, 201; natural order and, 61–62; political economy and, 62–63; religious origins, 4–5; resistance and philosophy, 12
governmentality, 142; conduct and, 7; of discipline, 168; genealogy, 103–4; liberal rule of law, 9–10; of security, 168; self-reflexivity and, 3; socialism, 146–47; subjectivity and, 3
Great Society, 170
Greek philosophy, 3; obedience, 173; soul, 190
Greeks, ethics of pleasure, 45–50

Habermas, Jürgen, 233n1
Hadot, Pierre, 227n14, 236n15

Hardt, Michael, 78, 232n18, 243n30; immaterial labor, 5; modern power, 137–38
Havel, Václav, 188, 252n19; *The Power of the Powerless*, 195–96
Hayek, Friedrich von, 144, 249nn27–28,30, 250n37; anti-Platonism, 175; catallaxy, 170; economic actors, 176; economics, coordination and, 171; Great Society, 170; historical realism, 175; judge-made law, 175–77; juridification of economics, 164–65; jurisprudence of, 11; *Law, Legislation and Liberty*, 175; liberal social order, 164; neoliberal project, 163; *nomos*, 175; normative order, 164–65; political organization and, 176–77; providentialism, 175; reconciliation of law and order, 174–78; social organization, 170; spontaneous social order, 164, 170, 174
Hegel, Georg Wilhelm Friedrich, 230n28
Heidegger, Martin, 194–95; *Introduction to Metaphysics*, 194; living-with-the-truth, 196
Heretical Essays (Patočka), 191–92
historicization, of regularities, 119–20
Hobbes, Thomas, 227n6
homo natura, 210
Homo Sacer: Sovereign Power and Bare Life (Agamben), 82–83
household as enterprise, 41–42
human body, biopolitics and, 78

identification: forms of sexuality, 115–16; objectification and, 114; subjectivization and, 115; way of life and, 116–17
identity: analytic of knowledges, 114; Foucault's critique, 113–18; inclusion in the system, 115; objectification, 115; self-identity, 113–14; sexual, 115–16
immunitas, 73, 214
imperial security, 19–20; paternal solicitude, 27

income tax, negative, 152–53
independence, mastery of self, 173
individualization, subjectivization and, 115
Introduction to Metaphysics (Heidegger), 194
Iranian Revolution: anti-imperialism predictions, 30–31; historical crisis and, 58; monothestic economics, 52–56; neoliberalism and, 7, 31–33; *nomos* and, 7; sexual politics, 43–44; Shi'ite Revolution, 34–40; women's service labor, 44–45, 53–54
Islamic Republic, 38; religio-sexual utopia, 39

juridical regression, neoliberalism as, 164–65
justice, principles of, 149–51
Justice as Fairness (Rawls), 151

Kantian constitutionalism, 166, 178
kitsch, 197–98
Kojève, Alexander, 237n16
Kundera, Milan: microphysics, 197; *The Unbearable Lightness of Being*, 196

Laches (Plato), 205
law: biologization, 171; of the household (*oikonomia*), 33; order and, 165–67, 174–78; nomocratic *versus* telocratic, 176–77; *versus* norms, 165–66; power-as-law, 166–68; as resistance, 181–84; self-mastery and, 167; sovereign state and, 166–67
Law, Legislation and Liberty (Hayek), 175
Lebensführung (conduct of life), 4, 171–72; religious origins of government, 4–5
leftist groups, Foucault and, 128–29
liberal reason, 131–32
liberal rule of law, *nomos* of governmentality, 9–10
liberalism: as art of governing humans, 61; biopolitics framework, 63; biopolitics origins and, 60–63; *The Birth of Biopolitics* (Foucault), 61; conduct of conducts, 5; conversion to, 3; culture of danger, 65; economic, 146; excess government, 131–32; freedom and, 64–65, 131–32, 143; government of life, 2; nature and, 62–63; neoliberalism and, 144–45; *nomos* of, 10; political rationality, 10; property distribution and, 10; rationality of government, 61; security and, 65–66; social order of, 164; *versus* state centralization, 57. See also neoliberalism

life: becoming thinkable, 80–81; biological, 82, 120; biologization of, 121; as biopolitical substance, 82–83; biopolitics and, 80–81; biopolitics as, 86–90; biopower and, 106; as *bios*, 9; creativity and, 121–24; dynamism of, 80–81, 84; exposure to power, 83; intelligence of anomaly, 85; mimesis of, biopower and, 86–88; naked life, 193; negative dimension, 85; polarity, 84–86; power and, 104–5; power over, 165–66; power relations and, 122; relationship with death, 191–93; as resistance to death, 80; salvation and, 203; sciences of the living, 84; subjectivity and, 81–82; subjectivization and, 122–23; surplus of life, 181–84; value of, 84–86; vehicle of truth, 210
"Life: Experience and Science" (Foucault), 81
logos: care of the soul and, 190; truth and, 221

Machiavelli, 132, 240n16
machinery of production, bodies in, 137
Madness and Civilization (Foucault), 113–14
Mahler, Margaret, 25
Malthus, 250n39
Marin, Louis, 136, 241nn21,25

market: natural order and legal order, 163–64; self-regulation, 62
Marx, Karl, 230n28
Marxism, 129; critique of political economy, 5; *The History of Sexuality* (Foucault) and, 129
mastery of self, independence, 173
Mayerne, Turquet de, *La monarchie aristodémocratique*, 102–3
Meade, James, 151, 245n18; property-owning democracy and, 159
medicine, economics and, 98–101
metaphysical Platonism, 193–4
metaphysics, nature and, 119
milieu, population and, 87, 90–3
millenarianism (Christian), 19–20
Mises, Ludwig von, 144
monotheistic economics in Iranian Revolution, 52–6
Montaigne, Michel de, 236n15
Mont-Pelerin Society, 144; negative income tax, 153

natural order, 84; conduct and, 8
natural sciences, classification in, 119–20
natural sciences *versus* sciences of the living, 84
naturalization, subjectivization and, 115
nature: biopolitics and, 118–21; discontinuity and, 119; as instrument of control, 120; liberalism, 62–63; metaphysics and, 119
Naudé, Gabriel, 133–34, 241nn17,19
necessities of life, 210; Cynics, 220
Negri, Antonio, 5, 78, 232n18, 239n7, 241n22, 243n30; immaterial labor, 5; modern power, 137–38
neoliberalism: Austrian School and, 174–75; biopolitics framework, 163–65; *The Birth of Biopolitics* (Foucault), 31–32, 132; Chicago School, 30, 144; economic rule of law and, 163–64; free market, 11; Freiburg School, 144; German model and, 146; government of life, 2; Iranian Revolution and, 7, 31–33; juridical regression, 164–65; juridification of politics, 174; law and order, 165–66; law and order reconciliation, 174–78; legal principles in economic order, 11; liberal government and, 144–45; Mont-Pelerin Society, 144; *nomos* and, 6; *nomos* in, 178–81; Ordoliberalism, 10, 40, 131, 144–45, 154; progressive liberals and, 153; Rawls, John, 152–54; socialists and, 153; state phobia and, 145–46. *See also* liberalism
new household economics, 32–33; Chicago School and, 40–45; conservatism, 56–58; medieval Islamic philosophers, 54; moral economy of pleasure, 57–58; *oikos* and, 46–47; wealth creation, 47; Western *versus* Islamic views, 43–44
Nietzsche, Friedrich, 254n5, 256nn13–14; ascetic ideal, 214; *Beyond Good and Evil*, 210; Cynics and, 12–13, 215–16; *The Gay Science*, 211; Plantonists and, 215–16; Platonic–Socratic model, 216–17; Stoics, 215; truth, 209–10
nomos, 5–6; Iranian Revolution and, 7; of liberalism, 10; medieval Islamic philosophers, 54–55; natural standard of conduct, 7–8; neoliberal governmentality as, 6; neoliberalism, 178–81; normative order, 9; republicanism, 177; Schmitt, Carl, 6–7; *Security, Territory, Population* and, 6; security as, 6–7; truth and, 221
normativity, 86; biological, 168–69; Canguilhem, Georges, 8; Hayek, 164–65; *nomos*, 9; of non-judgment, 202; norm and, 170–71; normalization, normation and 88–89; social, 168–69; *zoe*, 8

objectification: identification and, 114; identity and inclusion in system, 115
"Of Seditions and Troubles" (Bacon), 101–2

oikonomia (law of the household), 33, 45–52; economic theology, 56–58; Islamic economics, 54–55; virtuous exchange, 54
oikos, 46–47; use values, 51
On the Normal and the Pathological (Canguilhem), 81, 84–5
Ordoliberalism, 10, 40, 131, 144–45, 154; *The Birth of Biopolitics*, 31

Parallel Lives (Foucault), 122
parrhesia, 12, 173, 187–88; adulation of the powerful, 204; authentic, characteristics, 205; Cynics, 211–12; dissidence and, 188–207; Platonic-Socratic, 211–12; power and, 12; Socrates, 205–6
pastoral power, 172–73, 199–200; Christian, 173; examples, 198; new rights, 183; *versus* political power, 172–73; subordination and, 173
Patočka, Jan, 251nn5,8,12–13; a-subjective phenomenology, 189; *chorismos*, 194; death, 189; *Heretical Essays*, 191–92; *Plato and Europe*, 187, 190; revival of the soul, 190–91
people, *versus* population, 181–84
philosophical life, 208–9; the Cynics, 209–11; *logos*, 221; Nietzsche, 209–10; *nomos*, 221; opinion *versus* truth, 222; sovereign life, 221–22
philosophy, 12–13; resistance to government and, 12; reversal of values as political task, 211–12; security and, 18; Stoics, 215; as vehicle of community, 217–18
Physiological Researches upon Life and Death (Bichat), 84
Plato, 236n14; Christianized Platonism, 189; *Laches*, 205; *melethe thanatou*, 110; metaphysical Platonism, 193–94; negative Platonism, 193; Nietzsche, 215–16
Plato and Europe (Patočka), 187, 190
Platonic-Socratic model, 216–17; public/private life, 218–19

Platonic-Socratic *parrhesia*, 211–12
pleasure: ethics of with the Greeks, 45–50; fear and, 68; female, 50–51; lawfulness, 49
police: science of, 102–3; von Justi, 103
political economy, 56, 175; as form of knowledge, 61; government and, 62–63; market self-regulation, 62; political power and, 175
Political Liberalism (Rawls), 149, 156
political power: *versus* pastoral power, 172–73; political economy and, 175; *versus* sovereign power, 172
politics, happiness of individuals and, 103
politics of death, 104–7
population: biopolitics of, 79; identification, management and, 115; milieu and, 87, 90–93; *versus* people, 181–84; post-sovereign power and, 79–80
power: analytics, 129–30; descriptive approach, 142–47; discipline and, 136; economy of power, 67; genealogy of, 87; law and, 166–68; life and, 83, 104–5, 122, 165–66; modalities of dying, 108; modern, 137–38; *parrhesia* and, 12; pastoral, 172–73; prescriptive approach, 142–47; reduction of forms, 87–88; representation and, 135–36; resistance and, 3, 93–97; in sexuality, 104; state, limiting, 143; technology of, 136–37. *See also* biopower
property-owning democracy, 151–52, 158–59
public policy, Rawls on, 147–52
public reason: 10–11; content, 154–58; historical phenomenon, 157–58; institutional contexts, 158–60; nonpublic reason, 155–56; Rawls on, 147–52, 154–58

racism, 83
raison d'État, 21, 132, 135; definitions of reason of state, 101
Rancière, Jacques, 96, 248n14

288   Index

Rawls, John, 244n5, 245nn9,11, 17,21,24,27–28,30, 246nn37–38,41–42, 247nn48–49,54,60; egalitarianism, 152–54; Foucault comparison, 141–42; *Justice as Fairness*, 151; neoliberalism, 152–54; *Political Liberalism*, 149, 156; public policy, 147–52; public reason, 147–52, 154–58; *Theory of Justice*, 150, 152

reason: liberal, 131–32; public use, 10–11; of state, 10, 101–2, 131–32. *See also* raison d'État. *See also* public reason

Remnants of Auschwitz: The Witness and the Archive (Agamben), 82–3

representation, exercise of power and, 135–36

resistance: biopower and, 122–23; counter-conducts/discourses, 96; death as resistance to biopower, 107–11; to government, 12; law as, 181–84; power and, 3, 93–97

revolutionary conservatism, 35

revolutionary utopianism, 130

Ricardo, 250n39

risk-taking as public virtue, 68–69

Saint-Hilaire, Geoffroy, 119–20

salvation, 101, 203–4; Christian shepherd, 199–200; life and, 203; pastor, 201; truth and, 201–2

Schmitt, Carl, 226n10, 231n49, 241nn23–24; *nomos* and, 6–7; sovereignty, 133

security, 17; actors, redistribution, 24; autonomy and, 60; child psychology, 25; civil society and, 21–22; as control of flow, 25–26; *dispositifs*, 23, 27, 83, 90, 93; enemy and, 27; freedom and, 67–68; global age of security, 26–27; global security, 26; governmentality of, 168; hyperprevention, 70; industry, 69–71; liberalism and, 65–66; modalities, transformation, 25; moral experiences and, 19; nature of the threat, 26; *nomos*, 6–7; as non-juridical concept, 67; object of, 23–24; philosophy and, 18; political realism and, 22–23; as protection, 25–26; sovereign, 27; sovereign and, 6–7; spiritual meaning *versus* political, 18; surveillance technologies, 69–70; technology of, 7, 60–61, 63–66; total age of security, 26–27. *See also* four ages of security

Security, Territory, Population (Foucault), 6, 56, 131, 142, 198–200

self-identity, 113–14

sexual division of labor, 41–42

sexual ethics, 45–46; virginity, 50–51

sexual identity, 115

sexual immorality, Aristotle, 48–49

sexual revolution, 94

sexuality: art of exchange and, 47–48; identification with forms, 115–16; legislation in Islamic law, 38–39; power in, 104

Shi'ite Revolution, 34–40

Skeptics, security and, 18

smallpox, variolization and, 88–89

social movements, new household economics, 42–43

social security system, 59–60

socialism, governmentality, 146–47

La société punitive (Foucault), 139

society: public political culture, 156; security society, 65–66; well-ordered, 147–48

Society Must Be Defended (Foucault), 136; power analytics and, 138

Socrates, *First Alcibiades*, 205–6

Socratic philosophy, 11–12; Cynics, 12–13; Foucault's return to, 12–13; negative philosophy, 194; *parrhesia*, 205–6

Solidarnosc movement, 12, 167

somatocracy, 99, 105

soul: Greek philosophers and, 190; revival, Patočka, 190–91

sovereign power: appropriation and, 99–100; biopolitics and, 82–83; death

and, 104–5; economics and, 99–100; exception and, 133; law and 166–67; life and 221–22; *versus* political power, 172; politics and economics, 99–100; post-sovereign power, population and, 79–80; reason of state and, 101–2
sovereignty: bare life and, 82–83; coup d'état and, 135; of desire, 49–50; liberalism *versus* state centralization, 57; security and, 6–7
species body: biopolitics, 79; technology of power, 136–37
Spinoza, Benedict de, 227n4
spiritual security, 17–19; spiritual vigilance and, 27
state: biopolitics, 61; phobia, 145–46; problems, 129–30; limiting of, 143; reason of, 101–2, 131–32; reversal of relation with citizen, 69–70
Stoics: Nietzsche, 215; public/private life, 218–19; security and, 18–19
subjectivation, critique and desubjectivation, 72–74
subjectivity: affirmative biopolitics and, 9; governmentality and, 3; life and, 81–82; sexual identity, 115–16; technologies of the self, 3–4
subjectivization: becoming and, 117–18; identification, 115; individualization, 115; life, 122–23; naturalization, 115
suicide, 108–9
surplus of life, 170, 181–84

technology, of fear, 68; of power, 136–37, 168; of security, 7, 60, 63–66; biopower, 60; *The History of Sexuality*, 60; of self, 173
thanatopolitics, 9, 105; bare life, 78
Theory of Justice (Rawls), 150, 152
total age of security, 26–27
Treatise on the Family (Becker), 44
true life. *See* philosophical life
truth, 101, 208–9; alethurgy of, 210; Cynics, 210–11, 217–19; embodiment, 211–12; Heidegger, 195; living-within-the-truth, 196; Nietzsche, 209–10; reduction of *bios* to *zoe*, 209–10; salvation and, 201–2; vehicle of life, 210

value of life, 84–86
violence, political activites, 129
von Justi, Johann Heinrich Gottlob, 103

war, struggle and, 139
way of life, 116–17
Weber, Max: capitalism, 171–72; conduct of life, 171; *The Protestant Ethic and the Spirit of Capitalism*, 4
welfare state: feminization, 58; negative income tax and, 152–53; social security system and, 59–60
well-ordered society, 147–48
Wittgenstein, Ludwig, 227n1

zoe, 8, 107; philosophical life, 209–10; philosophy and, 13; reduction of *bios*, 209–10; social, individual *bios* and, 170

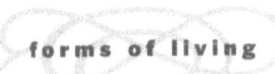

forms of living

Stefanos Geroulanos and Todd Meyers, *series editors*

Georges Canguilhem, *Knowledge of Life*. Translated by Stefanos Geroulanos and Daniela Ginsburg, Introduction by Paola Marrati and Todd Meyers.

Henri Atlan, *Selected Writings: On Self-Organization, Philosophy, Bioethics, and Judaism*. Edited and with an Introduction by Stefanos Geroulanos and Todd Meyers.

Catherine Malabou, *The New Wounded: From Neurosis to Brain Damage*. Translated by Steven Miller.

François Delaporte, *Chagas Disease: History of a Continent's Scourge*. Translated by Arthur Goldhammer, Foreword by Todd Meyers.

Jonathan Strauss, *Human Remains: Medicine, Death, and Desire in Nineteenth-Century Paris*.

Georges Canguilhem, *Writings on Medicine*. Translated and with an Introduction by Stefanos Geroulanos and Todd Meyers.

François Delaporte, *Figures of Medicine: Blood, Face Transplants, Parasites*. Translated by Nils F. Schott, Foreword by Christopher Lawrence.

Juan Manuel Garrido, *On Time, Being, and Hunger: Challenging the Traditional Way of Thinking Life*.

Pamela Reynolds, *War in Worcester: Youth and the Apartheid State*.

Vanessa Lemm and Miguel Vatter, eds., *The Government of Life: Foucault, Biopolitics, and Neoliberalism*.

www.ingramcontent.com/pod-product-compliance
Lightning Source LLC
Chambersburg PA
CBHW030435300426
44112CB00009B/1014